ENGLISH–ESPAÑOL

READING INVENTORY

FOR THE CLASSROOM

E. Sutton Flynt
Austin Peay State University

Robert B. Cooter, Jr.
Dallas Public Schools

Translations by Kathy Escamilla, Sally Nathenson-Mejia, Dora Alvarez, Patricia Garcia-Smith, and RosaMaria Rojo

Illustrations by Deborah S. Flynt

Merrill,
an imprint of Prentice Hall
Upper Saddle River, New Jersey   Columbus, Ohio

Library of Congress Cataloging-in-Publication Data

Flynt, E. Sutton.
    English–Espanol reading inventory for the classroom / E. Sutton
Flynt, Robert B. Cooter, Jr. : translations by Kathy Escamilla . . .
[et. al.] ; illustrations by Deborah S. Flynt.
        p.   cm.
    Includes bibliographical references.
    ISBN 0-13-955451-3
    1. English language—Study and teaching—Spanish speakers.
2. Hispanic American children—Education—Language arts.   3. English
language—Study and teaching—United States.   4. Hispanic American
children—Language.   5. Education, Bilingual—United States.
6. Reading—Ability testing.   I. Cooter, Robert B.   II. Title.
III. Title: Reading inventory.
PE1129.S8F55   1999
428'.007—dc21   98-32379
                                                                      CIP

Editor: *Bradley J. Potthoff*
Production Editor: *Mary Harlan*
Design Coordinator: *Diane C. Lorenzo*
Text Designer: *A. Colette Kelly*
Cover art: *©Melissa Taylor*
Production Manager: *Pamela D. Bennett*
Production Coordination: *Elm Street Publishing Services, Inc.*
Director of Marketing: *Kevin Flanagan*
Marketing Manager: *Suzanne Stanton*
Marketing Coordinator: *Krista Groshong*

This book was set in Times Roman by The Clarinda Company and was printed and bound by Courier/Kendallville, Inc. The cover was printed by Phoenix Color Corp.

©1999 by Prentice-Hall, Inc.
Simon & Schuster / A Viacom Company
Upper Saddle River, New Jersey 07458

Printed in the United States of America

10 9 8 7 6 5 4 3 2 1

ISBN 0-13-955451-3

Prentice-Hall International (UK) Limited, *London*
Prentice-Hall of Australia Pty. Limited, *Sydney*
Prentice-Hall of Canada, Inc., *Toronto*
Prentice-Hall Hispanoamericana, S.A., *Mexico*
Prentice-Hall of India Private Limited, *New Delhi*
Prentice-Hall of Japan, Inc., *Tokyo*
Simon & Schuster Asia Pte. Ltd., *Singapore*
Editora Prentice-Hall do Brasil, Ltda., *Rio de Janeiro*

Dedicated to the children of Dallas.
—ESF, RBC

ACKNOWLEDGMENTS

The *English–Español Reading Inventory for the Classroom (EERIC)* was developed to provide inservice and preservice teachers with a simple, straightforward means of assessing student reading development. The following individuals and groups provided a great deal of assistance during the development and fine-tuning of the inventory. As a result of their insight and suggestions, the *EERIC* is a better, more effective inventory.

We would like to extend our appreciation to Susie Emond, Saginaw Valley State University; Paula S. Currie, Southeastern Louisiana University; Maria Meyerson, University of Nevada–Las Vegas; Tim Campbell, University of Central Oklahoma; Kathy Escamilla, and Sally Nathenson-Mejia, University of Colorado, Denver; and Dora Alvarez, Patricia Garcia-Smith, and RosaMaria Rojo, Dallas Public Schools, as well as to Rosie Longoria, Sylvia Cambell, Paula Perez, the reviewers of the manuscript, and Laura Escalante-Brown, Dallas Public Schools, who reviewed the Spanish-language proofs; we appreciated their comments and insights. Also, thanks to Claudia Cornett, Wittenberg University; Shirley Freed, Andrews University; Carolyn M. Griffin, Mabee Reading Clinic; Victoria J. Risko, Vanderbilt University; M. K. Gillis, Southwest Texas State University; D. Ray Reutzel, Southern Utah University; Linda Gambrell, University of Maryland; MaryLou Curley, San Antonio Independent School District; Bill King, Westside Elementary School; the Chapter I Teachers, San Antonio Independent School District; the faculty and students at Westside Elementary School; and the faculty and students at George Nettels Elementary School. Special thanks to John Lidh and Laser Precision for the use of information about OTDRs.

E. Sutton Flynt
Robert B. Cooter, Jr.

CONTENTS

INTRODUCTION

The *English–Español Reading Inventory for the Classroom* is a new assessment tool intended for teachers of reading in regular, bilingual, and English as a Second Language (ESL) classrooms. Based on our best-selling assessment instrument in English, the Flynt–Cooter *Reading Inventory for the Classroom* (Flynt and Cooter, 1993, 1995, 1998), we have carefully constructed this new instrument with native Spanish-speaking children in mind. Before explaining how the *English–Español Reading Inventory for the Classroom* works, let us briefly describe the context of reading assessment in the United States as we see it.

In recent years a rather spirited dialogue has been taking place among reading educators regarding the role and nature of reading assessment. Valencia and Pearson (1987) captured an important point of consensus in the debate with the following statement:

> What we need are not just new and better tests. We need a new framework for thinking about assessment, one in which educators begin by considering types of decisions needed and the level of impact of those decisions. (729)

We attempted to use the spirit of this statement as a guide in the design of the *English–Español Reading Inventory for the Classroom.* Some important questions teachers ask (and their answers) helped guide the construction of this instrument.

We addressed the first question: *What decisions are required of classroom teachers, specialists, and clinicians in the initial assessment of students' reading development?* To answer this question candidly and consistently, one might first identify her or his theoretical and instructional orientation. Our view of learning is drawn from transactional theory (Rosenblatt, 1978; Smith, 1982), which is described by Reutzel and Cooter (1996) as emphasizing "that the reader, the text, and the social-situational context are inextricably linked and are transformed as a result of the reading event." Similarly we adopt a view of teaching compatible with that espoused by such process-oriented and balanced-reading educators as Holdaway (1979), Reutzel and Cooter (1999), and Clay (1985). Thus we feel that reading assessment should offer the teacher insights into student interests, attitudes, and motivation (affective considerations), background knowledge, types of text that students may have difficulty reading, and learning or teaching situations that may be problematic. This perspective contrasts sharply with more traditional views of reading assessment that tend to focus on the testing of discrete subskills with little or no attention to affective or social-situational contexts. In this instrument we only attempt to address a selected aspect of the affective domain, background knowledge, as well as the reader's ability to decode and comprehend narrative and expository texts.

We wish to note that at present many teachers may still be in a transitional mode of teaching (Reutzel and Cooter, 1996), moving gradually toward balanced literacy instruction while still using many traditional materials and practices. This inventory, therefore, retains some traditional methods and descriptions easily identifiable to teachers in an early stage of transition as well as naturalistic assessment methods and descriptions that are more consistent with current thinking about assessment.

The kinds of teaching and intervention decisions possible with the *English–Español Reading Inventory for the Classroom* (*EERIC*) relate to such areas as:

- needs of children in bilingual (Spanish) or English as a Second Language (ESL) classes

- assessment of prereading capabilities

- use of decoding strategies (phonemic awareness, phonics, etc.)
- reading aspects of print (selected words, punctuation, fluency)
- attention to story elements and content elements
- literal and higher order comprehension
- miscue recording and needs determination

From these and other data derived from the inventory, teachers working with normally developing and/or special needs students can begin to make decisions related to the kinds of reading materials that can be used, the pacing of instruction, the emphasis of instruction, and the need for student collaborative opportunities. Data gathered using the *EERIC* should of course be viewed only as one part of a comprehensive assessment. Results can be used as part of a student's portfolio, as a starting point for instruction, or as evidence to be shared in staffings that focus on whether students should be placed in special programs.

We also addressed the question for teachers that naturally follows: *What is the level of impact of these decisions?* This question has many interpretations based on the teacher's professional assignment. For the bilingual, ESL, or regular classroom reading teacher, the level of impact usually relates to the matching of reading materials and learning opportunities to the student's interests and performance abilities. For reading specialists and special program teachers, the level of impact involves the preceding decisions plus decision making related to the selection and retention of students in intervention programs.

In summary there are several important purposes of process-oriented reading assessment that can be addressed in part through use of this inventory. Reutzel and Cooter (1996) list several key points that summarize our subsidiary needs: (1) to show what stages students are in developmentally and to create an initial record of progress, (2) to determine areas of strength and need for planning instruction, and (3) to help teachers learn more about the reading process through interaction with students.

WHAT IS THE FLYNT–COOTER
ENGLISH–ESPAÑOL READING INVENTORY FOR THE CLASSROOM?

The *EERIC* is an informal reading inventory intended for determining Spanish or English reading levels from preprimer through grade 12. It was developed to meet the needs of professionals interested in assessing the reading competencies of students in public or private schools, intervention programs in English or Spanish, or clinical settings. The primary purpose of the inventory is to assist teachers in the placement of students with appropriate reading and instructional materials. Additionally the inventory can be used for educating preservice and in-service teachers in reading assessment and the interpretation of results.

DESCRIPTION OF THE *EERIC*

The inventory itself begins with an interest/attitude questionnaire designed to assist the examiner in establishing rapport with the student and to gather information about socially relevant factors that may be influencing the student's interest in reading. It also has the potential to suggest topics and/or materials for use in the classroom and/or remedial setting that may interest the student. Both a primary-level interview (pp. 27 and 223) and an upper-level interview (pp. 29 and 225) are provided.

The assessment portion of the inventory is divided into four forms: A, B, C, and D. Each of Forms A, B, and C, in turn, is composed of three sections: sentences to determine initial passage selection, the reading passages themselves, and the accompanying assessment protocols. Form D has no accompanying sentences for initial passage selection and will be discussed separately.

In Forms A, B, and C, the section entitled "Sentences for Initial Passage Selection" is a series of sentences designed to help examiners choose the initial passage, from Level 1 through Level 9, with which students will begin reading. (Instructions are provided later for administering the preprimer assessment to students who do not perform well on Level 1 sentences.) We have used sentences rather than the familiar word lists because reading sentences is closer to the actual act of reading than reading words in isolation. The sentences not only provide insights into how the reader approaches unfamiliar words but also provide a brief view of the reader's competence at varying levels of difficulty. If, as recommended, the examiner records the oral miscues (reading errors) students make while reading the sentences, then this information proves helpful in formulating ideas about the student's decoding and comprehension instructional needs. The words used in Form A sentences are drawn in part from the Form A narrative passages, as is true for Forms B and C. Thus, if an examiner is going to use Form A, then only sentences in Form A should be used to determine the starting point for reading the passages.

The reading selections were written or adapted by the authors and reflect what we perceive to be some of the interests of the students at the various age levels represented. Topics for the passages were selected based on our conversations with the school-age students we have worked with in recent years, as well as with our own children. The Spanish selections have been carefully written to take into account the cultural influences we have observed in southwestern schools in the United States. The *EERIC* now includes Levels PP and P in Forms A and B and also Form D, which includes grade levels 10, 11, and 12. Special instructions for administering these passages are provided in the next section. All passages are leveled such that Level PP corresponds to beginning first grade reading difficulty and Level 12 corresponds to twelfth grade difficulty. Forms A and B are narrative (story) passages, while Forms C and D are expository (factual/content-oriented) passages. Passage difficulty was determined using a combination of means including the Fry Readability Graph (1968), the Harris-Jacobson Readability Formula (1975), teacher input, and our own judgment. Notwithstanding the widely known limitations of readability formulas, the passages are within the assigned ranges and correspond closely with those associated with most commercial leveled materials. As with all assessment instruments and procedures, the examiner needs to use observation and judgment to interpret any findings concerning a student's reading level and abilities.

Following the reading selections in each of the forms are examiner's protocol forms for analysis of student reading ability. The protocols include an introductory prereading statement, comprehension questions, a miscue analysis grid, a section for analyzing results and determining whether or not to continue testing, and a listening comprehension assessment. For narrative passages, each of the comprehension questions is labeled according to story grammar element (balanced-reading/naturalistic) and hierarchical level (traditional view) of comprehension. For expository passages, each question is labeled by a designation we refer to as "expository grammar element" (based on the work of Meyer & Freedle, 1984) and traditional levels of comprehension.

A unique feature of the *EERIC* is the inclusion of a miscue analysis grid for each passage. Based on the seminal work of Goodman and Burke (1969, 1987), these grids, once completed by the examiner, will assist examiners in identifying error patterns made by students that will, in turn, lead to intervention decisions. Grids focus primarily on aspects of word identification and the use of context. Finally, a scoring chart is provided at the end of each protocol to assist in determining whether or not to continue the assessment.

The procedure for using these protocols is discussed more fully in the next section. A scored student example is provided on pages 15–20.

WHO SHOULD USE THE FLYNT–COOTER *EERIC*?

The *EERIC* is appropriate for both preservice (students enrolled in teacher education programs) and in-service teachers, and any other practicing professionals involved with students with reading needs. We feel it provides valuable insights into reading development, especially in the reading of connected text, word analysis, story and content comprehension, and miscue analysis. Classroom teachers using basal reading programs will find the inventory quite useful in basal placement. Teachers implementing literature-based reading programs will find the inventory helpful in planning collaborative learning activities involving reading, planning minilessons, and determining which non-negotiable skills (these are subskills necessary to teach because of state or local mandates, testing programs, and/or teacher judgment about reading development) (Reutzel and Cooter, 1996) need further development. The *EERIC* can also provide a valuable starting place for portfolio assessment profiles. In an intervention or clinical education setting, it can be used as part of an assessment training program as well as an investigative tool for research purposes.

HOW THE FLYNT–COOTER *EERIC* DIFFERS FROM OTHER INFORMAL READING INVENTORIES

From the outset, we wanted to create an inventory that is easy to use, focuses on identifying student strengths, helps teachers plan for instruction, and reflects the current state of knowledge concerning the assessment of reading processes. We also wanted to develop an instrument that is traditional in appearance and may be used by reading educators with a more traditional view of reading education. The *EERIC* has a number of features that help satisfy these goals.

- *Spanish reading passages*—A full range of interesting, leveled passages in Spanish are provided for ESL and bilingual educators.

- *Emergent reader rubric*—The *EERIC* contains a unique method for assessing prereading capabilities using balanced instructional procedures.

- *Miscue analysis grids*—Informed instruction is based on patterns of behavior, not onetime errors in oral reading. Each passage protocol includes a miscue analysis grid containing a facsimile of the passage, space for marking oral reading miscues, and columns for tallying numbers of miscue types. These grids facilitate efficient identification of error patterns and assist the teacher in planning intervention sessions based on student need.

- *Interest/attitude inventory*—This inventory is designed to gather affective information about students, whether native English speakers or learners of English as a second language.

- *High-interest passages*—The passages in this inventory reflect some of the prominent interests of students in elementary and secondary school settings.

- *Longer passages*—Passages are longer than typical instruments to allow for full development of story information and context. This creates more authentic ("real reading") situations to be observed.

- *Passage retellings*—Many authorities in reading complain that comprehension assessment has become an "interrogation." The use of passage retellings seems to be a more naturalistic approach to assessment, much less stressful for students and usually more informative for the examiner. Retellings are used at all levels of the inventory; then only those questions are asked that relate to text information not recounted by the student.

- *Story grammar analyses*—Recently introduced balanced views of reading comprehension have endorsed the story grammar perspective (for example, setting, characterization, story problem, resolution, theme). Each question in the silent reading/retelling section of Forms A and B (narrative selections) is keyed to story grammar categories, as well as to traditional hierarchical labels (literal, inferential, and so on).

- *Expository text grammars*—Just as narrative passages are keyed to the story grammar perspective, expository selections in Forms C and D are keyed to text-types (expository text grammars) based on the work of Meyer and Freedle (1984), as well as to traditional comprehension labels.

- *Intervention strategies*—Once error patterns are determined, a listing of possible instructional interventions is provided.

Administration and Scoring Procedures

STEP 1: INTEREST/ATTITUDE INTERVIEW

One of the most important, and often ignored, aspects of reading assessment is the affective domain. Affect involves interest, attitude, and motivational factors related to reading success. We include an Interest/Attitude Interview to assist examiners in learning more about students' background knowledge, interests, and motivations that may relate to reading success. Information from this brief survey should be used in the selection of reading materials that will be appealing to the student.

Two versions of the Interest/Attitude Interview are included: Primary Form and Upper Level Form. The Primary Form is intended for students in grades 1 and 2, and the Upper Level Form is intended for grades 3 through 12. In each case the examiner begins with the introductory statement provided on the form, then proceeds by asking each of the questions. It is the intention of the authors that examiners use these questions as a springboard for discussion, not simply as a rote exercise. Similarly, examiners should feel free to disregard any questions they feel are inappropriate.

Research on the affective domain and how it relates to reading success is rather sparse, and recommendations for using data derived from an interview of this sort are few. However, most teachers/examiners find that information derived from the Interest/Attitude Interview can be beneficial in several ways. First, information about reading interests can help the teacher select reading materials that are appealing to the student, and choose texts most likely matched to students' background knowledge and vocabulary. Second, information derived from questions related to reading and study habits at home can provide teachers with insights and appropriate suggestions for parents. Third, students' answers to such questions as "What makes a person a good reader?" and "What causes a person to not be a good reader?" often help teachers understand the students' strengths and needs. The Interest/Attitude Interview will not tell teachers everything they need to know about students' abilities, but it *will* help in finding an informed departure point for quality reading experiences.

STEP 2: INITIAL PASSAGE SELECTION SENTENCES

Begin by having students read the set of placement sentences at the beginning of the selected form of the inventory (A, B, or C). We suggest having students begin reading sentences two grade levels below their current grade placement, if possible. This will help avoid potential student frustration caused by starting with passages that are too difficult. If the student is in either grade 1, 2, or 3, begin with Level 1 sentences. (*Note:* If students do not perform well on the Level 1 sentences, see the instructions on pages 10–12 for administering the Preprimer and Primer passages.) **Have students continue reading sets of placement sentences until they miss two words or more, then stop. The highest level of placement sentences read with zero errors should be the level of the first passage to be read by the student.** For students who have no errors through Level 9, begin with Form D, Level 10.

STEP 3: READING PASSAGES

As mentioned previously, students should begin reading the passage indicated by their performance on the initial passage selection sentences. Examiners should place in front of the student a copy of the passage from which the student will read. In schools where a great deal of assessment takes place, we recommend that the student copies be laminated.

Examiners should turn to the corresponding protocol form for that passage and follow along. **Permission is granted to teachers purchasing the Flynt–Cooter *EERIC* to duplicate these protocol forms for their own classroom needs.** Note that each protocol is divided into Parts I, II, III, and IV (Parts I, II, and III in the Spanish section). A step-by-step description is offered for each section.

Part I: Silent Reading Comprehension

1. Read the background statement aloud and say that you will ask for a retelling of the passage after the student has read it silently. Then allow the student to read the passage once silently.

2. After the silent reading is complete, remove the passage and ask the student to retell what they remember about the passage. Check off each question in Part I that is answered during the student's retelling by placing "ua" in the appropriate blank to indicate the student was unaided. Ask all the remaining questions not covered in the student's retelling or that need clarification. Place "a" in the appropriate blank next to each question the student answers correctly to indicate the student was aided in recalling this information.

3. Because of the level of sophistication of students reading above the ninth grade, we recommend that students who are asked to read passages 10D, 11D, or 12D only read the passage silently. We feel it is unnecessary at these levels to assess students' oral reading behaviors. However, for those who wish to conduct oral reading at these levels, a grid has been provided.

Part II: Oral Reading and Analysis of Miscues

Next, have the student read the passage orally up to the *oral reading stop-marker* (*//*) noted on the protocol grid. Note any miscues on the passage facsimile portion of the grid. A description of miscues and how to mark them on the protocol is included in the next section. It is based on the work of Clay (1985) and Reutzel and Cooter (1996). Note that the grid should not be completed during the oral reading (completion is probably not possible in any case), but should be completed *after* the assessment session has been concluded with the student. Miscues should be marked on the passage facsimile during the oral reading, errors totaled, and a decision made (in Part III) as to whether or not to continue the assessment.

Miscues and Coding for Passages

- *Mispronunciation*

  Student incorrectly pronounces a word. Mispronunciations typically are non-words. Write the incorrect pronunciation above the word on the protocol.

  Student: *"The deg ran away."*

  Notation: The dȯg ran away.

- *Substitution*

  Student substitutes a real word or words for a word in the text. Draw a line through the word and write what the student said above it.

  Student: *"The tree was very high."*

  Notation: The ~~cloud~~ Tree was very high.

- *Self-correction*

  Student corrects a miscue himself. Self-corrections are noted by writing "SC," but should not be counted as errors in the final tally, unless the student never correctly pronounces the word.

Student: *"The money . . . the monkey was funny."*

Notation: The mo͡nkey was funny. [*SC* circled above "mo"]

- *Insertion*

  A word is added that is *not* in the text. An insertion symbol (^) is recorded between the two appropriate words, and the inserted word is written above the insertion symbol.

  Student: *He'll want to have a look in the mirror.*

  Notation: He'll want to ˄look in the mirror. [*have a* written above the ^]

- *Teacher assistance*

  The student is "stuck" on a word and the teacher pronounces it. Record the incident as "TA" (teacher-assisted). This error is also counted when the student asks for help during silent reading.

  Notation: auto͡mobile [*TA* circled above]

- *Repetition*

  The student repeats a word or series of words. A repetition is recorded by underlining the word(s) repeated. This category is recorded as additional observational data but *does not* figure in the determination of whether to continue testing or not. Therefore, in determining the number of miscues a student makes on a passage, repetitions are not a part of the final tally.

  Student: *The boy wanted to wanted to go to the show.*

  Notation: The boy <u>wanted to</u> go to the show.

- *Omission*

  If no word (or words) is given, the error is noted by circling the word(s) omitted on the protocol.

  Notation: The cloud was (very) high. ["very" circled]

- *Meaning disruption: A special consideration*

  Working with students, we have observed that some miscues are much more disruptive to comprehension than others. For instance, insertions often do not significantly alter reading comprehension, but mispronunciations typically do. Thus, we have included a Meaning Disruptions column on the Miscue Grid to encourage examiners to reflect on the severity of each miscue as it pertains to reading comprehension. Note that this is *not a miscue type;* rather, it is a point for the examiner to determine whether each miscue adversely affects the student's comprehension. If it does, a mark should be placed in this column to alert you that the student may be word calling rather than attending to the message of the passage. As you summarize a student's performance and begin to make instructional decisions about the student's needs, this column should provide you with additional information related to reading comprehension.

Oral reading miscues should be noted on the passage facsimile as the student is reading. We recommend that the student's voice also be tape recorded during the retelling and oral reading to allow for convenient review at a later time, and to establish permanent audio records of the child's reading development. As noted, miscue grids should be completed after the assessment session with the child has been concluded.

Interpreting Miscues on the Flynt–Cooter **EERIC**

After you have administered the oral reading section of the *English–Español Reading Inventory for the Classroom* and scored the grid, you will want to make some preliminary judgments about the student's instructional needs. Always remember that no single assessment procedure is adequate by itself and the *EERIC* is only a starting point. Teachers should look for *patterns* of behavior, not isolated occurrences. Do not assume that because a student makes a certain kind of error once that it is in fact a problem for her.

In order to provide some examples of how you can use miscue patterns as guides to instruction, we have included Table 1 on the following page. It describes a few common miscue types we have encountered with children, along with strategies that may be used to teach to demonstrated needs as described by Reutzel and Cooter (1996) in *Teaching Children to Read: From Basals to Books,* and Cooter and Flynt (1996) in *Teaching Reading in the Content Areas.* Here is a list of these books and other references offering intervention strategies:

Recommended Books Containing Reading Intervention Strategies

Cooter, R. B., & Flynt, E. S. (1996). *Teaching reading in the content areas.* Upper Saddle River, NJ: Merrill/Prentice Hall.

Reutzel, D. R., & Cooter, R. B. (1996). *Teaching children to read: From basals to books* (2nd Ed.). Upper Saddle River, NJ: Merrill/Prentice Hall.

Reutzel, D. R., & Cooter, R. B. (1999). *Balanced reading strategies and practices: Assessing and assisting readers with special needs.* Upper Saddle River, NJ: Merrill/Prentice Hall.

Yopp, R. H., & Yopp, H. K. (1992). *Literature-based reading activities.* Boston: Allyn & Bacon.

Part III: Developmental/Performance Summary

This section helps examiners determine whether or not to continue testing and identify the reading placement level. For silent reading comprehension and oral reading accuracy a three-tier system is used. In each case the examiner decides whether the passage appeared to be *easy, adequate,* or *too hard* for the student. These descriptors are based on the work of Powell (1969) and Betts (1946). *Easy* means that the passage can be read with few errors and the student requires no additional assistance from others in reading similar texts. The easy level is comparable to the independent reading level designation used in traditional informal reading inventories. *Adequate* means that students can read the passage effectively, but will likely require some help from another person to successfully comprehend the passage. The adequate level is comparable to the instructional designation used in traditional informal reading inventories. *Too hard* means that the passage difficulty is sufficient to cause the reader much anxiety and frustration. This level is sometimes called the frustration level in traditional inventories. We have used the designations easy, adequate, and too hard because we feel they describe the student's performance in simple terms that can be easily discussed with parents. **A student who scores at the too hard level in Silent Reading Comprehension should not proceed to any higher level passage.** Placement in reading material should be at the level just below the passage receiving a too hard judgment. Thus if a student first reaches a too hard score on Level 5 Silent Reading Comprehension, reading placement level for instructional purposes should be Level 4.

Part IV: Listening Comprehension

Having students listen to a passage and then respond to questions about it is a traditional method used by some reading specialists to estimate a student's listening comprehension level or reading capacity. According to some authorities (Durrell, 1969; Carroll, 1977; and Sinatra, 1990), establishing a student's listening comprehension level provides an indication

TABLE 1 Selected common miscues and intervention strategies.

MISCUE TYPE	EXAMPLES FROM THE FLYNT–COOTER *EERIC*	PROBLEM DESCRIPTION	POSSIBLE INTERVENTIONS
Mispronunciations (or possibly a substitution) **of Ending Sounds**	**Text:** *familiar* **Student reads as:** *family* or *famsom*	Student is decoding the first and middle part of the word, but not the ending.	If the student calls the word another word that doesn't make sense, then he is not using context clues. We suggest using story frames, discussion webs, or cloze/maze passages to emphasize the role of context in word identification (see Reutzel & Cooter, 1996).
Substitutions: Wrong Sounds	**Text:** *shoes* **Student reads as:** *feet*	Student reads as another word that fits the context, but not the correct word/ letter sounds.	In this case, the student is ready to learn the basic word identification strategy (Reutzel & Cooter, 1996): Context Clues + beginning sound(s) + medial sounds. Using enlarged text with stick-on notes revealing only the word parts you wish to emphasize (e.g., beginning sound), is a great way to model and practice.
Mispronunciations: No Use of Context	**Text:** *through* **Student reads as:** *primly*	Student is making up nonsense words without regard to the context of the passage.	This indicates that the student may not realize that reading is a meaning-based language activity. Cooter & Flynt (1996) recommend the guided listening procedure and lookback organizers. These strategies are equally useful with expository reading.
Self-corrections	**Text:** *loved* **Student reads as:** *lived, loved*	Student miscues on a word, then spontaneously self-corrects.	Self-corrections do not usually require intervention, but rather praise for reading strategically.
Insertions	**Text:** *Others who couldn't . . .* **Student reads as:** *Others who really couldn't . . .*	Student inserts words not actually in the text—a problem related to reading fluency.	Reutzel & Cooter (1996) recommend repeated readings, dialogue retellings, and student dramas as strategies that have students focus on accuracy.
Teacher assists	**Text:** *any text* **Student reads as:** *No response from student*	Teacher must say word(s) for the student.	Teachers should supply unknown words after about 5 seconds to preserve student's short-term memory of the sentence. If this happens frequently, then the passage may be too difficult or the student may not have learned the word identification strategy mentioned above.
Omissions	**Text:** *Some like ice cream, while others prefer soda.* **Student reads as:** *Some like ice cream, others prefer soda.*	Student leaves out a word(s) in the text.	This is usually a minor problem with accuracy or reading—a fluency type of miscue. See "Insertions" above for fluency strategies. (Note: Sometimes omissions are the result of a regional or cultural dialect.)

of a student's reading capacity. Reading capacity refers to the level a student has the potential of reaching if she receives appropriate reading experiences and instruction. The following details how one establishes a student's listening comprehension level using the *EERIC*. The listening comprehension section does not appear in the Spanish portion.

Once a student has reached the too hard level on silent reading comprehension, you can establish the student's listening comprehension level. Begin by using the passage that reached the too hard level criteria for your student in silent reading. Tell the student that now you are going to read a story to him. Encourage the student to listen carefully because you are going to ask him some questions when you are finished reading. Using the background statement for the passage, read the passage out loud to the student. When you finish reading the passage, ask each of the questions provided for the passage. A student who can answer 75% or more of the questions has adequate listening comprehension. Continue reading higher level passages to the student until he falls below the 75% criterion. The highest level to which the student can respond to 75% of the questions correctly is considered to be that student's listening comprehension level. This level could also indicate that student's reading capacity. However, you should be cautioned that this information should be coupled with careful observation of the student in the testing session as well as his performance in the classroom.

STEP 4: COMPLETING THE STUDENT SUMMARY

Immediately following the scored student sample is a copy of the *EERIC* Student Summary. Like other sections of this inventory, it may be duplicated by examiners for classroom assessment use. Examiners should complete this summary after the assessment session(s) has been completed in order to gather information and begin to develop initial classroom intervention plans, should they be necessary.

The *EERIC* is only a starting point in the assessment and intervention process. We encourage teachers and examiners embarking on intervention programs to begin with what students know, in order to continue sampling and gathering data about the student's reading abilities. This is what Marie Clay (1985) refers to as "roaming around the known." Clay suggests a two-week period of roaming around the known in her Reading Recovery Programme, the equivalent of about five hours spread over two weeks. This kind of continuing assessment, when used in conjunction with the *EERIC*, yields rich descriptive information about the student. As stated in the final section of the Student Summary, we feel that this process should help the teacher and examiner learn more about the student's reading abilities, confirm or reject initial findings drawn from this inventory, and discover ways of helping students continue to grow as successful readers.

INSTRUCTIONS FOR ADMINISTERING
THE PREPRIMER (PP) AND PRIMER (P) PASSAGES

Passages for emergent readers in Forms A and B of the *EERIC* have been given the conventional labels of Preprimer (PP) and Primer (P), but reflect a much more balanced view of early reading processes. We have drawn on recent research in emergent literacy (Clay, 1985; Sulzby, 1985, 1987; Morrow, 1993; Adams, 1994) to develop passages and procedures that can be used in beginning assessment in elementary classrooms. While information gained from administering these passages can be useful to teachers early in the school year and for periodic assessments, we feel that regular student–teacher interactions using authentic storybooks are necessary for more complete assessment profiles.

In developing these passages we have considered carefully the research of Cochrane and others (1984) and Sulzby (1985), who have attempted to chronicle the observable emergent reading developmental "milestones." To assist in the assessment of emergent readers, we have created checklists for the PP and P levels based on research findings in emergent literacy. The stages we have developed are listed on the following page.

Stage 1: Early Connections to Reading—Describing Pictures

- Attends to and describes (labels) pictures in books
- Has a limited sense of story
- Follows verbal directions for this activity
- Uses oral vocabulary appropriate for age/grade level
- Displays attention span appropriate for age/grade level
- Responds to questions in an appropriate manner
- Appears to connect pictures (sees them as being interrelated)

Stage 2: Connecting Pictures to Form a Story

- Attends to pictures and develops oral stories across the pages of the book
- Uses only childlike or descriptive (storyteller) language to tell the story, rather than book language (e.g., Once upon a time...; There once was a little boy...)

Stage 3: Transitional Picture Reading

- Attends to pictures as a connected story
- Mixes storyteller language with book language

Stage 4: Advanced Picture Reading

- Attends to pictures and develops oral stories across the pages of the book
- Speaks as though reading the story (uses book language)

Stage 5: Early Print Reading

- Tells a story using the pictures
- Knows print moves from left to right, top to bottom
- Creates part of the text using book language and knows some words on sight

Stage 6: Early Strategic Reading

- Uses context to guess at some unknown words (guesses make sense)
- Notices beginning sounds in words and uses them in guessing unknown words
- Seems to sometimes use syntax to help identify words in print
- Recognizes some word parts, such as root words and affixes

Stage 7: Moderate Strategic Reading

- Sometimes uses context and word parts to decode words
- Self-corrects when making an oral reading miscue
- Retells the passage easily and may embellish the storyline
- Shows some awareness of vowel sounds

In attempting to provide passages at emergent reading levels that correspond in some meaningful way with current knowledge of emergent literacy, we chose a simple but informative format. At the Preprimer (PP) level, we have provided a wordless picture book format. In each case there is a series of four illustrations that tell a story when read or retold sequentially. This format will enable examiners to learn whether the student has progressed through the first three or four stages of emergent reading as just outlined. Passages at the Primer (P) level also use the four-illustration format but include predictable text that tells the story. These passages enable the examiner to gain additional insights into the more advanced emergent reading stages outlined above.

We recommend that examiners begin with these passages if the student's performance on the placement sentences (see the following instructions) suggests that the Level 1 passages may be too difficult. Explain to students at both the PP and P levels that the four pictures tell a story. Ask the student to look at all four pictures first then retell the story by "reading" the pictures. We recommend that you transcribe the student's reading for later analysis. A tape recording of the session is quite helpful since you will probably have difficulty transcribing all that is said. If a student seems unable to tell a story from the pictures, ask the student to describe each picture. This will provide some insights into vocabulary knowledge, oral language skills, and whether a sense of story is developing. Further directions for administering Level PP and P passages and completing accompanying checklists are included with the assessment protocol forms (A & B) for each passage.

If the Student Cannot Read the Primer Level (P) Passage Adequately on the First Attempt . . . Then What?

Sometimes students making the developmental transition from advanced picture reading to early print reading are able to memorize text easily and repeat it verbatim, or nearly so. This sets up the opportunity for teaching them about one-to-one correspondence between spoken and written words and sounds. Therefore, if a student is unable to adequately read a passage aloud the first time, the examiner should read it aloud and then ask the student to try reading it again. If the student is able to do so, the examiner may assume that the student is transitioning into the early print reading stage. This would be a logical stopping point for the assessment.

INSTRUCTIONS FOR ADMINISTERING THE FORM D (FORMA D) PASSAGES

Form D passages are designed for students who read above the ninth-grade level. Each level (10, 11, 12) corresponds to that level of sophistication associated with high school reading. All three passages are expository in nature and are administered similarly to Form C passages. The one difference we recommend is that students not be required to read a portion of the passage orally. We believe that the oral reading skills of students in the 10th grade and above do not offer insightful assessment data. Rather, we believe that silent reading comprehension is the most important variable to be assessed at these levels. For those individuals who want to assess oral reading at these levels, however, we have provided a Miscue Grid for each passage. Assessment of oral reading using this grid follows the guidelines discussed earlier.

SELECTED REFERENCES

Adams, M. J. (1994). *Beginning to read.* Cambridge, MA: MIT Press.

Betts, E. A. (1946). *Foundation of reading instruction.* New York: Academic Book Company.

Burke, C. (1987). Burke reading interview. In Y. Goodman, D. Watson, & C. Burke (Eds.), *Reading miscue inventory: Alternative procedures.* New York: Richard C. Owen.

Clay, M. M. (1985). *The early detection of reading difficulties* (3rd ed.). Auckland, New Zealand: Heinemann Educational Books, Inc.

Cochrane, O., Cochrane, D., Scalena, D., & Buchanan, E. (1984). *Reading, writing, and caring.* New York: Richard C. Owen.

Farr, R., & Tone, B. (1994). *Portfolio and performance assessment.* Fort Worth: Harcourt Brace.

Freeman, Y. S, & Freeman, D. (1994). *Between worlds: Access to second language acquisition.* Portsmouth, NH: Heinemann.

Fry, E. (1968). Readability formula that saves time. *Journal of Reading, 11,* 513–516, 575–578.

Goodman, K. S. (1969). Analysis of oral reading miscues: Applied psycholinguistics. *Reading Research Quarterly, 5,* 9–30.

Harris, A. J., & Jacobson, M. D. (1975). The Harris–Jacobson readability formulas. In A. J. Harris & E. R. Sipay (Eds.), *How to increase reading ability* (pp. 712–729). New York: Longman, Inc.

Hill, B. C., & Ruptic, C. (1994). *Practical aspects of authentic assessment: Putting the pieces together.* Norwood, MA: Christopher-Gordon.

Holdaway, D. (1979). *Foundations of literacy.* Sydney: Ashton Scholastic.

Meyer, B. J. F., & Freedle, R. O. (1984). Effects of discourse type on recall. *American Educational Research Journal, 21*(1), 121–143.

Morrow, L. M. (1993). *Literacy development in the early years* (2nd ed.). Boston: Allyn and Bacon.

Newman, J. M. (Ed.). (1985). *Whole language: Theory in use.* Portsmouth, NH: Heinemann Educational Books, Inc.

Piaget, J. (1955). *The language and thought of the child.* New York: World.

Powell, W. R. (1969). Reappraising the criteria for interpreting informal inventories. In D. DeBoer (Ed.), *Reading diagnosis and evaluation* (pp. 100–109). Newark, DE: International Reading Association.

Puckett, M. B., & Black, J. K. (1994). *Authentic assessment of the young child.* Upper Saddle River, NJ: Merrill/Prentice Hall.

Reutzel, D. R., & Cooter, R. B. (1999). *Balanced reading strategies and practices: Assessing and assisting readers with special needs.* Upper Saddle River, NJ: Merrill/Prentice Hall.

Reutzel, D. R., & Cooter, R. B. (1996). *Teaching children to read: From basals to books* (2nd Ed.). Upper Saddle River, NJ: Merrill/Prentice Hall.

Rhodes, L. K., & Dudley-Marling, C. (1988). *Readers and writers with a difference.* Portsmouth, NH: Heinemann Educational Books, Inc.

Rosenblatt, L. M. (1978). *The reader, the text, and the poem.* Carbondale, IL: Southern Illinois University Press.

Smith, F. (1982). *Writing and the writer.* New York: Holt, Rinehart & Winston.

Sulzby, E. (1985). Children's emergent reading of favorite storybooks. *Reading Research Quarterly, 20,* 458–481.

Sulzby, E. (1987). *Simplified version of Sulzby's (1985) classification scheme for "Children's emergent reading of favorite storybooks."* Paper presented at the International Reading Association Conference, Anaheim, CA.

Sulzby, E. (1991). Assessment of emergent literacy: Storybook reading. *The Reading Teacher, 44*(7), 498–500.

Valencia, S., & Pearson, P. D. (1987). Reading assessment: Time for a change. *The Reading Teacher, 40*(8), 726–733.

SCORED STUDENT EXAMPLE

(pages 16–20)

The following pages provide an example of a completed student assessment. This particular example is based on the Level 5 passage found in Form A.

Hot Shoes (325 words)

PART I: SILENT READING COMPREHENSION

Background Statement: "This story is about how one group of boys feel about their athletic shoes. Read this story to find out how important special shoes are to playing sports. Read it carefully because I will ask you to tell me about it when you finish."

Teacher Directions: Once the student completes the silent reading, say, "Tell me about the story you just read." Answers to the questions below that the student provides during the retelling should be marked "ua" in the appropriate blank to indicate that this response was unaided. Ask all remaining questions not addressed during the retelling and mark those the student answers with an "a" to indicate that the correct response was given after prompting by the teacher.

Questions/Answers	*Story Grammar Element/ Level of Comprehension*
_____ 1. Where did the story take place? *(I. B. Belcher Elementary School or at a school)*	setting/literal I don't remember.
_ua_ 2. Who were the two main characters in the story? *(Jamie Lee and Josh Kidder)*	character-characterization/ literal Josh and Jamie
_a +_ 3. What was the problem between Jamie and Josh? *(Jamie didn't think Josh could be a good player because of his shoes, Josh didn't fit in, or other plausible response)*	story problem(s)/inferential Jamie didn't like Josh because he had old shoes and was different.
_____ 4. How did Josh solve his problem with the other boys? *(he outplayed all of them)*	problem resolution/ inferential He ignored them.
_____ 5. What kind of person was Jamie Lee? *(conceited, stuck-up, or other plausible responses)*	character-characterization/ evaluative Tall ... a big Tall boy
_ua_ 6. What happened after the game? *(the other boys gathered around and asked Josh his secret)*	problem resolution attempts/ literal Everyone wanted To know how Josh learned To play so good.
_a_ 7. Why did everyone laugh when Josh said, "Two things—lots of practice and cheap shoes"? *(because everything had happened because of his cheap shoes)*	problem resolution attempts/ inferential IT was funny. Because he played good even with lousy shoes.
_____ 8. What lesson does this story teach? *(responses will vary but should indicate a theme/moral related to "it's not what you wear that makes you good in a sport")*	theme/evaluative Josh was better than Jamie.

PART II: ORAL READING AND ANALYSIS OF MISCUES

Directions: Say, "Now I would like to hear you read this story out loud." Have the student read orally until the 100-word sample is completed. Follow along on the Miscue Grid, marking any oral reading errors as appropriate. *Remember to count miscues only up to the point in the story containing the oral reading stop-marker (//).* Then complete the Developmental/Performance Summary to determine whether to continue the assessment. (*Note:* The Miscue Grid should be completed *after* the assessment session has been concluded in order to minimize stress for the student.)

16   Scored Student Example

	MIS-PRONUN.	SUB-STITUTION	OMISSION	INSERTION	TCHR. ASSIST.	SELF-CORRECT.	MEANING DISRUPTION
Hot Shoes							
The guys at (the) I. B. Belcher			\				
Elementary School ~~loved~~ lived (sc) all the		\				\	
new sport shoes. Some ~~wore~~ wib the	\						\
"Sky High" model by Leader.							
Others who ^really couldn't ~~afford~~ buy Sky		\		\			
Highs would settle for a lesser							
shoe. Some ~~liked~~ have the "Street		\					\
Smarts" by Master, or (the)			\				
"Uptown-Downtown^s" by Beebop.				\			
The Belcher boys ~~got~~ get to the point		\					
with their shoes that they could							
~~identify~~ impea their friends just by	\						\
looking at their ~~feet~~ shoes (sc). But the boy		\				\	
who was the ~~envy~~ every of the entire fifth		\					\
grade was Jamie Lee. He had a							
pair of "High Five Pump 'em Ups"							
by Superior. The only thing Belcher							
boys loved as // *much as their*							
shoes was basketball.							
TOTALS	2	6	2	2	—	2	4

Notes:

The Total number of miscues is 12, not counting
The 2 self-corrections.

Examiner's Summary of Miscue Patterns:

The student had several repetitions and substitutions.
This might indicate he is using context to search for meaning.

PART III: DEVELOPMENTAL/PERFORMANCE SUMMARY

Silent Reading Comprehension

_____ 0–1 questions missed = Easy

_____ 2 questions missed = Adequate

✓ 3+ questions missed = Too hard

Continue to next assessment level passage? _____ Yes ✓ No

Oral Reading Accuracy

_____ 0–1 oral errors = Easy

_____ 2–5 oral errors = Adequate

✓ 6+ oral errors = Too hard

PART IV: LISTENING COMPREHENSION

Directions: If you have decided not to continue to have the student read any other passages, then use this passage to begin assessing the student's listening comprehension (see page 8). Begin by reading the background statement for this passage and then say, "I am going to read this story to you. Please listen carefully because I will be asking you some questions after I finish reading it to you." After reading the passage, ask the student the questions associated with the passage. If the student correctly answers more than six questions, you will need to move to the next level and repeat the procedure.

Listening Comprehension

_____ 0–2 questions missed = move to the next passage level

_____ more than two questions missed = stop assessment or move down a level

Examiner's Notes:

Very tough passage. Unaided recall was limited and he only
included the characters and the story problem. He couldn't remember
very much of the story. Every question required probing. He
doesn't seem to understand the concept of "Theme."

Student Summary

Student's Name: ___Frank Zeron___

Examiner: _____ Date: _____

Form(s) Used: (A)   B   C   D

PERFORMANCE LEVELS ON SENTENCES FOR INITIAL PASSAGE SELECTION

_____ _____ Highest level with zero (0) errors

_____ _____ First level with two (2) or more errors

OVERALL PERFORMANCE ON READING PASSAGES

_____ _____ Easy reading level (independent)

_____ _____ Adequate reading level (instructional)

_____ _____ Too hard reading level (frustration)

MISCUE SUMMARY CHART

	MISPRONUNCIATION	SUBSTITUTION	INSERTION	TEACHER ASSISTANCE	OMISSION	TOTALS
TOTALS	2	6	2	0	2	12
SELF-CORRECTION (no meaning disruption)	0	2	0	0	0	2
MEANING DISRUPTIONS	2	2	0	0	0	4

COMPREHENSION RESPONSE SUMMARY CHARTS

Narrative Passages (Forms A and B)

STORY GRAMMAR ELEMENT	UNAIDED RECALL	AIDED RECALL	NUMBER NOT RECALLED	% RECALLED
CHARACTER CHARACTERIZATION	1	—	1	50
SETTING	—	—	1	0
STORY PROBLEM	1	—	—	100
PROBLEM RESOLUTION ATTEMPT	—	2	—	100
RESOLUTION	—	—	1	0
THEME/MORAL	—	—	1	0

Expository Passages (Forms C and D)

EXPOSITORY GRAMMAR ELEMENT	UNAIDED RECALL	AIDED RECALL	NUMBER NOT RECALLED	% RECALLED
COLLECTIVE				
CAUSATIVE				
DESCRIPTIVE				
COMPARISON				
PROBLEM RESOLUTION				

SUMMARY TABLE OF PERCENTAGES

PASSAGE LEVEL	SILENT READING COMPREHENSION	ORAL READING ACCURACY
1		
2		
3		
4		
5	50% 4/8	90%
6		
7		
8		
9		
10		
11		
12		

LISTENING COMPREHENSION

HIGHEST LEVEL ACHIEVED 75%	6

THE ENGLISH PORTION
OF THE EERIC

Student Summary

Student's Name: _____

Examiner: _____ Date: _____

Form(s) Used: A B C D

PERFORMANCE LEVELS ON SENTENCES FOR INITIAL PASSAGE SELECTION

_____ _____ Highest level with zero (0) errors

_____ _____ First level with two (2) or more errors

OVERALL PERFORMANCE ON READING PASSAGES

_____ _____ Easy reading level (independent)

_____ _____ Adequate reading level (instructional)

_____ _____ Too hard reading level (frustration)

MISCUE SUMMARY CHART

	MISPRONUNCIATION	SUBSTITUTION	INSERTION	TEACHER ASSISTANCE	OMISSION	TOTALS
TOTALS						
SELF-CORRECTION (no meaning disruption)						
MEANING DISRUPTIONS						

COMPREHENSION RESPONSE SUMMARY CHARTS

Narrative Passages (Forms A and B)

STORY GRAMMAR ELEMENT	UNAIDED RECALL	AIDED RECALL	NUMBER NOT RECALLED	% RECALLED
CHARACTER CHARACTERIZATION				
SETTING				
STORY PROBLEM				
PROBLEM RESOLUTION ATTEMPT				
RESOLUTION				
THEME/MORAL				

Expository Passages (Forms C and D)

EXPOSITORY GRAMMAR ELEMENT	UNAIDED RECALL	AIDED RECALL	NUMBER NOT RECALLED	% RECALLED
COLLECTIVE				
CAUSATIVE				
DESCRIPTIVE				
COMPARISON				
PROBLEM RESOLUTION				

SUMMARY TABLE OF PERCENTAGES

PASSAGE LEVEL	SILENT READING COMPREHENSION	ORAL READING ACCURACY
1		
2		
3		
4		
5		
6		
7		
8		
9		
10		
11		
12		

LISTENING COMPREHENSION

HIGHEST LEVEL ACHIEVED 75%	

Briefly describe what you discovered about the student in the Interest/Attitude Interview.

ORAL READING SKILLS

Directions: Place an **X** by the characteristic(s) evident during this assessment.

_____ Reads in phrases (not word by word)	_____ Word-by-word reader
_____ Reads with expression	_____ Reads with little expression
_____ Attends to punctuation	_____ Ignores punctuation
_____ Uses word identification strategies	_____ Weak word identification ability
_____ Has few repetitions	_____ Has lots of repetitions

SUMMARY OF ABILITIES AND NEEDS IN *ORAL READING*

SUMMARY OF ABILITIES AND NEEDS IN *READING COMPREHENSION*

Directions: Include all information related to retellings, question/story grammar types, and use of comprehension strategies.

FIRST INTERVENTION STRATEGIES

Directions: Describe any intervention/teaching strategies you feel should be tried initially. These strategies should help you learn more about the student's reading abilities and confirm or reject findings drawn from this inventory and should also help the student continue to grow as a successful reader. Please see the table on page 9 for strategies.

Interest/Attitude Interview

PRIMARY FORM

Student's Name: _____ Age: _____

Date: _____ Examiner: _____

Introductory Statement: [*Student's name*], *before you read some stories for me I would like to ask you some questions.*

Home Life

1. Where do you live? Do you know your address? What is it?

2. Who lives in your house with you?

3. What kinds of jobs do you have at home?

4. What is one thing that you really like to do at home?

5. Do you ever read at home? [*If yes, ask:*] When do you read and what was the last thing you read? [*If no, ask:*] Does anyone ever read to you? [*If so, ask:*] Who, and how often?

6. Do you have a bedtime on school nights? [*If no, ask:*] When do you go to bed?

7. Do you have a TV in your room? How much TV do you watch every day? What are your favorite shows?

8. What do you like to do with your friends?

9. Do you have any pets? Do you collect things? Do you take any kinds of lessons?

10. When you make a new friend, what is something that your friend ought to know about you?

School Life

1. Besides recess and lunch, what do you like about school?

2. Do you get to read much in school?

3. Are you a good reader or a not-so-good reader?

   [*If a good reader, ask:*] What makes a person a good reader?

   [*If a not-so-good reader, ask:*] What causes a person to not be a good reader?

4. If you could pick any book to read, what would the book be about?

5. Do you like to write? What kind of writing do you do in school? What is the favorite thing you have written about?

6. Who has helped you the most in school? How did that person help you?

7. Do you have a place at home to study?

8. Do you get help with your homework? Who helps you?

9. What was the last book you read for school?

10. If you were helping someone learn to read, what could you do to help that person?

Interest/Attitude Interview

UPPER LEVEL FORM

Student's Name: _____ Age: _____

Date: _____ Examiner: _____

Introductory Statement: [*Student's name*], *before you read some stories for me I would like to ask you some questions.*

Home Life

1. How many people are there in your family?

2. Do you have your own room or do you share a room? [*Ask this only if it is apparent that the student has siblings.*]

3. Do your parent(s) work? What kinds of jobs do they have?

4. Do you have jobs around the house? What are they?

5. What do you usually do after school?

6. Do you have a TV in your room? How much time do you spend watching TV each day? What are your favorite shows?

7. Do you have a bedtime during the week? What time do you usually go to bed on a school night?

8. Do you get an allowance? How much?

9. Do you belong to any clubs at school or outside school? What are they?

10. What are some things that you really like to do? Do you collect things, have any hobbies, or take lessons outside school?

School Environment

1. Do you like school? What is your favorite class? Your least favorite class?

2. Do you have a special place to study at home?

3. How much homework do you have on a typical school night? Does anyone help you with your homework? Who?

4. Do you consider yourself a good reader or a not-so-good reader?

   [*If a good reader, ask:*] What has helped you most to become a good reader?

   [*If a not-so-good reader, ask:*] What causes someone to be a not-so-good reader?

5. If I gave you the choice of selecting a book about any topic, what would you choose to read about?

6. What is one thing you can think of that would help you become a better reader? Is there anything else?

7. Do you like to write? What kind of writing assignments do you like best?

8. If you went to a new school, what is one thing that you would want the teachers to know about you as a student?

9. If you were helping someone learn to read, what would be the most important thing you could do to help that person?

10. How will knowing how to read help you in the future?

SENTENCES FOR INITIAL
PASSAGE SELECTION........form **A**

FORM A: LEVEL 1

1. He wanted to fly.

2. The family got together.

3. The boy was jumping.

FORM A: LEVEL 2

1. I was walking fast to town.

2. She cried about going home.

3. I was pulled out of the hole.

FORM A: LEVEL 3

1. The forest was something to see.

2. I was enjoying sleeping when my Mom called.

3. I had to go to bed early last night.

FORM A: LEVEL 4

1. I dislike being the youngest.

2. I'm always getting into trouble.

3. They insisted on watching the show daily.

FORM A: LEVEL 5

1. Athletic shoes come in all kinds of colors.

2. Serious players manage to practice a lot.

3. A cheap pair of shoes doesn't last very long.

FORM A: LEVEL 6

1. He was searching for the evidence.

2. She realized the rock formations were too high.

3. The conservationist hoped to reforest the mountain.

FORM A: LEVEL 7

1. Unfortunately she was confused about the next activity.

2. The submerged rocks were dangerous.

3. She disappeared around the bend at a rapid rate.

FORM A: LEVEL 8

1. Ascending the mountain was rigorous and hazardous.

2. The cliff provided a panoramic view of the valley.

3. The incubation period lasted two weeks.

FORM A: LEVEL 9

1. The abduction made everyone suspicious.

2. The detective was besieged by the community.

3. Her pasty complexion made her look older.

NARRATIVE PASSAGES .... form A

1 I went swimming.

2 My dog jumped in the pool.

3 My friends came over and jumped in the pool too.

4 We had a great time swimming.

You Cannot Fly!

Once a boy named Sam wanted to fly.

His mother and father said, "You cannot fly."

His sister said, "You cannot fly."

Sam tried jumping off a box.

He tried jumping off his bed.

He fell down each time.

Sam still tried hard but he still could not fly.

Then one day a letter came for Sam.

The letter said, "Come and see me, Sam, on the next airplane."

It was from his grandfather.

Sam went to his family and read the letter.

Sam said, "Now I can fly."

Sam and his family all laughed together.

The Pig and the Snake

One day Mr. Pig was walking to town.

He saw a big hole in the road.

A big snake was in the hole.

"Help me," said the snake, "and I will be your friend."

"No, no," said Mr. Pig. "If I help you get out you will bite me. You are a snake!"

The snake cried and cried.

So Mr. Pig pulled the snake out of the hole.

Then the snake said, "Now I am going to bite you, Mr. Pig."

"How can you bite me after I helped you out of the hole?" said Mr. Pig.

The snake said, "You knew I was a snake when you pulled me out!"

The Big Bad Wolf

One day Mr. Wolf was walking through the forest. He was enjoying an afternoon walk and not bothering anyone. All of a sudden it started to rain and he became wet and cold.

Just when Mr. Wolf was about to freeze to death, he saw a small house in the woods. Smoke was coming from the chimney, so he knocked on the door. No one was home, but a note on the door said:

Come in and make yourself warm. I'll be back about 2:00 p.m.

> *Love,*
>
> *Granny*

The poor wet wolf came in and began to warm himself by the fire. He saw one of Granny's nightgowns on the bed, so he decided to put it on instead of his wet clothes. Since he was still very, very cold he decided to get into Granny's bed. Soon he was fast asleep.

Mr. Wolf fell into a deep sleep. When he awoke, Mr. Wolf found an old woman, a little girl wearing a red coat, and a woodcutter standing around the bed. The woodcutter was yelling at Mr. Wolf and saying something about how he was going to kill him with his axe. Mr. Wolf jumped out of the bed and ran for his life.

Later that day, Mr. Wolf was finally safe at home. His wife said, "Just you wait, those humans will make up a story about how big and bad *you* were."

New Clothes

Bobby was the youngest member of his family. He didn't like being the youngest because he couldn't stay up late and watch television. Most of all, he disliked having to wear hand me down clothes from his brother.

One day Bobby went to his mother and said, "Mom, I'm tired of wearing Brad's clothes. Why can't I have some more new clothes this school year?"

His mother replied, "Bobby, you know we can't afford to buy even more new clothes. You should be happy with the new clothes we have already bought. Besides, most of Brad's clothes are just like new."

As Bobby walked away, his mother said, "Bobby, if you can find a way to earn some money, I'll see what I can do to help you get what you want."

Bobby thought and thought. Finally, an idea hit him. Brad and his sister, Sara, had part-time jobs, and they didn't always have time to do their work around the house. What if he did some of their work for a small fee?

Bobby approached Brad and Sara about his idea. They liked his idea and agreed to pay Bobby for cleaning their rooms and making their beds.

As Bobby turned to leave the room, Sara said, "Bobby, do a good job or we will have to cut back how much we pay you."

Bobby took care of his brother's and sister's rooms for four weeks. Finally on the last Saturday before school started, Bobby's mom took him to the mall. Bobby got to pick out a cool pair of baggy jeans and a new shirt. On the first day of school, Bobby felt proud of his new clothes that he had worked so hard to buy. His mother was even prouder.

Hot Shoes

The guys at the I. B. Belcher Elementary School loved all the new sport shoes. Some wore the "Sky High" model by Leader. Others who couldn't afford Sky Highs would settle for a lesser shoe. Some liked the "Street Smarts" by Master, or the "Uptown-Downtown" by Beebop. The Belcher boys got to the point with their shoes that they could identify their friends just by looking at their feet. But the boy who was the envy of the entire fifth grade was Jamie Lee. He had a pair of "High Five Pump 'em Ups" by Superior. The only thing Belcher boys loved as much as their shoes was basketball. They would lace up their fancy athletic shoes and play basketball all afternoon. Everyone was sure that the shoes helped them jump higher and run faster.

One day a new student showed up on the playground. His name was Josh Kidder, and no one knew him. He lived in the poor part of town and wore a cheap pair of black hightop tennis shoes. They were made by an old fashioned company called White Dot. When Jamie Lee saw Josh's White Dot shoes, he said, "No serious basketball player wears White Dots. Where have you been, Kidder?" Josh said, "Well, I may not have a pair of shoes like yours but I would like to play basketball with you and the other guys."

Jamie Lee and the other boys kind of chuckled and said, "Sure kid, no problem." What happened next is a matter of history now at I. B. Belcher School. Josh ran faster, jumped higher, and scored more points (35 points to be exact) than anybody else that day. Jamie Lee, whom Josh guarded, only managed two points.

When it was all over the boys gathered around Josh. He was the hero of the day. "What's your secret weapon?" asked Randy. Josh just smiled and said, "Two things—lots of practice and cheap shoes." Everyone laughed.

Mountain Fire

One August afternoon Brad and Kevin went tracking with their fathers on Mount Holyoak. Brad's father was a conservationist for the Forest Service and was searching for evidence of cougars. Many people feared that the cougars were extinct on Mount Holyoak. The boys became excited when they found what appeared to be a partial cougar track near a stream. But as the day wore on, no new tracks were found.

After lunch Brad's father sent the boys upstream while he circled west. He told the boys to return to the lunch site in an hour. After about forty-five minutes, the boys found the stream's source and could follow it no more. They decided to search close to the stream before starting back. They saw interesting rock formations, eagles' nests on high ledges and, finally, two fresh cougar footprints. Both boys were very excited until they realized that they no longer could hear the stream. They were lost.

The boys searched an hour or more for the mountain stream, but without success. They were tired, dirty, and getting worried. Brad decided to start a small fire in hopes of his father seeing the smoke. Kevin reminded Brad of the danger of forest fires but finally agreed to help collect the twigs, branches, and brush. The moment Brad struck a match in the extra-dry mountain air and stuck it to the dry tinder, the fire exploded into a large fireball.

In a matter of minutes, trees all around the boys burst into flames. The fire spread quickly up the mountainside. The boys ran downhill as fast as they could.

Before the day was out, hotshot crews, airplanes carrying fire retardants, and bucket-loaded helicopters were on the scene trying to contain the fire. The fire raged for days, however, and by the time it was put out over 45,000 acres of timber had been consumed.

For several years Brad and Kevin spent every spare moment helping to reforest the mountain. One day the forest ranger commented, "Well, boys, it looks like things are about back to normal." Brad looked down at his feet and sadly replied, "Maybe, but no new cougar tracks have been seen since the fire."

The Canoe Trip

Katherine and her family like to spend their vacation camping out. Frequently they go to either Great Smoky Mountains National Park or Yellowstone National Park. Since they have camped out for many years, they have become quite accomplished. Katherine is able to start a fire with flint and steel, build a lean-to for shelter, and find food in the forest on which to live.

Katherine's favorite outdoor activity is canoeing. Although she is quite a good canoer, there is one canoe trip that she'll never forget. It was a canoe trip she took with her family and her friend Amy down the Madison River near West Yellowstone.

Katherine and Amy were in a canoe together following her parents down the river. The early going was fine and they didn't have any major problems. The girls did get confused once or twice in their steering and the boat would go sideways. But after about thirty minutes on the river, Katherine and Amy felt secure about their ability to navigate. Unfortunately their canoe could not keep up with Katherine's parents' canoe because they were carrying all the rations in two coolers. Slowly the lead canoe disappeared around a bend.

When the girls' canoe rounded a bend, not only could they not see the lead canoe but they were heading directly into some rough white water. The rough water was swift and there were a lot of rocks submerged below the surface. The swiftness and rocks were causing problems for the jittery canoe and the two inexperienced girls.

Just as the canoe was about to clear the rough water it struck a large boulder just beneath the surface. Before the girls knew what had happened the canoe had capsized, sending them into the icy cold river. Naturally they had on life jackets so they were not in much danger. But the two coolers full of food and the canoe started floating away from them at a rapid rate.

Katherine managed to grab hold of the canoe and one paddle. Amy swam over to the shore. After much effort both girls managed to pull in the canoe, empty the water, and start downstream after the lost coolers. But since they had only one paddle they limped along, unable to catch up to the now disappeared coolers.

Some forty-five minutes later, feeling cold and upset, the girls rounded a sharp bend in the river. To their surprise they saw the rest of the family sitting on the south-side shore of the river. Katherine's Dad had built a fire and was roasting hot dogs. Katherine's mother and little brother were sitting on the two coolers eating a hot dog and munching on potato chips. Dad said, "What took you two so long? We didn't know you were going to stop and take a swim, but thanks for sending the food on ahead." As cold as they were Katherine and Amy couldn't help but laugh.

The Eagle

There exists an old Native American legend about an eagle who thought he was a chicken. It seems that a Hopi farmer and his only son decided to climb a nearby mountain to observe an eagle's nest. The trip would take them all day, so they brought along some rations and water for the trek. The man and the boy crossed the enormous fields of maize and beans into the foothills. Soon thereafter they were ascending the mountain and the climb became rigorous and hazardous. They occasionally looked back toward their home and at the panoramic view of the entire valley.

Finally the farmer and son reached the mountain's summit. Perched on the highest point on a ledge was the eagle's nest. The farmer reached his hand into the nest after realizing that the mother had gone in search of food. He brought out a most precious prize, an eagle's egg. He tucked it into his tunic and the two descended the mount.

The egg was placed in the nest of a chicken for incubation. It soon hatched. The eaglet grew with the baby chicks and adopted their habits for gathering food in the barnyard; namely, scratching for feed the farmer threw out.

Some time later an Anasazi brave passed through the area and saw this enormous brown eagle scratching and walking about in the barnyard. He dismounted from his horse and went to the farmer. "Why do you have an eagle acting as a chicken? It is not right," queried the noble brave.

"That's no eagle, it's a chicken," retorted the farmer. "Can't you see that it scratches for food with the other chickens? No, it is indeed a chicken," exclaimed the farmer.

"I will show you that this is an eagle," said the brave.

The brave took the eagle on his arm and climbed to the top of the barn. Then saying, "You are an eagle, the most noble of birds. Fly and soar as you were destined!" He threw the eagle from the barn. But the startled eagle fluttered to the ground and began pecking for food.

"See," said the farmer. "I told you it is a chicken."

The brave replied, "I'll show you this is an eagle. It is clear what I must do."

Again the brave took the eagle on his arm and began walking toward the mountain. He climbed all day until he reached a high bluff overlooking the valley. Then the brave, with outstretched arm, held the bird out and said, "You are an eagle, the most noble of birds. Fly and soar as you were destined to."

Just then a mountain breeze washed across the eagle. His eyes brightened as he caught the wild scent of freedom. In a moment the eagle stretched his mighty wings and let out a magnificent screech. Leaping from the brave's arm, he flew high into the western sky.

The eagle saw more of the world in that one great moment than his barnyard friends would discover in a lifetime.

The Case of Angela Violet

Angela Violet was an elderly lady in our neighborhood who some people thought suspicious. She was rarely seen outside her spacious Victorian-styled home, and then only to retrieve the daily mail. Her pasty complexion and ancient dress made her appear like an apparition. Small children in the neighborhood speculated that she might be some sort of witch. It appeared that Miss Violet had no contact with the outside world.

One autumn day news spread through the community that a high school cheerleader, Katrina Bowers, had disappeared. It was feared by the police that Katrina had been abducted. State and local police joined forces with the Federal Bureau of Investigation in the massive search effort. In spite of all the best efforts of the constabulary, no trace of Katrina Bowers was uncovered. After ten days of suspense and worry, the search was called off.

Three weeks after Katrina's apparent abduction a break in the case occurred. An anonymous telephone caller informed the police that Miss Angela Violet had kidnapped Katrina. It was alleged that Miss Violet was holding her captive in her basement. Because of Miss Violet's unusual lifestyle, the police were inclined to give some credence to the tip. A search warrant was issued and the police converged on her house.

Detective Donna Jordan knocked on the shabby door of Miss Violet's residence. Two other officers attended Detective Jordan. Miss Violet showed surprise, but welcomed the police into her home graciously. She consented to having her home searched.

By the time the police had completed their search, two television news trucks had taken position outside her home. When the detectives came out of the house without Miss Violet, the anxious newspeople besieged them with queries.

Detective Jordan stepped forward and calmly said, "What we found was a kindly lady who is caring night and day for her ailing mother. There is no evidence whatsoever that Miss Violet has any involvement in the Katrina Bowers case."

People in the community began to reach out to Miss Violet and her mother from then on. They took food and sat with Miss Violet's mother so she could get out more. As for Katrina Bowers, she was located safe and sound in California with relatives. She had been a runaway case.

EXAMINER'S ASSESSMENT PROTOCOLS

form **A**

 **PREPRIMER (PP) LEVEL ASSESSMENT PROTOCOLS**
The Accident (Wordless picture story)

PART I: WORDLESS PICTURE STORY READING

Background Statement: "These pictures tell a story about a girl and something that happened to her. Look at each picture as I show it to you and think about the story the pictures tell. Later, I will want you to tell me the story using the pictures."

Teacher Directions: Refer the student to each picture slowly and in order as numbered. Do not comment on the pictures. Then repeat the procedure, asking the student to tell the story in the student's own words. Record the student's reading using a tape recorder, and transcribe the reading as it is being dictated. Replay the recording later to make sure that your transcription is accurate and complete.

PART II: EMERGENT READING BEHAVIOR CHECKLIST

Directions: Following are emergent reading behaviors identified through research and grouped according to broad developmental stages. Check all behaviors you have observed. *If the student progresses to Stage 3 or 4, continue your assessment using the Primer Level (P) passage.*

Stage 1: Early Connections to Reading—Describing Pictures

_____ Attends to and describes (labels) pictures in books

_____ Has a limited sense of story

_____ Follows verbal directions for this activity

_____ Uses oral vocabulary appropriate for age/grade level

_____ Displays attention span appropriate for age/grade level

_____ Responds to questions in an appropriate manner

_____ Appears to connect pictures (sees as being interrelated)

Stage 2: Connecting Pictures to Form Story

_____ Attends to pictures and develops oral stories across the pages of the book

_____ Uses only childlike or descriptive (storyteller) language to tell the story, rather than book language (i.e., Once upon a time...; There once was a little boy...)

Stage 3: Transitional Picture Reading

_____ Attends to pictures as a connected story

_____ Mixes storyteller language with book language

Stage 4: Advanced Picture Reading

_____ Attends to pictures and develops oral stories across the pages of the book

_____ Speaks as though reading the story (uses book language)

Examiner's Notes:

form A

PRIMER (P) LEVEL ASSESSMENT PROTOCOLS
Let's Go Swimming (25 words)

PART I: PICTURE STORY READING—ORAL READING AND ANALYSIS OF MISCUES

Background Statement: "This is a story about a child having fun. Let's look at each picture first. Now, read the story to yourself. Later, I will want you to read the story to me."

Teacher Directions: Refer the student to each frame of the story slowly and in order as numbered. Do not read the story or comment on the pictures. After the student has read the story silently, ask the student to read the story aloud. Record the student's reading using a tape recorder, and mark any miscues on the Miscue Grid provided. Following the oral reading, complete the Emergent Reading Behavior Checklist. Assessment information obtained from both the Miscue Grid and the Emergent Reading Behavior Checklist will help you determine whether to continue your assessment. If the student is unable to read the passage independently the first time, read it aloud, then ask the student to try to read the story again. This will help you understand whether the student is able to memorize and repeat text, an important developmental milestone (see the *Instructions for Administering the Preprimer (PP) and Primer (P) Passages* section in the front of this book for more information). The assessment should stop after this activity, if the child is unable to read the text independently. (*Note:* The Miscue Grid should be completed *after* the assessment session has been concluded in order to minimize stress for the student.)

	MIS-PRONUN.	SUB-STITUTION	OMISSION	INSERTION	TCHR. ASSIST.	SELF-CORRECT.	MEANING DISRUPTION
Let's Go Swimming							
I went swimming.							
My dog jumped in the							
pool. My friends came							
over and jumped in							
the pool too. We had							
a great time swimming.							
TOTALS							

Notes:

PART II: EMERGENT READING BEHAVIOR CHECKLIST

Directions: Following are emergent reading behaviors identified through research and grouped according to broad developmental stages. After the student has completed the oral reading, check each behavior observed below to help determine development level and whether to continue the assessment. *If the student seems to be at Stage 6 or 7 and the oral reading scored at an Easy or Adequate level, continue the assessment using the Level 1 passage.*

Stage 5: Early Print Reading

_____ Tells a story using the pictures

_____ Knows print moves from left to right, top to bottom

_____ Creates part of the text using book language and knows some words on sight

Stage 6: Early Strategic Reading

_____ Uses context to guess at some unknown words (guesses make sense)

_____ Notices beginning sounds in words and uses them in guessing unknown words

_____ Seems to sometimes use syntax to help identify words in print

_____ Recognizes some word parts, such as root words and affixes

Stage 7: Moderate Strategic Reading

_____ Sometimes uses context and word parts to decode words

_____ Self-corrects when making an oral reading miscue

_____ Retells the passage easily and may embellish the storyline

_____ Shows some awareness of vowel sounds

Examiner's Notes:

Examiner's Summary of Miscue Patterns:

PART III: DEVELOPMENTAL/PERFORMANCE SUMMARY

Oral Reading Accuracy

_____   0–1   oral errors = Easy

_____   2–5   oral errors = Adequate

_____   6+   oral errors = Too hard

Continue to next assessment level passage?   _____ Yes   _____ No

Examiner's Notes:

You Cannot Fly! (96 words)

PART I: SILENT READING COMPREHENSION

Background Statement: "Have you ever wished you could fly? A boy named Sam in this story wants to fly. Read this story to find out if Sam gets to fly. Read it carefully because when you're through I'm going to ask you to tell me about the story."

Teacher Directions: Once the student completes the silent reading, say, "Tell me about the story you just read." Answers to the questions below that the student provides during the retelling should be marked "ua" in the appropriate blank to indicate that this response was unaided. Ask all remaining questions not addressed during the retelling and mark those the student answers with an "a" to indicate that the correct response was given after prompting by the teacher.

Questions/Answers	*Story Grammar Element/ Level of Comprehension*
_____1. What was the name of the boy in the story? *(Sam)*	character-characterization/ literal
_____2. What did Sam really want to do? *(Sam wanted to fly, but couldn't)*	story problem(s)/literal
_____3. What were two ways Sam tried to fly? *(jumping off his bed and a box)*	problem resolution attempts/ literal
_____4. How was Sam's problem finally solved? *(Sam got to ride on an airplane)*	problem resolution/ inferential
_____5. What did the family and Sam do after reading the letter? *(laughed)*	problem resolution attempts/ literal
_____6. Where did the story take place? *(Sam's house)*	setting/inferential
_____7. What did Sam learn about being able to fly? *(people can't fly except in airplanes)*	theme/evaluative
_____8. What words would you use to tell someone what kind of boy Sam was? *(responses will vary; accept plausible ones)*	character-characterization/ evaluative

PART II: ORAL READING AND ANALYSIS OF MISCUES

Directions: Say, "Now I would like to hear you read this story out loud. Please start at the beginning and keep reading until I tell you to stop." Have the student read orally until the oral reading stop-marker (//) is reached. Follow along on the Miscue Grid, marking any oral reading errors as appropriate. Then complete the Developmental/Performance Summary to determine whether to continue the assessment. (*Note:* The Miscue Grid should be completed *after* the assessment session has been concluded in order to minimize stress for the student.)

	MIS-PRONUN.	SUB-STITUTION	OMISSION	INSERTION	TCHR. ASSIST.	SELF-CORRECT.	MEANING DISRUPTION
You Cannot Fly!							
Once a boy named Sam wanted to							
fly. His mother and father said,							
"You cannot fly." His sister said,							
"You cannot fly." Sam tried jumping							
off a box. He tried jumping off							
his bed. He fell down each time.							
Sam still tried hard but he still							
could not fly. Then one day							
a letter came for Sam. The letter							
said, "Come and see me, Sam, on							
the next airplane." It was from							
his grandfather. Sam went to his							
family and read the letter. Sam							
said, "Now I can fly." Sam and his							
family all laughed together. //							
TOTALS							

Notes:

Examiner's Summary of Miscue Patterns:

PART III: DEVELOPMENTAL/PERFORMANCE SUMMARY

Silent Reading Comprehension	*Oral Reading Accuracy*

_____ 0–1 questions missed = Easy   _____ 0–1 oral errors = Easy

_____ 2   questions missed = Adequate   _____ 2–5 oral errors = Adequate

_____ 3+   questions missed = Too hard   _____ 6+   oral errors = Too hard

Continue to next assessment level passage? _____ Yes _____ No

PART IV: LISTENING COMPREHENSION

Directions: If you have decided not to continue to have the student read any other passages, then use this passage to begin assessing the student's listening comprehension (see page 8). Begin by reading the background statement for this passage and then say, "I am going to read this story to you. Please listen carefully because I will be asking you some questions after I finish reading it to you." After reading the passage, ask the student the questions associated with the passage. If the student correctly answers more than six questions, you will need to move to the next level and repeat the procedure.

Listening Comprehension

_____ 0–2 questions missed   = move to the next passage level

_____ more than two questions missed = stop assessment or move down a level

Examiner's Notes:

The Pig and the Snake (111 words)

PART I: SILENT READING COMPREHENSION

Background Statement: "Read this story to find out what happened to Mr. Pig when he tried to help a snake in trouble. Be sure and read it carefully because I'm going to ask you to tell me about the story."

Teacher Directions: Once the student completes the silent reading, say, "Tell me about the story you just read." Answers to the questions below that the student provides during the retelling should be marked "ua" in the appropriate blank to indicate that this response was unaided. Ask all remaining questions not addressed during the retelling and mark those the student answers with an "a" to indicate that the correct response was given after prompting by the teacher.

<table>
<tr><td align="center">Questions/Answers</td><td>Story Grammar Element/
Level of Comprehension</td></tr>
<tr><td>_____1. Where did the story take place?
(on the road to town)</td><td>setting/literal</td></tr>
<tr><td>_____2. Who were the animals in the story?
(Mr. Pig and a snake)</td><td>character-characterization/
literal</td></tr>
<tr><td>_____3. What was the snake's problem?
(he was stuck in a hole and wanted help getting out)</td><td>story problem(s)/literal</td></tr>
<tr><td>_____4. How did the snake solve his problem?
(by getting the pig to help him by promising not to hurt him)</td><td>problem resolution/
inferential</td></tr>
<tr><td>_____5. What words would you use to describe the snake?
(sneaky, liar, or any other plausible response)</td><td>character-characterization/
evaluative</td></tr>
<tr><td>_____6. What lesson did Mr. Pig learn?
(responses will vary but should indicate a theme/moral related to "you can't always trust what someone says")</td><td>theme/evaluative</td></tr>
<tr><td>_____7. How did Mr. Pig feel after he helped pull the snake out of the hole?
(surprised, upset, etc.)</td><td>character-characterization/
inferential</td></tr>
<tr><td>_____8. What was one thing the snake did to get Mr. Pig to help him out of the hole?
(cried or said he would be his friend)</td><td>problem resolution attempts/
literal</td></tr>
</table>

PART II: ORAL READING AND ANALYSIS OF MISCUES

Directions: Say, "Now I would like to hear you read this story out loud." Have the student read orally until the 100-word sample is completed. Follow along on the Miscue Grid, marking any oral reading errors as appropriate. *Remember to count miscues only up to the point in the story containing the oral reading stop-marker (//).* Then complete the Developmental/Performance Summary to determine whether to continue the assessment. (*Note:* The Miscue Grid should be completed *after* the assessment session has been concluded in order to minimize stress for the student.)

	MIS-PRONUN.	SUB-STITUTION	OMISSION	INSERTION	TCHR. ASSIST.	SELF-CORRECT.	MEANING DISRUPTION
The Pig and the Snake							
One day Mr. Pig was walking to							
town. He saw a big hole in the							
road. A big snake was in the							
hole. "Help me," said the snake,							
"and I will be your friend." "No, no,"							
said Mr. Pig. "If I help you get							
out you will bite me. You are							
a snake!" The snake cried and							
cried. So Mr. Pig pulled the							
snake out of the hole.							
Then the snake said, "Now I am							
going to bite you, Mr. Pig."							
"How can you bite me after							
I helped you out of the hole?"							
said Mr. Pig. The snake said, //							
"You knew I was a snake							
when you pulled me out!"							
TOTALS							

Notes:

Examiner's Summary of Miscue Patterns:

PART III: DEVELOPMENTAL/PERFORMANCE SUMMARY

Silent Reading Comprehension

_____ 0–1 questions missed = Easy

_____ 2 questions missed = Adequate

_____ 3+ questions missed = Too hard

Oral Reading Accuracy

_____ 0–1 oral errors = Easy

_____ 2–5 oral errors = Adequate

_____ 6+ oral errors = Too hard

Continue to next assessment level passage? _____ Yes _____ No

PART IV: LISTENING COMPREHENSION

Directions: If you have decided not to continue to have the student read any other passages, then use this passage to begin assessing the student's listening comprehension (see page 8). Begin by reading the background statement for this passage and then say, "I am going to read this story to you. Please listen carefully because I will be asking you some questions after I finish reading it to you." After reading the passage, ask the student the questions associated with the passage. If the student correctly answers more than six questions, you will need to move to the next level and repeat the procedure.

Listening Comprehension

_____ 0–2 questions missed = move to the next passage level

_____ more than two questions missed = stop assessment or move down a level

Examiner's Notes:

LEVEL 3 ASSESSMENT PROTOCOLS
The Big Bad Wolf (235 words)

PART I: SILENT READING COMPREHENSION

Background Statement: "Have you ever had someone say something about you that wasn't true? Mr. Wolf thinks he has. Read and find out what really happened. Read it carefully because I'm going to ask you to tell me about the story."

Teacher Directions: Once the student completes the silent reading, say, "Tell me about the story you just read." Answers to the questions below that the student provides during the retelling should be marked "ua" in the appropriate blank to indicate that this response was unaided. Ask all remaining questions not addressed during the retelling and mark those the student answers with an "a" to indicate that the correct response was given after prompting by the teacher.

Questions/Answers	*Story Grammar Element/ Level of Comprehension*
_____1. Who was the story about? *(Mr. Wolf, Granny, little girl, woodcutter)*	character-characterization/ literal
_____2. Where was Mr. Wolf when he saw the house? *(in the forest)*	setting/literal
_____3. Why did Mr. Wolf need to get into the house? *(he was wet and freezing)*	story problem(s)/literal
_____4. What made Mr. Wolf think it was OK to go into the house? *(the note on the door)*	problem resolution attempts/ inferential
_____5. What did Mr. Wolf do after entering the house? *(began to warm himself and changed into a nightgown)*	problem resolution attempts/ literal
_____6. Why did Mr. Wolf have to run for his life? *(woodcutter was going to kill him)*	problem resolution attempts/ literal
_____7. What lesson did Mr. Wolf learn? *(responses will vary but should indicate a theme/moral related to not doing things without permission)*	theme/evaluative
_____8. What did Mrs. Wolf say that would make you think she didn't trust humans? *(she said the humans would make up a story about her husband)*	character-characterization/ inferential

PART II: ORAL READING AND ANALYSIS OF MISCUES

Directions: Say, "Now I would like to hear you read this story out loud." Have the student read orally until the 100-word sample is completed. Follow along on the Miscue Grid, marking any oral reading errors as appropriate. *Remember to count miscues only up to the point in the story containing the oral reading stop-marker (//).* Then complete the Developmental/Performance Summary to determine whether to continue the assessment. (*Note:* The Miscue Grid should be completed *after* the assessment session has been concluded in order to minimize stress for the student.)

	MIS-PRONUN.	SUB-STITUTION	OMISSION	INSERTION	TCHR. ASSIST.	SELF-CORRECT.	MEANING DISRUPTION
The Big Bad Wolf							
One day Mr. Wolf was walking							
through the forest. He was enjoying							
an afternoon walk and not bothering							
anyone. All of a sudden it started							
to rain and he became wet and cold.							
Just when Mr. Wolf was about							
to freeze to death, he saw a small							
house in the woods. Smoke was							
coming from the chimney, so he							
knocked on the door. No one was							
home, but a note on the door said:							
Come in and make yourself warm.							
I'll be back about 2:00 p.m.							
Love,							
Granny							
The poor wet wolf came in and							
began to warm himself by // *the*							
fire.							
TOTALS							

Notes:

Examiner's Summary of Miscue Patterns:

PART III: DEVELOPMENTAL/PERFORMANCE SUMMARY

Silent Reading Comprehension

_____ 0–1 questions missed = Easy

_____ 2 questions missed = Adequate

_____ 3+ questions missed = Too hard

Oral Reading Accuracy

_____ 0–1 oral errors = Easy

_____ 2–5 oral errors = Adequate

_____ 6+ oral errors = Too hard

Continue to next assessment level passage? _____ Yes _____ No

PART IV: LISTENING COMPREHENSION

Directions: If you have decided not to continue to have the student read any other passages, then use this passage to begin assessing the student's listening comprehension (see page 8). Begin by reading the background statement for this passage and then say, "I am going to read this story to you. Please listen carefully because I will be asking you some questions after I finish reading it to you." After reading the passage, ask the student the questions associated with the passage. If the student correctly answers more than six questions, you will need to move to the next level and repeat the procedure.

Listening Comprehension

_____ 0–2 questions missed = move to the next passage level

_____ more than two questions missed = stop assessment or move down a level

Examiner's Notes:

LEVEL 4 ASSESSMENT PROTOCOLS
New Clothes (295 words)

PART I: SILENT READING COMPREHENSION

Background Statement: "Read this story to find out what happens when Bobby decides he wants some new clothes. Be sure and read it carefully because I'm going to ask you to tell me about the story when you finish."

Teacher Directions: Once the student completes the silent reading, say, "Tell me about the story you just read." Answers to the questions below that the student provides during the retelling should be marked "ua" in the appropriate blank to indicate that this response was unaided. Ask all remaining questions not addressed during the retelling and mark those the student answers with an "a" to indicate that the correct response was given after prompting by the teacher.

Questions/Answers	*Story Grammar Element/ Level of Comprehension*
_____1. Who are the characters in this story? *(Bobby, Mother, Sara, & Brad)*	character-characterization/ literal
_____2. Where does the story mainly take place? *(Bobby's home)*	setting/literal
_____3. Besides being the youngest, what is Bobby's big problem in the story? *(earning money to buy new clothes)*	story problem/literal
_____4. What did Bobby do to earn money? *(he cleaned his brother's and sister's rooms)*	problem resolution/literal
_____5. Besides hand-me-down clothes, what was one other thing that Bobby disliked about being the youngest? *(couldn't stay up late and watch TV)*	story problem/literal
_____6. What does Bobby do at the end of the story? *(buy some new clothes)*	problem resolution/literal
_____7. What would be some words, other than proud, that would describe how Bobby felt on the first day of school? *(happy, cool, other plausible responses)*	character-characterization/ evaluative
_____8. Why do you think Bobby's Mother was "even prouder?" *(responses should indicate that Bobby's mother was proud that her son had worked hard and found a way to earn money)*	character-characterization

PART II: ORAL READING AND ANALYSIS OF MISCUES

Directions: Say, "Now I would like to hear you read some of this story out loud." Have the student read orally until the 100-word sample is completed. Follow along on the Miscue Grid, marking any oral reading errors as appropriate. *Remember to count miscues only up to the point in the story containing the oral reading stop-marker (//).* Then complete the Developmental/Performance Summary to determine whether to continue the assessment. (*Note:* The Miscue Grid should be completed *after* the assessment session has been concluded in order to minimize stress for the student.)

	MIS-PRONUN.	SUB-STITUTION	OMISSION	INSERTION	TCHR. ASSIST.	SELF-CORRECT.	MEANING DISRUPTION
New Clothes							
Bobby was the youngest member							
of his family. He didn't like being							
the youngest because he couldn't							
stay up late and watch television.							
Most of all, he disliked having to							
wear hand me down clothes from							
his brother. One day Bobby went							
to his mother and said, "Mom,							
I'm tired of wearing Brad's							
clothes. Why can't I have							
some more new clothes this							
school year?" His mother replied,							
"Bobby, you know we can't							
afford to buy even more new clothes.							
You should be happy with the new							
clothes we have already bought.							
Besides, most of Brad's clothes							
are just like // *new.*"							
TOTALS							

Notes:

Examiner's Summary of Miscue Patterns:

PART III: DEVELOPMENTAL/PERFORMANCE SUMMARY

Silent Reading Comprehension

_____ 0–1 questions missed = Easy

_____ 2 questions missed = Adequate

_____ 3+ questions missed = Too hard

Oral Reading Accuracy

_____ 0–1 oral errors = Easy

_____ 2–5 oral errors = Adequate

_____ 6+ oral errors = Too hard

Continue to next assessment level passage? _____ Yes _____ No

PART IV: LISTENING COMPREHENSION

Directions: If you have decided not to continue to have the student read any other passages, then use this passage to begin assessing the student's listening comprehension (see page 8). Begin by reading the background statement for this passage and then say, "I am going to read this story to you. Please listen carefully because I will be asking you some questions after I finish reading it to you." After reading the passage, ask the student the questions associated with the passage. If the student correctly answers more than six questions, you will need to move to the next level and repeat the procedure.

Listening Comprehension

_____ 0–2 questions missed = move to the next passage level

_____ more than two questions missed = stop assessment or move down a level

Examiner's Notes:

LEVEL 5 ASSESSMENT PROTOCOLS
Hot Shoes (324 words)

PART I: SILENT READING COMPREHENSION

Background Statement: "This story is about how one group of boys feel about their athletic shoes. Read this story to find out how important special shoes are to playing sports. Read it carefully because I will ask you to tell me about it when you finish."

Teacher Directions: Once the student completes the silent reading, say, "Tell me about the story you just read." Answers to the questions below that the student provides during the retelling should be marked "ua" in the appropriate blank to indicate that this response was unaided. Ask all remaining questions not addressed during the retelling and mark those the student answers with an "a" to indicate that the correct response was given after prompting by the teacher.

	Questions/Answers	*Story Grammar Element/ Level of Comprehension*
_____	1. Where did the story take place? *(I. B. Belcher Elementary School or at a school)*	setting/literal
_____	2. Who were the two main characters in the story? *(Jamie Lee and Josh Kidder)*	character-characterization/ literal
_____	3. What was the problem between Jamie and Josh? *(Jamie didn't think Josh could be a good player because of his shoes, Josh didn't fit in, or other plausible response)*	story problem(s)/inferential
_____	4. How did Josh solve his problem with the other boys? *(he outplayed all of them)*	problem resolution/ inferential
_____	5. What kind of person was Jamie Lee? *(conceited, stuck-up, or other plausible responses)*	character-characterization/ evaluative
_____	6. What happened after the game? *(the other boys gathered around and asked Josh his secret)*	problem resolution attempts/ literal
_____	7. Why did everyone laugh when Josh said, "Two things—lots of practice and cheap shoes"? *(because everything had happened because of his cheap shoes)*	problem resolution attempts/ inferential
_____	8. What lesson does this story teach? *(responses will vary but should indicate a theme/moral related to "it's not what you wear that makes you good in a sport")*	theme/evaluative

PART II: ORAL READING AND ANALYSIS OF MISCUES

Directions: Say, "Now I would like to hear you read this story out loud." Have the student read orally until the 100-word sample is completed. Follow along on the Miscue Grid, marking any oral reading errors as appropriate. *Remember to count miscues only up to the point in the story containing the oral reading stop-marker (//).* Then complete the Developmental/Performance Summary to determine whether to continue the assessment. (*Note:* The Miscue Grid should be completed *after* the assessment session has been concluded in order to minimize stress for the student.)

	MIS-PRONUN.	SUB-STITUTION	OMISSION	INSERTION	TCHR. ASSIST.	SELF-CORRECT.	MEANING DISRUPTION
Hot Shoes							
The guys at the I. B. Belcher							
Elementary School loved all the							
new sport shoes. Some wore the							
"Sky High" model by Leader.							
Others who couldn't afford Sky							
Highs would settle for a lesser							
shoe. Some liked the "Street							
Smarts" by Master, or the							
"Uptown-Downtown" by Beebop.							
The Belcher boys got to the point							
with their shoes that they could							
identify their friends just by							
looking at their feet. But the boy							
who was the envy of the entire fifth							
grade was Jamie Lee. He had a							
pair of "High Five Pump 'em Ups"							
by Superior. The only thing Belcher							
boys // *loved as much as their*							
shoes was basketball.							
TOTALS							

Notes:

Examiner's Summary of Miscue Patterns:

PART III: DEVELOPMENTAL/PERFORMANCE SUMMARY

Silent Reading Comprehension

_____ 0–1 questions missed = Easy

_____ 2 questions missed = Adequate

_____ 3+ questions missed = Too hard

Oral Reading Accuracy

_____ 0–1 oral errors = Easy

_____ 2–5 oral errors = Adequate

_____ 6+ oral errors = Too hard

Continue to next assessment level passage?   _____ Yes   _____ No

PART IV: LISTENING COMPREHENSION

Directions: If you have decided not to continue to have the student read any other passages, then use this passage to begin assessing the student's listening comprehension (see page 8). Begin by reading the background statement for this passage and then say, "I am going to read this story to you. Please listen carefully because I will be asking you some questions after I finish reading it to you." After reading the passage, ask the student the questions associated with the passage. If the student correctly answers more than six questions, you will need to move to the next level and repeat the procedure.

Listening Comprehension

_____ 0–2 questions missed   = move to the next passage level

_____ more than two questions missed = stop assessment or move down a level

Examiner's Notes:

PART I: SILENT READING COMPREHENSION

Background Statement: "This story is about two boys who are lost on a mountain. Read the story to find out what they did to find their way home and what were the results of their problem resolution attempts. Read it carefully because I will ask you to tell me about what you read."

Teacher Directions: Once the student completes the silent reading, say, "Tell me about the story you just read." Answers to the questions below that the student provides during the retelling should be marked "ua" in the appropriate blank to indicate that this response was unaided. Ask all remaining questions not addressed during the retelling and mark those the student answers with an "a" to indicate that the correct response was given after prompting by the teacher.

Questions/Answers	*Story Grammar Element/ Level of Comprehension*
_____1. Where did the story take place? *(Mount Holyoak)*	setting/literal
_____2. Who were the two boys in the story? *(Brad, Kevin)*	character-characterization/ literal
_____3. Why were the boys sent upstream by Brad's father? *(to look for cougar tracks)*	problem resolution attempts/ inferential
_____4. What was Brad's and Kevin's problem after going upstream? *(they became lost)*	story problem(s)/literal
_____5. What did the boys do to be found? *(they started a fire)*	problem resolution/ literal
_____6. What happened after their fire got out of hand? *(people came and put the fire out; other specifics related to this question are acceptable)*	problem resolution attempts/ literal
_____7. After the forest fire was put out, what did the boys do? *(helped reforest the area)*	problem resolution attempts/ literal
_____8. What new problem resulted from the forest fire? *(cougars were no longer in the area)*	story problem(s)/inferential

PART II: ORAL READING AND ANALYSIS OF MISCUES

Directions: Say, "Now I would like to hear you read this story out loud." Have the student read orally until the 100-word sample is completed. Follow along on the Miscue Grid, marking any oral reading errors as appropriate. *Remember to count miscues only up to the point in the story containing the oral reading stop-marker (//).* Then complete the Developmental/Performance Summary to determine whether to continue the assessment. (*Note:* The Miscue Grid should be completed *after* the assessment session has been concluded in order to minimize stress for the student.)

	MIS-PRONUN.	SUB-STITUTION	OMISSION	INSERTION	TCHR. ASSIST.	SELF-CORRECT.	MEANING DISRUPTION
Mountain Fire							
One August afternoon Brad and							
Kevin went tracking with their							
fathers on Mount Holyoak. Brad's							
father was a conservationist for the							
Forest Service and was searching							
for evidence of cougars. Many people							
feared that the cougars were extinct on							
Mount Holyoak. The boys became							
excited when they found what appeared							
to be a partial cougar track near							
a stream. But as the day wore on, no							
new tracks were found. After lunch							
Brad's father sent the boys upstream							
while he circled west. He told the							
boys to return to the lunch site							
in an hour. After about forty-five							
minutes, // *the boys found the stream's*							
source and could follow it no							
more.							
TOTALS							

Notes:

Examiner's Summary of Miscue Patterns:

PART III: DEVELOPMENTAL/PERFORMANCE SUMMARY

Silent Reading Comprehension

_____ 0–1 questions missed = Easy

_____ 2   questions missed = Adequate

_____ 3+   questions missed = Too hard

Oral Reading Accuracy

_____ 0–1 oral errors = Easy

_____ 2–5 oral errors = Adequate

_____ 6+   oral errors = Too hard

Continue to next assessment level passage?   _____ Yes   _____ No

PART IV: LISTENING COMPREHENSION

Directions: If you have decided not to continue to have the student read any other passages, then use this passage to begin assessing the student's listening comprehension (see page 8). Begin by reading the background statement for this passage and then say, "I am going to read this story to you. Please listen carefully because I will be asking you some questions after I finish reading it to you." After reading the passage, ask the student the questions associated with the passage. If the student correctly answers more than six questions, you will need to move to the next level and repeat the procedure.

Listening Comprehension

_____ 0–2 questions missed   = move to the next passage level

_____ more than two questions missed = stop assessment or move down a level

Examiner's Notes:

LEVEL 7 ASSESSMENT PROTOCOLS
The Canoe Trip (490 words)

PART I: SILENT READING COMPREHENSION

Background Statement: "This story is about two girls who take a canoe trip. Read the story and find out what happens to the girls while canoeing. Read it carefully because I'm going to ask you to tell me about it when you finish."

Teacher Directions: Once the student completes the silent reading, say, "Tell me about the story you just read." Answers to the questions below that the student provides during the retelling should be marked "ua" in the appropriate blank to indicate that this response was unaided. Ask all remaining questions not addressed during the retelling and mark those the student answers with an "a" to indicate that the correct response was given after prompting by the teacher.

Questions/Answers	*Story Grammar Element/ Level of Comprehension*
_____1. Where did this story take place? *(West Yellowstone)*	setting/literal
_____2. Who was the story mainly about? *(Katherine and Amy)*	character-characterization/ literal
_____3. What was the girls' problem? *(they capsized their canoe)*	story problem(s)/literal
_____4. What happened after they capsized? *(they lost their food but saved the canoe)*	problem resolution attempts/ inferential
_____5. Why couldn't the girls catch up with the floating coolers? *(because of the time it took to empty the canoe and the swiftness of the water)*	problem resolution attempts/ inferential
_____6. How did the problem of the lost food turn out? *(Katherine's parents caught the floating coolers)*	story solution/literal
_____7. How did Katherine and Amy feel after reaching Katherine's parents? *(relieved, embarrassed, or other plausible response)*	character-characterization/ evaluative
_____8. Why is "all's well that ends well" a good theme for this story? *(responses will vary but should reflect the fact that the girls didn't give up and everything turned out fine when they reached Katherine's parents)*	theme/evaluative

PART II: ORAL READING AND ANALYSIS OF MISCUES

Directions: Say, "Now I would like to hear you read this story out loud." Have the student read orally until the 100-word sample is completed. Follow along on the Miscue Grid, marking any oral reading errors as appropriate. *Remember to count miscues only up to the point in the story containing the oral reading stop-marker (//).* Then complete the Developmental/Performance Summary to determine whether to continue the assessment. (*Note:* The Miscue Grid should be completed *after* the assessment session has been concluded in order to minimize stress for the student.)

	MIS-PRONUN.	SUB-STITUTION	OMISSION	INSERTION	TCHR. ASSIST.	SELF-CORRECT.	MEANING DISRUPTION
The Canoe Trip							
Katherine and her family like to							
spend their vacation camping out.							
Frequently they go to either							
Great Smoky Mountains National							
Park or Yellowstone National Park.							
Since they have camped out							
for many years, they have become							
quite accomplished. Katherine is able							
to start a fire with flint and steel,							
build a lean-to for shelter, and							
find food in the forest on							
which to live. Katherine's favorite							
outdoor activity is canoeing. Although							
she is quite a good canoer, there is							
one canoe trip that she'll never forget.							
It was a canoe trip she took with							
her family and her friend // *Amy*							
down the Madison River near							
West Yellowstone.							
TOTALS							

Notes:

Examiner's Summary of Miscue Patterns:

PART III: DEVELOPMENTAL/PERFORMANCE SUMMARY

Silent Reading Comprehension

_____ 0–1 questions missed = Easy

_____ 2 questions missed = Adequate

_____ 3+ questions missed = Too hard

Continue to next assessment level passage? _____ Yes _____ No

Oral Reading Accuracy

_____ 0–1 oral errors = Easy

_____ 2–5 oral errors = Adequate

_____ 6+ oral errors = Too hard

PART IV: LISTENING COMPREHENSION

Directions: If you have decided not to continue to have the student read any other passages, then use this passage to begin assessing the student's listening comprehension (see page 8). Begin by reading the background statement for this passage and then say, "I am going to read this story to you. Please listen carefully because I will be asking you some questions after I finish reading it to you." After reading the passage, ask the student the questions associated with the passage. If the student correctly answers more than six questions, you will need to move to the next level and repeat the procedure.

Listening Comprehension

_____ 0–2 questions missed = move to the next passage level

_____ more than two questions missed = stop assessment or move down a level

Examiner's Notes:

The Eagle (504 words)

PART I: SILENT READING COMPREHENSION

Background Statement: "This story is an old Native American tale about an eagle. Read the passage and try to identify the message the story tells. Read it carefully because I'm going to ask you to tell me about it when you finish."

Teacher Directions: Once the student completes the silent reading, say, "Tell me about the story you just read." Answers to the questions below that the student provides during the retelling should be marked "ua" in the appropriate blank to indicate that this response was unaided. Ask all remaining questions not addressed during the retelling and mark those the student answers with an "a" to indicate that the correct response was given after prompting by the teacher.

Questions/Answers	*Story Grammar Element/ Level of Comprehension*
_____1. Where does the story take place? *(mountain and farm)*	setting/literal
_____2. Who were the people in the story? *(Hopi farmer, his son, and Anasazi brave)*	character-characterization/ literal
_____3. What was the problem presented in the story? *(convincing the eagle that he wasn't a chicken)*	story problem(s)/inferential
_____4. What did the eagle do that was like a chicken? *(scratching, pecking at food, wouldn't fly)*	problem resolution attempts/ literal
_____5. What was the brave's first attempt to convince the bird it was an eagle? *(tried to get it to fly from barn)*	problem resolution attempts/ literal
_____6. How did the brave finally get the bird to recognize it could fly? *(by taking it up to a high bluff so that it could see the valley and sense freedom)*	problem resolution/ literal
_____7. What words would you use to describe the farmer? *(responses will vary but should relate to the farmer being deceitful, uncaring, or a liar)*	character-characterization/ evaluative
_____8. What lesson does this story teach? *(responses will vary but should indicate a theme/ moral related to "you are what you think you are")*	theme/evaluative

PART II: ORAL READING AND ANALYSIS OF MISCUES

Directions: Say, "Now I would like to hear you read this story out loud." Have the student read orally until the 100-word sample is completed. Follow along on the Miscue Grid, marking any oral reading errors as appropriate. *Remember to count miscues only up to the point in the story containing the oral reading stop-marker (//).* Then complete the Developmental/Performance Summary to determine whether to continue the assessment. (*Note:* The Miscue Grid should be completed *after* the assessment session has been concluded in order to minimize stress for the student.)

	MIS-PRONUN.	SUB-STITUTION	OMISSION	INSERTION	TCHR. ASSIST.	SELF-CORRECT.	MEANING DISRUPTION
The Eagle							
There exists an old Native American							
legend about an eagle who thought							
he was a chicken. It seems that							
a Hopi farmer and his only son							
decided to climb a nearby mountain							
to observe an eagle's nest.							
The trip would take them all							
day, so they brought along some							
rations and water for the trek.							
The man and the boy crossed the							
enormous fields of maize and beans							
into the foothills. Soon thereafter							
they were ascending the mountain							
and the climb became rigorous							
and hazardous. They occasionally							
looked back toward their home and							
at the panoramic view of the entire //							
valley. Finally the farmer and son							
reached the mountain's summit.							
TOTALS							

Notes:

Examiner's Summary of Miscue Patterns:

PART III: DEVELOPMENTAL/PERFORMANCE SUMMARY

Silent Reading Comprehension

_____ 0–1 questions missed = Easy

_____ 2 questions missed = Adequate

_____ 3+ questions missed = Too hard

Oral Reading Accuracy

_____ 0–1 oral errors = Easy

_____ 2–5 oral errors = Adequate

_____ 6+ oral errors = Too hard

Continue to next assessment level passage?   _____ Yes   _____ No

PART IV: LISTENING COMPREHENSION

Directions: If you have decided not to continue to have the student read any other passages, then use this passage to begin assessing the student's listening comprehension (see page 8). Begin by reading the background statement for this passage and then say, "I am going to read this story to you. Please listen carefully because I will be asking you some questions after I finish reading it to you." After reading the passage, ask the student the questions associated with the passage. If the student correctly answers more than six questions, you will need to move to the next level and repeat the procedure.

Listening Comprehension

_____ 0–2 questions missed   = move to the next passage level

_____ more than two questions missed = stop assessment or move down a level

Examiner's Notes:

LEVEL 9 ASSESSMENT PROTOCOLS
The Case of Angela Violet (378 words)

PART I: SILENT READING COMPREHENSION

Background Statement: "This story is about a young girl's disappearance. Read the story carefully because I will ask you to tell it to me when you finish."

Teacher Directions: Once the student completes the silent reading, say, "Tell me about the story you just read." Answers to the questions below that the student provides during the retelling should be marked "ua" in the appropriate blank to indicate that this response was unaided. Ask all remaining questions not addressed during the retelling and mark those the student answers with an "a" to indicate that the correct response was given after prompting by the teacher.

Questions/Answers   **Story Grammar Element/ Level of Comprehension**

_____1. What time of year did the story take place?
   (autumn)

setting/literal

_____2. What was the main problem in the story?
   (Katrina Bowers had disappeared)

story problem(s)/inferential

_____3. What problem resolution attempts did the
   authorities take when they received the
   telephone tip?
   *(got a search warrant and went to Miss Violet's
   house)*

problem resolution attempts/ literal

_____4. How was Katrina's case finally solved?
   (she was found in California)

problem resolution/literal

_____5. What was Miss Violet's reaction
   to the police wanting to search her house?
   (she didn't mind, she welcomed the search)

problem resolution attempts/ literal

_____6. What kind of person was Miss Violet?
   *(responses will vary but should suggest
   kind, caring, gentle, lonely)*

character-characterization/ inferential

_____7. What did the people in the community
   do after Miss Violet was proved innocent?
   (began to do things for and with her)

problem resolution attempts/ literal

_____8. What is the lesson of this story?
   *(responses will vary but should indicate
   a theme/moral related to "you can't judge a
   book by its cover")*

theme/evaluative

PART II: ORAL READING AND ANALYSIS OF MISCUES

Directions: Say, "Now I would like to hear you read this story out loud." Have the student read orally until the 100-word sample is completed. Follow along on the Miscue Grid, marking any oral reading errors as appropriate. *Remember to count miscues only up to the point in the story containing the oral reading stop-marker (//).* Then complete the Developmental/Performance Summary to determine whether to continue the assessment. (*Note:* The Miscue Grid should be completed *after* the assessment session has been concluded in order to minimize stress for the student.)

	MIS-PRONUN.	SUB-STITUTION	OMISSION	INSERTION	TCHR. ASSIST.	SELF-CORRECT.	MEANING DISRUPTION
The Case of Angela Violet							
Angela Violet was an elderly lady in							
our neighborhood who some people							
thought suspicious. She was rarely seen							
outside her spacious Victorian-styled							
home, and then only to retrieve the daily							
mail. Her pasty complexion and ancient							
dress made her appear like an apparition.							
Small children in the neighborhood							
speculated that she might be some							
sort of witch. It appeared that Miss							
Violet had no contact with the outside							
world. One autumn day news spread							
through the community that a high							
school cheerleader, Katrina Bowers,							
had disappeared. It was feared by the							
police that Katrina had been abducted.							
State and // *local police joined forces*							
with the Federal Bureau of Investigation							
in the massive search effort.							
TOTALS							

Notes:

Examiner's Summary of Miscue Patterns:

PART III: DEVELOPMENTAL/PERFORMANCE SUMMARY

Silent Reading Comprehension

_____ 0–1 questions missed = Easy

_____ 2 questions missed = Adequate

_____ 3+ questions missed = Too hard

Continue to next assessment level passage? _____ Yes _____ No

Oral Reading Accuracy

_____ 0–1 oral errors = Easy

_____ 2–5 oral errors = Adequate

_____ 6+ oral errors = Too hard

PART IV: LISTENING COMPREHENSION

Directions: If you have decided not to continue to have the student read any other passages, then use this passage to begin assessing the student's listening comprehension (see page 8). Begin by reading the background statement for this passage and then say, "I am going to read this story to you. Please listen carefully because I will be asking you some questions after I finish reading it to you." After reading the passage, ask the student the questions associated with the passage. If the student correctly answers more than six questions, you will need to move to the next level and repeat the procedure.

Listening Comprehension

_____ 0–2 questions missed = move to the next passage level

_____ more than two questions missed = stop assessment or move down a level

Examiner's Notes:

SENTENCES FOR INITIAL PASSAGE SELECTION

form B

FORM B: LEVEL 1

1. Today is my birthday.

2. I wanted to have a party.

3. She stopped at the trees.

FORM B: LEVEL 2

1. We have extra leaves to rake.

2. I need some extra money.

3. She heard me in the kitchen.

FORM B: LEVEL 3

1. I was beginning to get afraid.

2. He could hear the voice get closer.

3. Tomorrow I will finish my work.

FORM B: LEVEL 4

1. She walked carefully into the darkness.

2. I know it is important to eat vegetables.

3. He slipped as he reached up into the oak tree.

FORM B: LEVEL 5

1. The tree withered away after the storm.

2. The neighborhood was shaken after the fire.

3. I was frightened by my dream.

FORM B: LEVEL 6

1. By not participating, he was barely passing in school.

2. I allowed the gifted students extra time.

3. Especially high achievement is a result of good instruction.

FORM B: LEVEL 7

1. I made an appointment to purchase the bike.

2. The plastic covering the application form was especially thick.

3. His robust legs made a difference in his overall physical strength.

FORM B: LEVEL 8

1. He was provoked because he was small in stature.

2. The familiar mockery led to the fight.

3. His bruised ego never really recovered.

FORM B: LEVEL 9

1. Her nontraditional dress improved her appearance.

2. The anonymous letter wasn't taken seriously.

3. He was a formidable-looking person, even wearing a sleazy coat.

NARRATIVE PASSAGES......form B

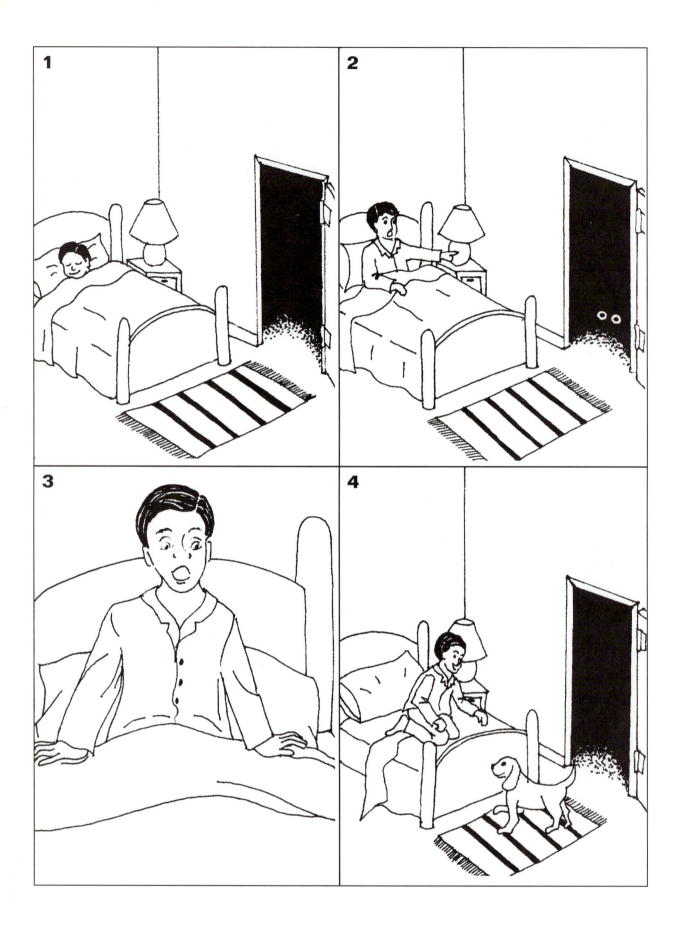

Form B   Level PP Wordless Picture Story

1. I like to play T-ball at school.

2. On Friday we played the big game.

3. I got a hit at the end of the game.

4. I made it home and won the game.

Birthday at the Zoo

It was Sunday.

I got out of bed and went to eat.

Mom said, "Today is your birthday, Pat. What do you want to do?"

I wanted a party but I did not tell Mom.

I said, "I just want to play."

Mom said, "Come take a ride with me."

I got in the car and soon we were in the city.

The car stopped. We got out.

We walked past some trees and I saw a sign that said "City Zoo."

All my friends were at the gate.

I was all smiles. Mom had planned a party for me.

It was the best birthday ever.

Mary's New Bike

Mary wanted a new bike. She helped around the house to make money. She had even helped her Father rake leaves for extra money. But she still didn't have the money for the new ten-speed bike.

One day her Aunt Deb came to visit Mary's family. Aunt Deb heard that Mary wanted a new bike. She told Mary that she had some work for her. Mary walked over to Aunt Deb's house the very next day.

Aunt Deb had Mary mop her kitchen floor. Mary cleaned out the flower beds. Mary swept out the carport. Finally Aunt Deb asked Mary to fold her clean clothes. Mary was tired by the end of the day. But when Aunt Deb paid Mary her money, Mary smiled and hugged Aunt Deb. She hurried home to tell her parents the good news. They smiled and told her how proud they were.

The next day Mary went to the store.

Bedtime

The sun was going down. The air was hot and Wild Willie was afraid. Never had he been in such a dry, hot place. His horse, Wizard, was trying to find a few blades of grass. Wild Willie was beginning to fall asleep from staying awake so long. Then he heard the sound again—the same sound he had been hearing for days. What could it be? Why was it following him? How could he find out what or who it was?

Slowly Wizard turned around. Willie stood up in the stirrups to see over the sand dune. He saw no one. Again he heard the sound. This time it came from behind. It was a slow rumbling sound. He got off his horse. He took his gun and got ready. Slowly the sound came closer and closer. Willie raised his gun. . . .

Then the TV went off and a voice said, "Beth, it's time to go to bed. Tomorrow is a school day and it's getting late." "Aw, Mom, can't I finish seeing the show?" I asked. "No, you can watch it another time," my mother replied.

As I went slowly upstairs to bed, I wondered what Wild Willie had seen. Maybe it had been some kind of animal or just a person in a wagon. But it was probably the Ghost of the Sand Wind. Yeah, that had to be it. Other people had claimed to have seen it. But I won't know until the reruns.

A Different Time

Marlo lived in a different time and a different place. He lived in a time of darkness and gloom. Marlo lived in a small hut with his poor parents. He didn't have nice clothes and he didn't have much to eat. But neither of these things bothered Marlo. There was only one thing he wanted. But he couldn't have it because the ruler would not let any of his people have it. This most important thing was to be able to read. Today this may seem like a dumb wish, but to Marlo it wasn't.

One day Marlo's father sent him to the castle with a cart of vegetables. On the way Marlo met an old man who had strange eyes. The old man's head was hooded, but his eyes were deep blue and sparkled. The old man asked Marlo if he could please have a few vegetables to eat. Marlo agreed even though he knew he would get into trouble. When the old man finished, he said, "Come to the old oak tree tonight and the future will be yours." Marlo walked away wondering what the old man meant.

That night Marlo slipped out of the hut. He ran up the road until he reached the old oak tree. There he found the old man sitting on the ground.

The old man stood up and handed Marlo a box. He said, "Marlo, inside this box is what you want. Your life will never be the same."

Marlo took the box, looked down for a second, and then the old man was nowhere to be seen. Marlo rushed home. He carefully opened the box. And there in the light of his one candle Marlo saw what was in the box. It was a book.

Laser Boy

My name is Bob and I'm a teacher. Several years ago I knew a student that I'd like to tell you about.

Matthew was a 13-year-old who never seemed to do well in school. Some say that he was a misfit, someone who doesn't quite fit in with the other kids his age. Not only that, Matthew had trouble in school nearly his whole life. He failed to complete his homework even when it was an easy assignment. By not participating in class, not turning in homework, and only doing a fair job on tests, Matthew always seemed to be just barely passing.

One day when Matthew was in seventh grade his teacher decided to find out what Matthew's problem was in school. The teacher had him tested and found out from the special education teacher that Matthew was gifted in the areas of science and mathematics! The special education teacher said, "Oh, yes, sometimes students who do poorly in school are quite gifted. They just haven't been allowed to show what they can do. Also, some gifted students are not especially strong in some school subjects. But they are excellent in music, working with mechanical objects, or even athletics."

After Matthew's discovery was made, he was asked what he was interested in studying. Matthew answered that he wanted to study lasers. For the rest of that year, Matthew read everything he could find in the library at the university having to do with lasers. Later, a professor in California was found who was an expert on laser technology. The professor agreed to talk with Matthew on a regular basis to help answer questions or solve any problems Matthew had.

During the last part of seventh grade, Matthew worked on a special science project. He built a model laser. It was fantastic! Matthew's model was accurate to the last detail. Everyone was very impressed with his project. All the kids at school began calling him "laser boy." He found new friends and his life at school and home greatly improved.

Since that very special year when I got to know "laser boy," I've looked at students who are experiencing trouble in a new way. I'm convinced that everyone has special talents. We only need to discover what they are.

The Paper Route

Scott had a chance to earn his own money for the first time. Answering an advertisement for newspaper carriers, he set up an appointment with Mr. Miley, the distribution manager. Mr. Miley was a rather short and stocky man who spoke with a loud voice.

After reviewing Scott's application, Mr. Miley said, "You look like a dependable young man to me. Do your parents approve of your becoming a paperboy?" "Yes, sir," replied Scott, "and I have a letter from my Dad saying it's OK with him."

"You can have the job, Scott," said Mr. Miley. "However, I want you to realize that this is a long route and you will have to get up very early. You will also have to have robust legs and a good bike," warned Mr. Miley.

Getting started was not easy. Scott had to be out of bed by 4:30 A.M. Next he had to pick up the papers and roll them up for placement in a plastic bag. He would usually finish that much by 5:30 A.M. Then it was time to deliver the papers.

Most days Scott could deliver all his newspapers in just two trips. His father had purchased a new bike for Scott and attached an enormous basket to it. The really hard days were Thursday and Sunday. Newspapers were especially large on those days. Scott would have to make as many as five trips to get the papers delivered on those days.

The good part of the job was, of course, the money. Scott found that he was making about 250 dollars a month. He was also developing his physical strength. But the negative side of the job was bad weather and cranky customers. When it rained, Scott got drenched. When it snowed, Scott froze. Scott's biggest complaint was his cranky customers, particularly Mr. Gripper. Mr. Gripper insisted on his paper being put in his mailbox, rain or shine. If Scott failed to do this, Mr. Gripper always called the newspaper office and complained. But Scott avoided most complaints by going out of his way to please his customers.

After one year on the job, Scott was called into Mr. Miley's office for an end-of-year conference. During the year Scott had managed to save 1,300 dollars and pay back his father for the bike. So when Mr. Miley asked him if he wanted to continue working for the paper, Scott said, "Yes." But he added, "It was a lot more work than I counted on and I could live without the Mr. Grippers of the world. But I really like the work."

Riley and Leonard

At times Leonard felt like the most unpopular boy in school. No matter what he did he was constantly ridiculed by his classmates. Maybe it was because he was small in stature and wore thick bifocals. Or maybe it was because he didn't like sports. Possibly it was because he couldn't afford the designer clothes the other kids seemed to live for. Regardless, Leonard felt like a loser and was unhappy with his situation.

One day, while putting his books in his locker, the familiar mockery began. A small covey of classmates formed a semicircle around Leonard. Each began to taunt him and call him names. Most joined in after Riley McClure made Leonard drop his books. They all laughed and called him *bozo*, *nerd*, and *dweeb*. But Leonard tried not to be provoked; that is, until Riley made horrible slurs about Leonard's family and particularly Leonard's mother. Leonard couldn't resist. He lunged at Riley but Riley was much bigger and Leonard's attack ended in disaster. Riley slammed him into the lockers, grabbed Leonard by the throat, and made Leonard holler "calf rope," a sign of total submission.

As the group disbanded, so they wouldn't be late for their next class, Lorrie Warner approached Leonard. She apologized for the group's behavior and tried to comfort Leonard's hurt pride. She said, "What goes around, comes around." But her consoling didn't help Leonard's bruised ego.

Twenty years later Leonard found himself president of the largest bank in town. He was well respected in the community and was quite generous when it came to civic projects. Although he had never married, he had recently begun dating Lorrie Warner, his old classmate.

One Friday evening Leonard and Lorrie were eating at a fancy restaurant. They had finished their meal and were heading out the door when a beggar approached. The beggar requested money to buy food. There was something curious about the beggar that Leonard could not place. But being generous, Leonard gave the man ten dollars. The beggar was so surprised by the large amount that he shook Leonard's hand vigorously before quickly backing away into the street. Lorrie screamed a word of caution but it was too late. The beggar had stepped into the path of a truck and was struck broadside. Leonard and Lorrie waited for the ambulance to carry the man away.

The next morning the headlines carried the story of the beggar. He had died from internal injuries early that morning. As Leonard read the details, he suddenly dropped the paper and turned pale. The beggar's name was Riley McClure.

The Long Night

I arrived late at the New Orleans International Airport because of delays in St. Louis. The night was descending on the Crescent City as I entered the cab for the short ride to city center. As the cab headed toward the city, the cabbie engaged me in an informative conversation about the Crescent City. She had an island accent and her multicolored dress was very nontraditional. After I told her I wanted to go to Rampart in the French Quarter, she abruptly turned left and headed southwest.

Fifteen minutes later, without a word, I got out of the cab and proceeded up Rampart. I had gone only two blocks when I noticed that a bleak little man was following me. I say bleak because when I saw his silhouette under a fluorescent street light, he looked as if something mean and cruel had happened in his early life. You know, a kind of woebegone appearance. Every time I stopped, he stopped. If I sped up my pace, his pace quickened. Finally I slipped into an anonymous doorway. As he approached I swiftly reached out and grabbed him by his grimy coat. I asked him why he was following me but all he did was whimper and hand me a crumpled-up note. As my eyes fell on the note, he slipped out of my grasp and ran into the eerily approaching fog.

The note contained the following message: "Your death is behind you. Run if you value your life." I didn't think, I ran.

As I rounded the corner of Rampart and Royal, I ran straight into a policeman. I felt relief. I told him my story. He chuckled and didn't take me seriously. As he walked away I saw a set of eyes from behind a refuse container in an alleyway. I ran again.

As I cut through an alley I was accosted by two large, burly men. They said they had been sent by Nero. They asked me where I had put the package. I told them I had no idea of what they were referring to. They gathered me up and forced me into a dingy building.

As soon as my eyes adjusted to the glow of the incandescent lights, I saw a large, rotund man at a table. He looked formidable. I was forced to sit across the table from the man. He leaned forward and I could see his face. A face of evil. He studied me carefully, and then he looked at my assailants. "This isn't Mouser, you idiots. Get him out of here." They blindfolded me and walked me out of the building a different way. An hour later I found myself on a deserted street.

Two days later I left the Crescent City. I never told anyone about my experience, and I've never been back.

EXAMINER'S ASSESSMENT PROTOCOLS

form **B**

 **PREPRIMER (PP) LEVEL ASSESSMENT PROTOCOL**

Eyes in My Closet (Wordless picture story)

PART I: WORDLESS PICTURE STORY READING

Background Statement: "These pictures tell a story about a child who is going to bed. Look at each picture as I show it to you and think about the story the pictures tell. Later, I will want you to tell me the story using the pictures."

Teacher Directions: Refer the student to each picture slowly and in order as numbered. Do not comment on the pictures. Then repeat the procedure, asking the student to tell the story in the student's own words. Record the student's reading using a tape recorder, and transcribe the reading as it is being dictated. Replay the recording later to make sure that your transcription is accurate and complete.

PART II: EMERGENT READING BEHAVIOR CHECKLIST

Directions: Following are emergent reading behaviors identified through research and grouped according to broad developmental stages. Check all behaviors you have observed. *If the student progresses to Stage 3 or 4, continue your assessment using the Primer Level (P) passage.*

Stage 1: Early Connections to Reading—Describing Pictures

_____ Attends to and describes (labels) pictures in books

_____ Has a limited sense of story

_____ Follows verbal directions for this activity

_____ Uses oral vocabulary appropriate for age/grade level

_____ Displays attention span appropriate for age/grade level

_____ Responds to questions in an appropriate manner

_____ Appears to connect pictures (sees as being interrelated)

Stage 2: Connecting Pictures to Form Story

_____ Attends to pictures and develops oral stories across the pages of the book

_____ Uses only childlike or descriptive (storyteller) language to tell the story, rather than book language (i.e., Once upon a time...; There once was a little boy...)

Stage 3: Transitional Picture Reading

_____ Attends to pictures as a connected story

_____ Mixes storyteller language with book language

Stage 4: Advanced Picture Reading

_____ Attends to pictures and develops oral stories across the pages of the book

_____ Speaks as though reading the story (uses book language)

Examiner's Notes:

PRIMER (P) LEVEL ASSESSMENT PROTOCOLS
The T-Ball Game (32 words)

PART I: PICTURE STORY READING—ORAL READING AND ANALYSIS OF MISCUES

Background Statement: "This is a story about a child who is playing a game. Let's look at each picture first. Now, read the story to yourself. Later, I will want you to read the story to me."

Teacher Directions: Refer the student to each frame of the story slowly and in order as numbered. Do not read the story or comment on the pictures. After the student has read the story silently, ask the student to read the story aloud. Record the student's reading using a tape recorder, and mark any miscues on the Miscue Grid provided. Following the oral reading, complete the Emergent Reading Behavior Checklist. Assessment information obtained from both the Miscue Grid and the Emergent Reading Behavior Checklist will help you to determine whether to continue your assessment. If the student is unable to read the passage independently the first time, read it aloud, then ask the student to try to read the story again. This will help you to understand whether the student is able to memorize and repeat text, an important developmental milestone (see the *Instructions for Administering the Preprimer (PP) and Primer (P) Passages* section in the front of this book for more information). The assessment should stop after this activity, if the child is unable to read the text independently. (Note: The Miscue Grid should be completed *after* the assessment session has been concluded in order to minimize stress for the student.)

	MIS-PRONUN.	SUB-STITUTION	OMISSION	INSERTION	TCHR. ASSIST.	SELF-CORRECT.	MEANING DISRUPTION
The T-Ball Game							
I like to play T-ball							
at school. On Friday							
we played the big							
game. I got a							
hit at the end of							
the game. I made							
it home and won							
the game.							
TOTALS							

Notes:

PART II: EMERGENT READING BEHAVIOR CHECKLIST

Directions: Following are emergent reading behaviors identified through research and grouped according to broad developmental stages. After completing the oral reading, check each behavior observed below to help determine development level and whether to continue the assessment. *If the student seems to be at Stage 6 or 7 and the oral reading scored at an Easy or Adequate level, continue the assessment using the Level 1 passage.*

Stage 5: Early Print Reading

_____ Tells a story using the pictures

_____ Knows print moves from left to right, top to bottom

_____ Creates part of the text using book language and knows some words on sight

Stage 6: Early Strategic Reading

_____ Uses context to guess at some unknown words (guesses make sense)

_____ Notices beginning sounds in words and uses them in guessing unknown words

_____ Seems to sometimes use syntax to help identify words in print

_____ Recognizes some word parts, such as root words and affixes

Stage 7: Moderate Strategic Reading

_____ Sometimes uses context and word parts to decode words

_____ Self-corrects when making an oral reading miscue

_____ Retells the passage easily and may embellish the storyline

_____ Shows some awareness of vowel sounds

Examiner's Notes

Examiner's Summary of Miscue Patterns:

PART III: DEVELOPMENTAL/PERFORMANCE SUMMARY

Silent Reading Comprehension

_____ 0–1 questions missed = Easy

_____ 2 questions missed = Adequate

_____ 3+ questions missed = Too hard

Oral Reading Accuracy

_____ 0–1 oral errors = Easy

_____ 2–5 oral errors = Adequate

_____ 6+ oral errors = Too hard

Continue to next assessment level passage? _____ Yes _____ No

Examiner's Notes:

LEVEL 1 ASSESSMENT PROTOCOLS
Birthday at the Zoo (106 words)

PART I: SILENT READING COMPREHENSION

Background Statement: "What do you like to do on your birthday? Read this story carefully to find out what special thing a girl wanted for her birthday. I'm going to ask you to tell me about the story when you're through reading it."

Teacher Directions: Once the student completes the silent reading, say, "Tell me about the story you just read." Answers to the questions below that the student provides during the retelling should be marked "ua" in the appropriate blank to indicate that this response was unaided. Ask all remaining questions not addressed during the retelling and mark those the student answers with an "a" to indicate that the correct response was given after prompting by the teacher.

Questions/Answers	*Story Grammar Element/ Level of Comprehension*
_____1. Who were the people in the story? *(Pat and her Mom)*	character-characterization/ literal
_____2. What was Pat's wish? *(Pat wanted to have a party)*	story problem(s)/literal
_____3. What did Pat say she wanted to do for her birthday? *(just play)*	problem resolution attempts/ literal
_____4. Did Pat get her wish? How do you know? *(yes, she had a surprise party at the zoo)*	problem resolution/ literal
_____5. How did Pat and her Mom get to the zoo? *(drove in by car)*	problem resolution attempts/ literal
_____6. What words would you use to describe how Pat felt at the zoo? *(surprised, happy, etc.)*	character-characterization/ inferential
_____7. Where was Pat when the story began? *(in her bedroom or house)*	setting/inferential
_____8. When did Pat first know that she was going to have a birthday party? *(when she got to the zoo and saw her friends)*	problem resolution attempts/ inferential

PART II: ORAL READING AND ANALYSIS OF MISCUES

Directions: Say, "Now I would like to hear you read this story out loud." Have the student read orally until the 100-word sample is completed. Follow along on the Miscue Grid, marking any oral reading errors as appropriate. *Remember to count miscues only up to the point in the story containing the oral reading stop-marker (//).* Then complete the Developmental/Performance Summary to determine whether to continue the assessment. (*Note:* The Miscue Grid should be completed *after* the assessment session has been concluded in order to minimize stress for the student.)

	MIS-PRONUN.	SUB-STITUTION	OMISSION	INSERTION	TCHR. ASSIST.	SELF-CORRECT.	MEANING DISRUPTION
Birthday at the Zoo							
It was Sunday.							
I got out of bed and went							
to eat. Mom said, "Today							
is your birthday, Pat. What							
do you want to do?" I wanted							
a party but I did not tell Mom.							
I said, "I just want to play."							
Mom said, "Come take							
a ride with me." I got							
in the car and soon we							
were in the city.							
The car stopped. We got							
out. We walked past some							
trees and I saw a sign that							
said "City Zoo." All my friends							
were at the gate. I was all smiles.							
Mom had planned a party for me. //							
It was the best birthday ever.							
TOTALS							

Notes:

Examiner's Summary of Miscue Patterns:

PART III: DEVELOPMENTAL/PERFORMANCE SUMMARY

Silent Reading Comprehension

_____ 0–1 questions missed = Easy

_____ 2 questions missed = Adequate

_____ 3+ questions missed = Too hard

Oral Reading Accuracy

_____ 0–1 oral errors = Easy

_____ 2–5 oral errors = Adequate

_____ 6+ oral errors = Too hard

Continue to next assessment level passage? _____ Yes _____ No

PART IV: LISTENING COMPREHENSION

Directions: If you have decided not to continue to have the student read any other passages, then use this passage to begin assessing the student's listening comprehension (see page 8). Begin by reading the background statement for this passage and then say, "I am going to read this story to you. Please listen carefully because I will be asking you some questions after I finish reading it to you." After reading the passage, ask the student the questions associated with the passage. If the student correctly answers more than six questions, you will need to move to the next level and repeat the procedure.

Listening Comprehension

_____ 0–2 questions missed = move to the next passage level

_____ more than two questions missed = stop assessment or move down a level

Examiner's Notes:

Mary's New Bike (156 words)

PART I: SILENT READING COMPREHENSION

Background Statement: "Have you ever tried to earn money for something special? Read this story to find out how Mary was able to earn something special. Read it carefully because I am going to ask you to tell me about the story when you finish."

Teacher Directions: Once the student completes the silent reading, say, "Tell me about the story you just read." Answers to the questions below that the student provides during the retelling should be marked "ua" in the appropriate blank to indicate that this response was unaided. Ask all remaining questions not addressed during the retelling and mark those the student answers with an "a" to indicate that the correct response was given after prompting by the teacher.

Questions/Answers	*Story Grammar Element/ Level of Comprehension*
_____1. Who was this story about? *(Mary)*	character-characterization/ literal
_____2. What was Mary's problem in the story? *(she wanted a new bike but she didn't have enough money)*	story problem(s)/literal
_____3. What had Mary done to earn money in the past? *(rake leaves and help around the house)*	problem resolution attempts/ literal
_____4. Besides Mary, who were the people in the story? *(Aunt Deb, Mary's family)*	character-characterization/ literal
_____5. How did Mary finally solve her problem? *(worked hard for Aunt Deb and earned enough money)*	problem resolution/ inferential
_____6. What were two things Mary did for Aunt Deb? *(mopped floor, swept carport, cleaned out flower beds)*	problem resolution attempts/ literal
_____7. What lesson did Mary learn about getting something you really want? *(it takes time and hard work)*	theme/evaluative
_____8. Why did Mary go to the store the next day? *(to buy her bike)*	problem resolution attempts/ inferential

PART II: ORAL READING AND ANALYSIS OF MISCUES

Directions: Say, "Now I would like to hear you read this story out loud." Have the student read orally until the 100-word sample is completed. Follow along on the Miscue Grid, marking any oral reading errors as appropriate. *Remember to count miscues only up to the point in the story containing the oral reading stop-marker (//).* Then complete the Developmental/Performance Summary to determine whether to continue the assessment. (*Note:* The Miscue Grid should be completed *after* the assessment session has been concluded in order to minimize stress for the student.)

	MIS-PRONUN.	SUB-STITUTION	OMISSION	INSERTION	TCHR. ASSIST.	SELF-CORRECT.	MEANING DISRUPTION
Mary's New Bike							
Mary wanted a new bike. She							
helped around the house to make							
money. She had even helped her							
Father rake leaves for extra money.							
But she still didn't have the							
money for the new ten-speed bike.							
One day her Aunt Deb came to							
visit Mary's family. Aunt Deb							
heard that Mary wanted a new							
bike. She told Mary that she							
had some work for her. Mary							
walked over to Aunt Deb's house							
the very next day. Aunt Deb							
had Mary mop her kitchen floor.							
Mary cleaned out the flower beds.							
Mary swept out the carport. Finally							
Aunt Deb asked //							
Mary to fold her clean clothes.							
TOTALS							

Notes:

	MIS-PRONUN.	SUB-STITUTION	OMISSION	INSERTION	TCHR. ASSIST.	SELF-CORRECT.	MEANING DISRUPTION
Bedtime							
The sun was going down.							
The air was hot and Wild Willie							
was afraid. Never had he been							
in such a dry, hot place. His							
horse, Wizard, was trying to find							
a few blades of grass. Wild Willie							
was beginning to fall asleep							
from staying awake so long. Then							
he heard the sound again—the							
same sound he had been hearing for							
days. What could it be?							
Why was it following him? How							
could he find out what or who							
it was? Slowly Wizard turned							
around. Willie stood up in							
the stirrups to see over							
the sand dune. He							
saw // *no one.*							
TOTALS							

Notes:

Examiner's Summary of Miscue Patterns:

PART III: DEVELOPMENTAL/PERFORMANCE SUMMARY

Silent Reading Comprehension

_____ 0–1 questions missed = Easy

_____ 2 questions missed = Adequate

_____ 3+ questions missed = Too hard

Oral Reading Accuracy

_____ 0–1 oral errors = Easy

_____ 2–5 oral errors = Adequate

_____ 6+ oral errors = Too hard

Continue to next assessment level passage? _____ Yes _____ No

PART IV: LISTENING COMPREHENSION

Directions: If you have decided not to continue to have the student read any other passages, then use this passage to begin assessing the student's listening comprehension (see page 8). Begin by reading the background statement for this passage and then say, "I am going to read this story to you. Please listen carefully because I will be asking you some questions after I finish reading it to you." After reading the passage, ask the student the questions associated with the passage. If the student correctly answers more than six questions, you will need to move to the next level and repeat the procedure.

Listening Comprehension

_____ 0–2 questions missed = move to the next passage level

_____ more than two questions missed = stop assessment or move down a level

Examiner's Notes:

A Different Time (294 words)

PART I: SILENT READING COMPREHENSION

Background Statement: "This story is about a boy who lived a long time ago. Read the story to find out what Marlo wanted and why he couldn't have it. Read it carefully because I will ask you to tell me about it when you finish."

Teacher Directions: Once the student completes the silent reading, say, "Tell me about the story you just read." Answers to the questions below that the student provides during the retelling should be marked "ua" in the appropriate blank to indicate that this response was unaided. Ask all remaining questions not addressed during the retelling and mark those the student answers with an "a" to indicate that the correct response was given after prompting by the teacher.

Questions/Answers	**Story Grammar Element/ Level of Comprehension**
_____1. Where did Marlo live? *(in a hut)*	setting/literal
_____2. What was Marlo's problem? *(he wanted to read)*	story problem(s)/literal
_____3. What did Marlo do that caused the old man to help him? *(gave him some vegetables)*	problem resolution attempts/ inferential
_____4. Where did Marlo have to meet the old man? *(old oak tree)*	setting/literal
_____5. How was Marlo's problem solved? *(the old man gave him a book so he could learn to read)*	problem resolution attempts/ inferential
_____6. How would you describe Marlo? *(kind, nice, thankful, other plausible response)*	character-characterization/ evaluative
_____7. How do you know that this story took place in olden times and not today? *(castle, they lived in hut, used a cart, lots of people couldn't read, and other plausible responses)*	setting/inferential
_____8. Why is "be kind to others and they'll be kind to you" a good theme for this story? *(responses will vary but should indicate that Marlo got his wish because of his kindness)*	theme/evaluative

PART II: ORAL READING AND ANALYSIS OF MISCUES

Directions: Say, "Now I would like to hear you read this story out loud." Have the student read orally until the 100-word sample is completed. Follow along on the Miscue Grid, marking any oral reading errors as appropriate. *Remember to count miscues only up to the point in the story containing the oral reading stop-marker (//).* Then complete the Developmental/Performance Summary to determine whether to continue the assessment. (*Note:* The Miscue Grid should be completed *after* the assessment session has been concluded in order to minimize stress for the student.)

	MIS- PRONUN.	SUB- STITUTION	OMISSION	INSERTION	TCHR. ASSIST.	SELF- CORRECT.	MEANING DISRUPTION
A Different Time							
Marlo lived in a different time							
and a different place. He lived							
in a time of darkness and gloom.							
Marlo lived in a small hut with							
his poor parents. He didn't have							
nice clothes and he didn't have							
much to eat. But neither of these							
things bothered Marlo. There was							
only one thing he wanted. But							
he couldn't have it because the							
ruler would not let any of							
his people have it. This most							
important thing was to be able							
to read. Today this may							
seem like a dumb wish, but to							
Marlo it wasn't. One day							
Marlo's father sent // *him*							
to the castle with a cart of vegetables.							
TOTALS							

Notes:

Examiner's Summary of Miscue Patterns:

PART III: DEVELOPMENTAL/PERFORMANCE SUMMARY

Silent Reading Comprehension

_____ 0–1 questions missed = Easy

_____ 2   questions missed = Adequate

_____ 3+   questions missed = Too hard

Oral Reading Accuracy

_____ 0–1 oral errors = Easy

_____ 2–5 oral errors = Adequate

_____ 6+   oral errors = Too hard

Continue to next assessment level passage?   _____ Yes   _____ No

PART IV: LISTENING COMPREHENSION

Directions: If you have decided not to continue to have the student read any other passages, then use this passage to begin assessing the student's listening comprehension (see page 8). Begin by reading the background statement for this passage and then say, "I am going to read this story to you. Please listen carefully because I will be asking you some questions after I finish reading it to you." After reading the passage, ask the student the questions associated with the passage. If the student correctly answers more than six questions, you will need to move to the next level and repeat the procedure.

Listening Comprehension

_____ 0–2 questions missed   = move to the next passage level

_____ more than two questions missed = stop assessment or move down a level

Examiner's Notes:

LEVEL 5 ASSESSMENT PROTOCOLS
Afternoon Walk (390 words)

PART I: SILENT READING COMPREHENSION

Background Statement: "This story is about a young girl who goes walking in woods that are supposed to be haunted. Read the story to find out what happens to Allison when she ventures into the haunted woods. Read it carefully because I will ask you to tell me about it when you finish."

Teacher Directions: Once the student completes the silent reading, say, "Tell me about the story you just read." Answers to the questions below that the student provides during the retelling should be marked "ua" in the appropriate blank to indicate that this response was unaided. Ask all remaining questions not addressed during the retelling and mark those the student answers with an "a" to indicate that the correct response was given after prompting by the teacher.

Questions/Answers	*Story Grammar Element/ Level of Comprehension*
_____1. Who is the main character in this story? *(Allison)*	character-characterization/ literal
_____2. Where was Allison when she first met the old lady? *(in the woods or under an elm tree)*	setting/literal
_____3. Where did the old woman take Allison? *(to the old woman's hut)*	setting/literal
_____4. What was Allison's problem with the old woman? *(getting away before being sold to the dwarf or not acting tired)*	story problem(s)/inferential
_____5. How did Allison escape from the old woman? *(she ran out the door while the woman was looking for her dog)*	problem resolution/literal
_____6. What happened after Allison couldn't run any farther and fell asleep? *(her brother woke her up)*	problem resolution attempts/ literal
_____7. What happened after Allison was safely back home? *(she found a small metal tag with "Spirit" printed on it)*	problem resolution attempts/ literal
_____8. Why, in the story, did Allison always tell the old woman that she was not tired? *(because she didn't want to be sold)*	problem resolution attempts/ inferential

PART II: ORAL READING AND ANALYSIS OF MISCUES

Directions: Say, "Now I would like to hear you read this story out loud." Have the student read orally until the 100-word sample is completed. Follow along on the Miscue Grid, marking any oral reading errors as appropriate. *Remember to count miscues only up to the point in the story containing the oral reading stop-marker (//).* Then complete the Developmental/Performance Summary to determine whether to continue the assessment. (*Note:* The Miscue Grid should be completed *after* the assessment session has been concluded in order to minimize stress for the student.)

	MIS-PRONUN.	SUB-STITUTION	OMISSION	INSERTION	TCHR. ASSIST.	SELF-CORRECT.	MEANING DISRUPTION
Afternoon Walk							
One day Allison was walking in							
the woods behind her house. Some of							
the other children in the neighborhood							
liked to tease her by saying that the							
woods were haunted. "There's an							
old, withered, witch-like woman							
in those woods who comes							
out at two o'clock every day to							
catch children," they'd say.							
"She makes them do housework							
and things like that. Then							
she sells them to a grim looking							
dwarf from far away when they are							
too tired to work. Once captured they							
are never seen again." Allison knew her							
friends were only telling stories,							
but it still frightened //							
her sometimes when she went							
into the woods.							
TOTALS							

Notes:

Examiner's Summary of Miscue Patterns:

PART III: DEVELOPMENTAL/PERFORMANCE SUMMARY

Silent Reading Comprehension

_____ 0–1 questions missed = Easy

_____ 2   questions missed = Adequate

_____ 3+   questions missed = Too hard

Oral Reading Accuracy

_____ 0–1 oral errors = Easy

_____ 2–5 oral errors = Adequate

_____ 6+   oral errors = Too hard

Continue to next assessment level passage? _____ Yes _____ No

PART IV: LISTENING COMPREHENSION

Directions: If you have decided not to continue to have the student read any other passages, then use this passage to begin assessing the student's listening comprehension (see page 8). Begin by reading the background statement for this passage and then say, "I am going to read this story to you. Please listen carefully because I will be asking you some questions after I finish reading it to you." After reading the passage, ask the student the questions associated with the passage. If the student correctly answers more than six questions, you will need to move to the next level and repeat the procedure.

Listening Comprehension

_____ 0–2 questions missed   = move to the next passage level

_____ more than two questions missed = stop assessment or move down a level

Examiner's Notes:

PART I: SILENT READING COMPREHENSION

Background Statement: "This story is about a boy who had problems in school. Read the story to find out how the boy's problems were solved. Read it carefully because I'm going to ask you to tell me about it when you finish."

Teacher Directions: Once the student completes the silent reading, say, "Tell me about the story you just read." Answers to the questions below that the student provides during the retelling should be marked "ua" in the appropriate blank to indicate that this response was unaided. Ask all remaining questions not addressed during the retelling and mark those the student answers with an "a" to indicate that the correct response was given after prompting by the teacher.

Questions/Answers	*Story Grammar Element/ Level of Comprehension*
_____1. Who was the story mainly about? *(Matthew)*	character-characterization/ literal
_____2. What was Matthew's problem? *(he wasn't doing well in school, or other plausible response)*	story problem(s)/inferential
_____3. What did Matthew's teacher decide to do about Matthew's problem? *(have Matthew tested for a learning problem)*	problem resolution attempts/ literal
_____4. Summarize what the school found out about Matthew's problem. *(he was gifted in math and science)*	problem resolution/inferential
_____5. How did the school try to solve the problem? *(it allowed Matthew to study what interested him the most)*	problem resolution attempts/ inferential
_____6. How was Matthew affected by being allowed to study what most interested him? *(he improved as a student and made friends)*	character-characterization/ inferential
_____7. How did Matthew's story affect the writer of this story? *(the writer believes everyone has special talents if you look for them)*	theme/evaluative
_____8. Why were the phone calls with the professor set up for Matthew? *(so he could ask the professor about lasers when he needed to)*	problem resolution attempts/ literal

PART II: ORAL READING AND ANALYSIS OF MISCUES

Directions: Say, "Now I would like to hear you read this story out loud." Have the student read orally until the 100-word sample is completed. Follow along on the Miscue Grid, marking any oral reading errors as appropriate. *Remember to count miscues only up to the point in the story containing the oral reading stop-marker (//).* Then complete the Developmental/Performance Summary to determine whether to continue the assessment. (*Note:* The Miscue Grid should be completed *after* the assessment session has been concluded in order to minimize stress for the student.)

	MIS-PRONUN.	SUB-STITUTION	OMISSION	INSERTION	TCHR. ASSIST.	SELF-CORRECT.	MEANING DISRUPTION
Laser Boy							
My name is Bob and I'm a teacher.							
Several years ago I knew a student							
that I'd like to tell you about.							
Matthew was a 13-year-old who never							
seemed to do well in school. Some							
say that he was a misfit, someone							
who doesn't quite fit in with the							
other kids his age.							
Not only that, Matthew							
had trouble in school nearly							
his whole life.							
He failed to complete his							
homework even when it was							
an easy assignment.							
By not participating in class,							
not turning in homework, and							
only doing a fair job on tests,							
Matthew always seemed							
to // *be just barely passing.*							
TOTALS							

Notes:

Examiner's Summary of Miscue Patterns:

PART III: DEVELOPMENTAL/PERFORMANCE SUMMARY

Silent Reading Comprehension

_____ 0–1 questions missed = Easy

_____ 2 questions missed = Adequate

_____ 3+ questions missed = Too hard

Oral Reading Accuracy

_____ 0–1 oral errors = Easy

_____ 2–5 oral errors = Adequate

_____ 6+ oral errors = Too hard

Continue to next assessment level passage? _____ Yes _____ No

PART IV: LISTENING COMPREHENSION

Directions: If you have decided not to continue to have the student read any other passages, then use this passage to begin assessing the student's listening comprehension (see page 8). Begin by reading the background statement for this passage and then say, "I am going to read this story to you. Please listen carefully because I will be asking you some questions after I finish reading it to you." After reading the passage, ask the student the questions associated with the passage. If the student correctly answers more than six questions, you will need to move to the next level and repeat the procedure.

Listening Comprehension

_____ 0–2 questions missed = move to the next passage level

_____ more than two questions missed = stop assessment or move down a level

Examiner's Notes:

The Paper Route (435 words)

PART I: SILENT READING COMPREHENSION

Background Statement: "This story is about a boy who begins his first job as a paperboy. Read it to find out what his first year as a paperboy was like. Read it carefully because I will ask you to tell me about it when you finish."

Teacher Directions: Once the student completes the silent reading, say, "Tell me about the story you just read." Answers to the questions below that the student provides during the retelling should be marked "ua" in the appropriate blank to indicate that this response was unaided. Ask all remaining questions not addressed during the retelling and mark those the student answers with an "a" to indicate that the correct response was given after prompting by the teacher.

Questions/Answers	*Story Grammar Element/ Level of Comprehension*
_____1. Who were the main characters in the story? *(Scott and Mr. Miley)*	character-characterization/ literal
_____2. How did Scott get a chance to earn money? *(by answering an ad for newspaper carriers)*	problem resolution attempts/ literal
_____3. What did Scott have to do each morning after picking up his newspapers? *(roll them and put them in plastic bags)*	problem resolution attempts/ literal
_____4. Why were Thursdays and Sundays problems for Scott? *(papers were extra large and it took many trips to get them delivered)*	story problem(s)/inferential
_____5. What were the two main problems Scott faced with his job? *(bad weather and cranky customers)*	story problem(s)/literal
_____6. How did Scott handle the problem of cranky customers? *(by going out of his way to please them)*	problem resolution/literal
_____7. What words would you use to describe Scott? *(responses will vary but should reflect the idea of hardworking, conscientious)*	character-characterization/ evaluative
_____8. What lessons would a job like Scott's teach? *(responses will vary but should indicate a theme related to benefits of hard work)*	theme/evaluative

PART II: ORAL READING AND ANALYSIS OF MISCUES

Directions: Say, "Now I would like to hear you read this story out loud." Have the student read orally until the 100-word sample is completed. Follow along on the Miscue Grid, marking any oral reading errors as appropriate. *Remember to count miscues only up to the point in the story containing the oral reading stop-marker (//).* Then complete the Developmental/Performance Summary to determine whether to continue the assessment. (*Note:* The Miscue Grid should be completed *after* the assessment session has been concluded in order to minimize stress for the student.)

	MIS-PRONUN.	SUB-STITUTION	OMISSION	INSERTION	TCHR. ASSIST.	SELF-CORRECT.	MEANING DISRUPTION
The Paper Route							
Scott had a chance to earn his own							
money for the first time. Answering							
an advertisement for newspaper							
carriers, he set up an appointment							
with Mr. Miley, the distribution							
manager. Mr. Miley was a rather							
short and stocky man who spoke							
with a loud voice. After reviewing							
Scott's application, Mr. Miley							
said, "You look like a dependable							
young man to me. Do your							
parents approve of your becoming							
a paperboy?" "Yes, sir," replied							
Scott, "and I have a letter from							
my Dad saying it's OK with him."							
"You can have the job, Scott," said Mr.							
Miley. "However, I want you to //							
realize that this is a long route and							
you will have to get up very early.							
TOTALS							

Notes:

Examiner's Summary of Miscue Patterns:

PART III: DEVELOPMENTAL/PERFORMANCE SUMMARY

Silent Reading Comprehension

_____ 0–1 questions missed = Easy

_____ 2 questions missed = Adequate

_____ 3+ questions missed = Too hard

Oral Reading Accuracy

_____ 0–1 oral errors = Easy

_____ 2–5 oral errors = Adequate

_____ 6+ oral errors = Too hard

Continue to next assessment level passage? _____ Yes _____ No

PART IV: LISTENING COMPREHENSION

Directions: If you have decided not to continue to have the student read any other passages, then use this passage to begin assessing the student's listening comprehension (see page 8). Begin by reading the background statement for this passage and then say, "I am going to read this story to you. Please listen carefully because I will be asking you some questions after I finish reading it to you." After reading the passage, ask the student the questions associated with the passage. If the student correctly answers more than six questions, you will need to move to the next level and repeat the procedure.

Listening Comprehension

_____ 0–2 questions missed = move to the next passage level

_____ more than two questions missed = stop assessment or move down a level

Examiner's Notes:

Examiner's Summary of Miscue Patterns:

PART III: DEVELOPMENTAL/PERFORMANCE SUMMARY

Silent Reading Comprehension

_____ 0–1 questions missed = Easy

_____ 2   questions missed = Adequate

_____ 3+   questions missed = Too hard

Oral Reading Accuracy

_____ 0–1 oral errors = Easy

_____ 2–5 oral errors = Adequate

_____ 6+   oral errors = Too hard

Continue to next assessment level passage?   _____ Yes   _____ No

PART IV: LISTENING COMPREHENSION

Directions: If you have decided not to continue to have the student read any other passages, then use this passage to begin assessing the student's listening comprehension (see page 8). Begin by reading the background statement for this passage and then say, "I am going to read this story to you. Please listen carefully because I will be asking you some questions after I finish reading it to you." After reading the passage, ask the student the questions associated with the passage. If the student correctly answers more than six questions, you will need to move to the next level and repeat the procedure.

Listening Comprehension

_____ 0–2 questions missed   = move to the next passage level

_____ more than two questions missed = stop assessment or move down a level

Examiner's Notes:

The Long Night (474 words)

PART I: SILENT READING COMPREHENSION

Background Statement: "This story is about mistaken identity. Read it carefully because I will ask you to tell me about the story when you finish reading."

Teacher Directions: Once the student completes the silent reading, say, "Tell me about the story you just read." Answers to the questions below that the student provides during the retelling should be marked "ua" in the appropriate blank to indicate that this response was unaided. Ask all remaining questions not addressed during the retelling and mark those the student answers with an "a" to indicate that the correct response was given after prompting by the teacher.

Questions/Answers	*Story Grammar Element/ Level of Comprehension*
_____1. Where and at what time of day did this story take place? *(nighttime in New Orleans)*	setting/literal
_____2. What was the problem facing the writer of this story while he walked up Rampart? *(he was being followed and someone gave him a note that said he was going to die)*	story problem(s)/inferential
_____3. How did the policeman react to his story? *(didn't really believe him)*	problem resolution attempts/ literal
_____4. What happened after he left the policeman? *(he was taken into a building by two men)*	problem resolution attempts/ literal
_____5. How did the writer of this story solve the problem(s)? *(it turned out to be a case of mistaken identity)*	problem resolution/ inferential
_____6. Who was Nero, and how would you describe him? *(he was the boss, a criminal, and a nasty kind of character)*	character-characterization/ inferential
_____7. What series of events got the person in this story into such trouble? *(flight delay, walking alone at night, and he looked like someone else)*	story problem(s)/inferential
_____8. What did the author do after he was released? *(stayed two more days and never returned)*	problem resolution attempts/ literal

PART II: ORAL READING AND ANALYSIS OF MISCUES

Directions: Say, "Now I would like to hear you read this story out loud." Have the student read orally until the 100-word sample is completed. Follow along on the Miscue Grid, marking any oral reading errors as appropriate. *Remember to count miscues only up to the point in the story containing the oral reading stop-marker (//).* Then complete the Developmental/Performance Summary to determine whether to continue the assessment. (*Note:* The Miscue Grid should be completed *after* the assessment session has been concluded in order to minimize stress for the student.)

	MIS-PRONUN.	SUB-STITUTION	OMISSION	INSERTION	TCHR. ASSIST.	SELF-CORRECT.	MEANING DISRUPTION
The Long Night							
I arrived late at the New Orleans							
International Airport because of							
delays in St. Louis. The night							
was descending on the							
Crescent City as I entered							
the cab for the short ride to							
city center. As the cab headed							
toward the city, the cabbie engaged							
me in an informative conversation							
about the Crescent City. She had an							
island accent and her multicolored							
dress was very nontraditional.							
After I told her I wanted to							
go to Rampart in the							
French Quarter, she abruptly turned							
left and headed southwest.							
Fifteen minutes later, without a word,							
I got out of the cab // *and proceeded*							
up Rampart.							
TOTALS							

Notes:

Examiner's Summary of Miscue Patterns:

PART III: DEVELOPMENTAL/PERFORMANCE SUMMARY

Silent Reading Comprehension

_____ 0–1 questions missed = Easy

_____ 2 questions missed = Adequate

_____ 3+ questions missed = Too hard

Oral Reading Accuracy

_____ 0–1 oral errors = Easy

_____ 2–5 oral errors = Adequate

_____ 6+ oral errors = Too hard

Continue to next assessment level passage? _____ Yes _____ No

PART IV: LISTENING COMPREHENSION

Directions: If you have decided not to continue to have the student read any other passages, then use this passage to begin assessing the student's listening comprehension (see page 8). Begin by reading the background statement for this passage and then say, "I am going to read this story to you. Please listen carefully because I will be asking you some questions after I finish reading it to you." After reading the passage, ask the student the questions associated with the passage. If the student correctly answers more than six questions, you will need to move to the next level and repeat the procedure.

Listening Comprehension

_____ 0–2 questions missed = move to the next passage level

_____ more than two questions missed = stop assessment or move down a level

Examiner's Notes:

SENTENCES FOR INITIAL PASSAGE SELECTION .... **form**

FORM C: LEVEL 1

1. Some animals are fun.

2. I eat lots of food.

3. He can smell good.

FORM C: LEVEL 2

1. It was a very clear night.

2. I get hot when the sun shines bright.

3. We can't see air moving.

FORM C: LEVEL 3

1. Many insects are very helpful.

2. Some adults are slender, some are fat.

3. I agree that it is the most beautiful flower.

FORM C: LEVEL 4

1. A famous man would know what to do.

2. The invention was very important.

3. Instead of jam I like syrup on my food.

FORM C: LEVEL 5

1. The estimate for my car was not acceptable.

2. Various people came immediately to the fire.

3. The amount of water you drink is important.

FORM C: LEVEL 6

1. He considered it carefully, but it was too expensive.

2. The new method of raising the temperature got good results.

3. What is common today is the result of many years of experimenting.

FORM C: LEVEL 7

1. Scientists hope to transform the industrial site before the end of the year.

2. Foreign minerals are used to develop usable compounds.

3. The presence of impurities lowers the value of all gems.

FORM C: LEVEL 8

1. Scientists are always looking for advancements to improve the world.

2. The prearranged site was eliminated.

3. To compress hundreds of wires into one is called "fiber optics."

FORM C: LEVEL 9

1. He moved in a circular motion, then ran off laterally.

2. The vertical object couldn't be viewed easily.

3. At the intersection, a series of accidents occurred.

EXPOSITORY PASSAGES......form

Bears

There are many kinds of bears.

Some bears are brown. Others are black.

Still others are white and are called polar bears.

The biggest bears are called grizzly bears.

Bears can smell and hear very well.

Bears have small eyes and cannot see very well.

They eat all kinds of food.

They eat small animals, plants, and berries.

Most bears sleep during the winter.

When they wake up they are hungry.

Bears can run very fast.

They can climb trees.

They are not safe animals to be around.

The best place to be around bears is at the zoo.

The Night Sky

Look up at the sky at night. If it is a clear night, you will see stars. How many stars are there? No one knows for sure. But there is one star that you know by name. You can see it in the daytime. It is our sun. The sun is a star. All stars are suns. Our sun is so close that we cannot see other stars in the day. We only see the other suns at night.

Stars are made up of very hot gas and they seem to twinkle because of the air moving across them. Even though we can't always see them, they are always in the sky, even in the daytime.

Flying Flowers

There are many kinds of insects. There are big ones, little ones, ugly ones, biting ones, and helpful ones. But there is one kind of insect that most people agree is the most beautiful one. This insect is often called the flying flower. It is the butterfly.

Butterflies are insects that have two pairs of wings. The wings are covered with tiny scales. The scales are different colors. These scales give the butterfly its beautiful colors. Butterflies smell and hear by using their long, thin antennae. Butterflies can't bite or chew. They use long, tube-like tongues to get at the food they eat from flowers.

Butterflies begin as eggs. Then they hatch into caterpillars. A caterpillar forms a hard skin. When they finally break out of the hard skin, they are butterflies with colorful wings. Adult butterflies must lay eggs soon. They do not live very long.

Butterflies and moths are different. Butterflies like the day. Moths like the night. Moths are not as colorful as butterflies. Butterfly bodies are slender, while moths tend to have large, fat bodies. Moths

Most of the medicine that cures headaches was taken out of Coca-Cola as time went on. But Dr. Pemberton's drink is still one of the world's favorite soft drinks.

Popcorn

There are three major types of corn grown in this country. First, there is the type of corn people eat most of the time. It is called sweet corn because of its flavor. Second, there is field corn, which is used mainly for feeding livestock. Sometimes people eat field corn too. However, its taste is not as good as sweet corn and its kernels are not as full. The third type of corn, often called Indian corn, is popcorn. Popcorn is grown commercially in the United States because the average American eats almost two pounds of popcorn a year, according to various estimates.

When America was discovered by Columbus, Native Americans had been eating popcorn for thousands of years. They prepared it several different ways. One way was to stick the ear of corn on a stick and place it over a campfire. Any kernels that popped out of the fire were gathered up and eaten. Another method was to scrape the cob and throw the kernels into the fire. Any kernels that popped out of the fire were immediately eaten. Since these methods limited how many kernels could actually be eaten, the Native Americans began to use small clay bowls that they would heat sand in. When the sand got really hot, they placed the popcorn in the bowls and waited for the kernels to pop.

Popcorn is popcorn because of the amount of water content of the kernel. Most experts agree that, ideally, a kernel should have at least fourteen percent water content to be good corn for popping. If the corn kernels have less than twelve percent water content, then the kernels will be duds. They won't pop right.

Cooking Without Fire: The Microwave Oven

Microwave cooking is very common today. It is, however, a recent invention. The microwave oven one uses today was developed from the invention of the magnetron tube in 1940. The invention of the magnetron tube, by Sir John Randall and Dr. H. A. Boot, was a very important part of the radar defense of England during World War II. Neither man considered it as a means of preparing food after they invented it.

It wasn't until the late 1940s that Dr. Percy Spencer discovered the magnetron's ability to heat and cook food from the inside out. Spencer experimented with many different foods, all with the same results: The inside got hot first.

It took several years for the company Spencer worked for to develop what we know today as the microwave oven. Not until around 1952 could a person purchase a microwave oven, then called a Radar Range, for home use. These early models were expensive and bulky.

Today's microwave ovens are inexpensive and come with a variety of features. The features include: defrost, constant temperature cooking, and automatic reheat. Microwave cooking, many claim, was the first completely new method of cooking food since early humans discovered fire. Why? Because microwave cooking requires no fire or element of fire to cook food. The food is cooked by electromagnetic energy.

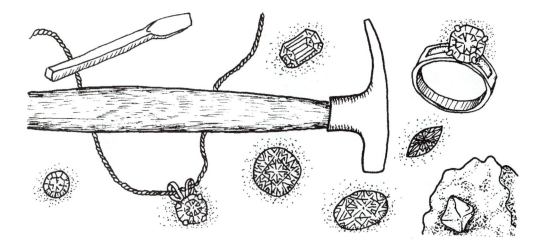

Diamonds

A diamond is one of the most beautiful treasures that nature ever created, and one of the rarest. It takes thousands of years for nature to transform a chunk of carbon into a rough diamond. Only three important diamond fields have been found in the world—in India, South America, and Africa.

The first diamonds were found in the sand and gravel of stream beds. These types of diamonds are called alluvial diamonds. Later, diamonds were found deep in the earth in rock formations called pipes. These formations resemble extinct volcanoes. The rock in which diamonds are found is called blue ground. Yet even where diamonds are plentiful, it takes digging and sorting through tons of rock and gravel to find enough diamonds for a one-carat ring.

Gem diamonds' quality is based on weight, purity, color, and cut. The weight of a diamond is measured by the carat. Its purity is determined by the presence or absence of impurities, such as foreign minerals and uncrystallized carbon. The color of diamonds varies, but most diamonds are tinged yellow or brown. The cut of a diamond also figures into its value. A fully cut diamond, often called flawless, would have fifty-eight facets. Facets, or sides, cause the brilliance that is produced when a diamond is struck by light.

Humans have learned how to make artificial diamonds. Manufactured diamonds are placed in a machine that creates the same pressure that exists about two hundred and fifty miles beneath the surface of the earth. Besides intense pressure, the carbon compounds are heated to temperatures over five thousand degrees Fahrenheit. Unfortunately, the created diamonds are small and are used mainly in industrial settings. They have no value as gems.

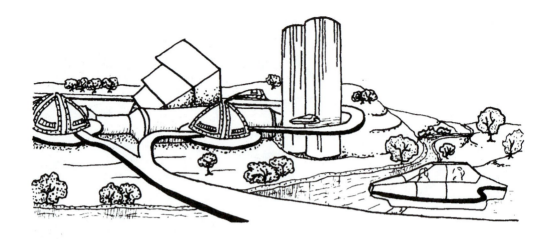

The Future Is Here

What will the twenty-first century bring in terms of new inventions and space-age technologies? No one knows for sure. But scientists, inventors, and futurists are predicting a variety of new inventions. These new advancements will affect the way we live and play. Some of them are already on the drawing board.

One example is the levitation vehicle. The idea of a vertical take-off and landing aircraft that can also be driven on the road is the invention of Paul Moeller. He named his version of this type of craft the Moeller 400. People involved in this type of technology see increases in population and crowded highways as reasons that a levitation vehicle will be needed. Imagine flying into the city, hovering over a prearranged landing site, landing, and then driving the rest of the way to work.

Another innovation that will be refined during the 1990s is the dental laser. Researchers have developed a laser that they hope will replace the much feared dental drill. The laser basically vaporizes the cavity without affecting the surrounding enamel. As a bonus, the laser will eliminate the need of a shot for deadening surrounding tissue.

Probably one of the most significant new technologies that will affect people in the near future is the advent of fiber optics. Fiber optics compress hundreds of wires into one, thus allowing for the communication of huge amounts of information over very thin wires. One example of the application of fiber optics will be the development of full-motion, color video telephones. These will be particularly important to the deaf.

Another advancement that is on the horizon is high-definition television. The average consumer will be able to upgrade his or her current televiewing dramatically when high-definition television becomes widely available. The color of these televisions will have the vividness of 35-millimeter movies and the sound quality of compact discs. This refinement will lead to improvements in at-home movies and video games, both of which will be available in three-dimensional formats.

Regardless of new advancements in technology, people must be prepared to face the challenges of the future: namely, to assist each other as we travel through time, and to help preserve our home, the earth.

Visual Illusions

A visual illusion is an unreal or misleading appearance or image, according to *Webster's* dictionary. In other words, visual illusions are sometimes caused by ideas one holds about what one expects to see. In other instances, the illusion is caused by the brain's difficulty in choosing from two or more visual patterns.

If you look at a bull's-eye and move it slowly in circular motions, you should see spokes moving. The spokes, if you see them, aren't really there. This type of visual illusion is called lateral inhibition.

Another type of visual illusion occurs when a person tries to estimate the height of a vertical object. It is referred to as length distortion. The famous Gateway Arch in St. Louis is an example of length distortion, because the arch seems much higher than it is wide. In reality the height and width of the arch are identical. Length distortion occurs because our eyes move more easily from side to side than up and down. This greater effort to look up causes the brain to over-interpret the height of vertical objects.

If you look at a series of squares, you should see small gray spots at each intersection. If you look directly at one intersection the spots should disappear. This illusion is known as Hermann's Grid. It is often seen in modern high-rise office buildings. Many of these buildings have windows separated by crossing strips of metal or concrete.

The above are only three examples of the many ways that our eyes can deceive us. But they do reinforce the old axiom, "Don't believe everything you see."

EXAMINER'S ASSESSMENT PROTOCOLS

PROTOCOLS form C

LEVEL 1 ASSESSMENT PROTOCOLS
Bears (99 words)

PART I: SILENT READING COMPREHENSION

Background Statement: "This story is about bears. Read this story to find out information about the different kinds of bears. Read it carefully because I'm going to ask you to tell me about what you read."

Teacher Directions: Once the student completes the silent reading, say, "Tell me about the story you just read." Answers to the questions below that the student provides during the retelling should be marked "ua" in the appropriate blank to indicate that this response was unaided. Ask all remaining questions not addressed during the retelling and mark those the student answers with an "a" to indicate that the correct response was given after prompting by the teacher.

Questions/Answers	**Expository Grammar Element/ Level of Comprehension**
_____1. What kinds of bears did you read about? *(brown, black, polar, and grizzly)*	collection/literal
_____2. What kind of bear is the biggest of all? *(grizzly bear)*	description/literal
_____3. Explain why bears are not safe to be around. *(plausible responses related to they are wild animals, don't like humans, can run fast and climb trees)*	problem resolution attempts/ inferential
_____4. What are some things bears can do very well? *(smell, hear, run, climb—any three)*	collection/literal
_____5. How do bears find their food? *(smelling and hearing)*	problem resolution attempts/ inferential
_____6. Why are bears often hungry after winter? *(because they sleep most of the winter)*	causation/inferential
_____7. Can you name two things that bears eat? *(plants, berries, and small animals)*	collection/literal
_____8. Where did the story say was the best place to be around bears? *(at the zoo)*	description/literal

PART II: ORAL READING AND ANALYSIS OF MISCUES

Directions: Say, "Now I would like to hear you read this story out loud." Have the student read orally until the passage is completed. Follow along on the Miscue Grid, marking any oral reading errors as appropriate. Then complete the Developmental/Performance Summary to determine whether to continue the assessment. (*Note:* The Miscue Grid should be completed *after* the assessment session has been concluded in order to minimize stress for the student.)

	MIS- PRONUN.	SUB- STITUTION	OMISSION	INSERTION	TCHR. ASSIST.	SELF- CORRECT.	MEANING DISRUPTION
Bears							
There are many kinds of bears.							
Some bears are brown. Others are							
black. Still others are white and							
are called polar bears. The biggest							
bears are called grizzly bears.							
Bears can smell and hear very							
well. Bears have small eyes and							
cannot see very well. They eat all							
kinds of food. They eat							
small animals, plants, and							
berries. Most bears sleep during							
the winter. When they wake up							
they are hungry. Bears can run							
very fast. They can climb trees.							
They are not safe animals to							
be around. The best place							
to be around bears is							
at the zoo. //							
TOTALS							

Notes:

Examiner's Summary of Miscue Patterns:

PART III: DEVELOPMENTAL/PERFORMANCE SUMMARY

Silent Reading Comprehension

_____ 0–1 questions missed = Easy

_____ 2 questions missed = Adequate

_____ 3+ questions missed = Too hard

Continue to next assessment level passage? _____ Yes _____ No

Oral Reading Accuracy

_____ 0–1 oral errors = Easy

_____ 2–5 oral errors = Adequate

_____ 6+ oral errors = Too hard

PART IV: LISTENING COMPREHENSION

Directions: If you have decided not to continue to have the student read any other passages, then use this passage to begin assessing the student's listening comprehension (see page 8). Begin by reading the background statement for this passage and then say, "I am going to read this story to you. Please listen carefully because I will be asking you some questions after I finish reading it to you." After reading the passage, ask the student the questions associated with the passage. If the student correctly answers more than six questions, you will need to move to the next level and repeat the procedure.

Listening Comprehension

_____ 0–2 questions missed = move to the next passage level

_____ more than two questions missed = stop assessment or move down a level

Examiner's Notes:

The Night Sky (116 words)

PART I: SILENT READING COMPREHENSION

Background Statement: "This story is about stars. Read it and try to remember some of the important facts about stars because I'm going to ask you to tell me about what you have read."

Teacher Directions: Once the student completes the silent reading, say, "Tell me about the story you just read." Answers to the questions below that the student provides during the retelling should be marked "ua" in the appropriate blank to indicate that this response was unaided. Ask all remaining questions not addressed during the retelling and mark those the student answers with an "a" to indicate that the correct response was given after prompting by the teacher.

Questions/Answers	*Expository Grammar Element/ Level of Comprehension*
_____1. What kind of night is best for seeing stars? *(clear night)*	description/literal
_____2. What are stars made of? *(hot gases)*	description/literal
_____3. What star can you see only in the daytime? *(the sun)*	causation/literal
_____4. What causes stars to twinkle? *(the air moving across them)*	causation/literal
_____5. Why can't people on earth see other stars during the day? *(the sun is so close and bright)*	collection/literal
_____6. If one night you looked up at the sky and could see no stars, what could be the reason? *(cloudy night)*	problem resolution attempts/ evaluative
_____7. Explain why saying "look at all the suns in the night sky" is not a wrong statement. *(because all stars are suns)*	causation/literal
_____8. Can you name one reason why the earth cannot be called a star? *(it is not made up of hot gases, it is a planet not a star, it has water, and any other plausible responses)*	comparison/evaluative

PART II: ORAL READING AND ANALYSIS OF MISCUES

Directions: Say, "Now I would like to hear you read this story out loud." Have the student read orally until the 100-word sample is completed. Follow along on the Miscue Grid, marking any oral reading errors as appropriate. *Remember to count miscues only up to the point in the story containing the oral reading stop-marker (//).* Then complete the Developmental/Performance Summary to determine whether to continue the assessment. (*Note:* The Miscue Grid should be completed *after* the assessment session has been concluded in order to minimize stress for the student.)

	MIS-PRONUN.	SUB-STITUTION	OMISSION	INSERTION	TCHR. ASSIST.	SELF-CORRECT.	MEANING DISRUPTION
The Night Sky							
Look up at the sky at night.							
If it is a clear night, you will							
see stars. How many stars are							
there? No one knows for							
sure. But there is one star that							
you know by name. You							
can see it in the daytime. It							
is our sun. The sun is a star.							
All stars are suns. Our sun							
is so close that we cannot see other							
stars in the day. We only see							
the other suns at night. Stars are							
made up of very hot gas and							
they seem to twinkle because of							
the air moving across them.							
Even // *though we can't always see*							
them, they are always in the sky,							
even in the daytime.							
TOTALS							

Notes:

Examiner's Summary of Miscue Patterns:

PART III: DEVELOPMENTAL/PERFORMANCE SUMMARY

Silent Reading Comprehension

_____ 0–1 questions missed = Easy

_____ 2 questions missed = Adequate

_____ 3+ questions missed = Too hard

Oral Reading Accuracy

_____ 0–1 oral errors = Easy

_____ 2–5 oral errors = Adequate

_____ 6+ oral errors = Too hard

Continue to next assessment level passage?   _____ Yes   _____ No

PART IV: LISTENING COMPREHENSION

Directions: If you have decided not to continue to have the student read any other passages, then use this passage to begin assessing the student's listening comprehension (see page 8). Begin by reading the background statement for this passage and then say, "I am going to read this story to you. Please listen carefully because I will be asking you some questions after I finish reading it to you." After reading the passage, ask the student the questions associated with the passage. If the student correctly answers more than six questions, you will need to move to the next level and repeat the procedure.

Listening Comprehension

_____ 0–2 questions missed = move to the next passage level

_____ more than two questions missed = stop assessment or move down a level

Examiner's Notes:

LEVEL 3 ASSESSMENT PROTOCOLS
Flying Flowers (194 words)

PART I: SILENT READING COMPREHENSION

Background Statement: "This selection is about a special kind of insect. It is about butterflies. Read this selection to find out some interesting facts about butterflies. I will ask you to tell me about what you read, so read carefully."

Teacher Directions: Once the student completes the silent reading, say, "Tell me about the story you just read." Answers to the questions below that the student provides during the retelling should be marked "ua" in the appropriate blank to indicate that this response was unaided. Ask all remaining questions not addressed during the retelling and mark those the student answers with an "a" to indicate that the correct response was given after prompting by the teacher.

Questions/Answers	*Expository Grammar Element/Level of Comprehension*
_____1. What kind of insect was the passage mainly about? *(butterfly)*	description/literal
_____2. Why is the butterfly referred to as the flying flower? *(because of its many different colors)*	collection/inferential
_____3. What gives the butterfly its colors? *(scales)*	causation/literal
_____4. Can you name two ways in which a butterfly and a moth are different? *(butterflies like the day, are more colorful, are thinner, and most don't form cocoons—moths are the opposite)*	comparison/literal
_____5. Can you name two ways in which a butterfly and a moth are alike? *(they fly, lay eggs, have scales, have wings, etc.)*	comparison/inferential
_____6. What are the antennae of a butterfly used for? *(to smell and hear)*	collection/literal
_____7. Why do grown-up butterflies have to lay eggs as soon as possible? *(they don't live very long)*	problem resolution attempts/inferential
_____8. What happens after a butterfly egg becomes a caterpillar? *(it forms a hard skin that it has to break out of)*	causation/literal

PART II: ORAL READING AND ANALYSIS OF MISCUES

Directions: Say, "Now I would like to hear you read this story out loud." Have the student read orally until the 100-word sample is completed. Follow along on the Miscue Grid, marking any oral reading errors as appropriate. *Remember to count miscues only up to the point in the story containing the oral reading stop-marker (//).* Then complete the Developmental/Performance Summary to determine whether to continue the assessment. (*Note:* The Miscue Grid should be completed *after* the assessment session has been concluded in order to minimize stress for the student.)

	MIS-PRONUN.	SUB-STITUTION	OMISSION	INSERTION	TCHR. ASSIST.	SELF-CORRECT.	MEANING DISRUPTION
Flying Flowers							
There are many kinds of insects.							
There are big ones, little ones, ugly							
ones, biting ones, and helpful ones.							
But there is one kind of insect							
that most people agree is the most							
beautiful one. This insect is often							
called the flying flower. It is							
the butterfly. Butterflies are insects							
that have two pairs of wings.							
The wings are covered with tiny							
scales. The scales are different							
colors. These scales give the							
butterfly its beautiful colors.							
Butterflies smell and hear by using							
their long, thin antennae. Butterflies							
can't bite or chew. They use long,							
tube-like tongues to get at // *the food*							
they eat from flowers.							
TOTALS							

Notes:

Examiner's Summary of Miscue Patterns:

PART III: DEVELOPMENTAL/PERFORMANCE SUMMARY

Silent Reading Comprehension

_____ 0–1 questions missed = Easy

_____ 2 questions missed = Adequate

_____ 3+ questions missed = Too hard

Oral Reading Accuracy

_____ 0–1 oral errors = Easy

_____ 2–5 oral errors = Adequate

_____ 6+ oral errors = Too hard

Continue to next assessment level passage? _____ Yes _____ No

PART IV: LISTENING COMPREHENSION

Directions: If you have decided not to continue to have the student read any other passages, then use this passage to begin assessing the student's listening comprehension (see page 8). Begin by reading the background statement for this passage and then say, "I am going to read this story to you. Please listen carefully because I will be asking you some questions after I finish reading it to you." After reading the passage, ask the student the questions associated with the passage. If the student correctly answers more than six questions, you will need to move to the next level and repeat the procedure.

Listening Comprehension

_____ 0–2 questions missed = move to the next passage level

_____ more than two questions missed = stop assessment or move down a level

Examiner's Notes:

LEVEL 4 ASSESSMENT PROTOCOLS
The Story of Coca-Cola (253 words)

PART I: SILENT READING COMPREHENSION

Background Statement: "This selection is about the history of Coca-Cola. Read it carefully and try to find out some facts about Coca-Cola, because I'm going to ask you to tell me about what you find."

Teacher Directions: Once the student completes the silent reading, say, "Tell me about the story you just read." Answers to the questions below that the student provides during the retelling should be marked "ua" in the appropriate blank to indicate that this response was unaided. Ask all remaining questions not addressed during the retelling and mark those the student answers with an "a" to indicate that the correct response was given after prompting by the teacher.

Questions/Answers	Expository Grammar Element/ Level of Comprehension
_____1. Who invented Coca-Cola? *(Mr./Dr. Pemberton)*	causation/literal
_____2. What was Dr. Pemberton trying to invent when he invented Coca-Cola? *(headache medicine)*	description/literal
_____3. Besides drugs for headaches, what other things were put into Dr. Pemberton's new medicine? *(leaves, fruits, and nuts)*	description/literal
_____4. Why didn't the medicine sell very well at first? *(because the syrup was mixed with regular water)*	causation/inferential
_____5. Why could one say that Coca-Cola became popular because of a mistake? *(because a clerk accidentally mixed the syrup with carbonated water)*	problem resolution attempts/ inferential
_____6. In which city did the original Coca-Cola become a hit? *(Atlanta)*	description/literal
_____7. Explain what is different between today's Coca-Cola and the original version. *(no headache medicine, or other plausible response)*	comparison/inferential
_____8. What's the difference between regular water and carbonated water? *(regular water doesn't have bubbles in it)*	comparison/inferential

PART II: ORAL READING AND ANALYSIS OF MISCUES

Directions: Say, "Now I would like to hear you read this story out loud." Have the student read orally until the 100-word sample is completed. Follow along on the Miscue Grid, marking any oral reading errors as appropriate. *Remember to count miscues only up to the point in the story containing the oral reading stop-marker (//).* Then complete the Developmental/Performance Summary to determine whether to continue the assessment. (*Note:* The Miscue Grid should be completed *after* the assessment session has been concluded in order to minimize stress for the student.)

	MIS-PRONUN.	SUB-STITUTION	OMISSION	INSERTION	TCHR. ASSIST.	SELF-CORRECT.	MEANING DISRUPTION
The Story of Coca-Cola							
Lots of people all over the world							
have heard of the soft drink							
called Coca-Cola. But not many							
people know the real story about							
how this drink was invented.							
Coca-Cola was the invention of							
a Mr. John Pemberton. Although he							
wasn't a doctor, most people called							
him Dr. Pemberton. He was a							
druggist in a town in the South.							
Dr. Pemberton liked to invent new							
things. He lived during the time							
just after the Civil War. One day							
Dr. Pemberton decided to make a							
headache medicine. He made it from							
nuts, fruits, and leaves. He also							
added the // *drugs necessary*							
to cure a headache.							
TOTALS							

Notes:

Examiner's Summary of Miscue Patterns:

PART III: DEVELOPMENTAL/PERFORMANCE SUMMARY

Silent Reading Comprehension

_____ 0–1 questions missed = Easy

_____ 2 questions missed = Adequate

_____ 3+ questions missed = Too hard

Oral Reading Accuracy

_____ 0–1 oral errors = Easy

_____ 2–5 oral errors = Adequate

_____ 6+ oral errors = Too hard

Continue to next assessment level passage?   _____ Yes   _____ No

PART IV: LISTENING COMPREHENSION

Directions: If you have decided not to continue to have the student read any other passages, then use this passage to begin assessing the student's listening comprehension (see page 8). Begin by reading the background statement for this passage and then say, "I am going to read this story to you. Please listen carefully because I will be asking you some questions after I finish reading it to you." After reading the passage, ask the student the questions associated with the passage. If the student correctly answers more than six questions, you will need to move to the next level and repeat the procedure.

Listening Comprehension

_____ 0–2 questions missed = move to the next passage level

_____ more than two questions missed = stop assessment or move down a level

Examiner's Notes:

LEVEL 5 ASSESSMENT PROTOCOLS
Popcorn (282 words)

PART I: SILENT READING COMPREHENSION

Background Statement: "This selection is about corn, and *popcorn* in particular. Read the passage to discover some interesting facts about corn. Read it carefully because I'm going to ask you to tell me about what you read."

Teacher Directions: Once the student completes the silent reading, say, "Tell me about the story you just read." Answers to the questions below that the student provides during the retelling should be marked "ua" in the appropriate blank to indicate that this response was unaided. Ask all remaining questions not addressed during the retelling and mark those the student answers with an "a" to indicate that the correct response was given after prompting by the teacher.

Questions/Answers	Expository Grammar Element/ Level of Comprehension
_____1. Which type of corn is this passage mainly about? *(Indian corn or popcorn)*	description/inferential
_____2. Explain how sweet corn differs from field corn. *(sweet corn is not used to feed livestock, tastes better, and has fuller kernels)*	comparison/inferential
_____3. What makes popcorn pop? *(water in the kernel)*	causation/inferential
_____4. What does the term *duds* mean when talking about popcorn? *(unpopped kernels)*	description/literal
_____5. Which of the methods to pop corn used by the Native Americans was the most effective, and why? *(the hot sand/clay bowl method because more kernels could be saved)*	problem resolution attempts/ inferential
_____6. How many pounds of popcorn did the passage say that the typical person in this country eats per year? *(two pounds)*	description/literal
_____7. How long did the passage say popcorn has been eaten by humans? *(thousands of years)*	description/literal
_____8. What is one limitation or problem associated with all three methods used by the Native Americans to pop corn? *(all lost kernels)*	problem resolution attempts/ inferential

PART II: ORAL READING AND ANALYSIS OF MISCUES

Directions: Say, "Now I would like to hear you read this story out loud." Have the student read orally until the 100-word sample is completed. Follow along on the Miscue Grid, marking any oral reading errors as appropriate. *Remember to count miscues only up to the point in the story containing the oral reading stop-marker (//).* Then complete the Developmental/Performance Summary to determine whether to continue the assessment. (*Note:* The Miscue Grid should be completed *after* the assessment session has been concluded in order to minimize stress for the student.)

	MIS-PRONUN.	SUB-STITUTION	OMISSION	INSERTION	TCHR. ASSIST.	SELF-CORRECT.	MEANING DISRUPTION
Popcorn							
There are three major types of							
corn grown in this country.							
First, there is the type of							
corn people eat most of the							
time. It is called sweet corn							
because of its flavor. Second,							
there is field corn, which							
is used mainly for feeding							
livestock. Sometimes people eat field							
corn too. However, its taste							
is not as good as sweet							
corn and its kernels are not							
as full. The third type of corn,							
often called Indian corn, is popcorn.							
Popcorn is grown commercially in the							
United States because the average							
American eats almost two pounds of							
popcorn a year, according //							
to various estimates.							
TOTALS							

Notes:

Examiner's Summary of Miscue Patterns:

PART III: DEVELOPMENTAL/PERFORMANCE SUMMARY

Silent Reading Comprehension

_____ 0–1 questions missed = Easy

_____ 2   questions missed = Adequate

_____ 3+   questions missed = Too hard

Oral Reading Accuracy

_____ 0–1 oral errors = Easy

_____ 2–5 oral errors = Adequate

_____ 6+   oral errors = Too hard

Continue to next assessment level passage?   _____ Yes   _____ No

PART IV: LISTENING COMPREHENSION

Directions: If you have decided not to continue to have the student read any other passages, then use this passage to begin assessing the student's listening comprehension (see page 8). Begin by reading the background statement for this passage and then say, "I am going to read this story to you. Please listen carefully because I will be asking you some questions after I finish reading it to you." After reading the passage, ask the student the questions associated with the passage. If the student correctly answers more than six questions, you will need to move to the next level and repeat the procedure.

Listening Comprehension

_____ 0–2 questions missed   = move to the next passage level

_____   more than two questions missed = stop assessment or move down a level

Examiner's Notes:

LEVEL 6 ASSESSMENT PROTOCOLS
Cooking Without Fire: The Microwave Oven (219 words)

PART I: SILENT READING COMPREHENSION

Background Statement: "This passage is about microwave ovens. Read the selection to find out how microwave ovens were developed. Read it carefully because I'm going to ask you to tell me about what you read."

Teacher Directions: Once the student completes the silent reading, say, "Tell me about the story you just read." Answers to the questions below that the student provides during the retelling should be marked "ua" in the appropriate blank to indicate that this response was unaided. Ask all remaining questions not addressed during the retelling and mark those the student answers with an "a" to indicate that the correct response was given after prompting by the teacher.

Questions/Answers	*Expository Grammar Element/ Level of Comprehension*
_____1. What invention led to the development of the microwave oven? *(magnetron tube)*	causation/literal
_____2. For what was the magnetron tube first used? *(radar)*	description/literal
_____3. What did Dr. Percy Spencer discover about the magnetron tube? *(it could heat food from the inside out)*	description/literal
_____4. What was the name given to the first microwave oven? *(Radar Range)*	description/literal
_____5. Name two ways that today's microwave ovens differ from the first ones. *(not as bulky, more features, less expensive)*	comparison/inferential
_____6. Explain why some people consider microwave cooking the first new method of cooking since the discovery of fire. *(it requires no fire or element of fire to cook food)*	causation/literal
_____7. What type of energy is used by the microwave to cook food? *(electromagnetic)*	description/literal
_____8. What are two features found on most microwave ovens, according to the passage? *(defrost, reheat, constant temperature cooking)*	description/literal

PART II: ORAL READING AND ANALYSIS OF MISCUES

Directions: Say, "Now I would like to hear you read this story out loud." Have the student read orally until the 100-word sample is completed. Follow along on the Miscue Grid, marking any oral reading errors as appropriate. *Remember to count miscues only up to the point in the story containing the oral reading stop-marker (//).* Then complete the Developmental/Performance Summary to determine whether to continue the assessment. (*Note:* The Miscue Grid should be completed *after* the assessment session has been concluded in order to minimize stress for the student.)

	MIS-PRONUN.	SUB-STITUTION	OMISSION	INSERTION	TCHR. ASSIST.	SELF-CORRECT.	MEANING DISRUPTION
Cooking Without Fire: The							
Microwave Oven							
Microwave cooking is very common							
today. It is, however, a recent invention.							
The microwave oven one uses today							
was developed from the invention							
of the magnetron tube							
in 1940. The invention of							
the magnetron tube, by							
Sir John Randall and Dr. H. A. Boot,							
was a very important part of							
the radar defense of England							
during World War II. Neither man							
considered it as a means of							
preparing food after they invented it.							
It wasn't until the late							
1940s that Dr. Percy Spencer							
discovered the magnetron's ability to							
heat and cook food from							
the inside out. Spencer experimented							
with many different // *foods,*							
all with the same results:							
The inside got hot first.							
TOTALS							

Notes:

Examiner's Summary of Miscue Patterns:

PART III: DEVELOPMENTAL/PERFORMANCE SUMMARY

Silent Reading Comprehension

_____ 0–1 questions missed = Easy

_____ 2   questions missed = Adequate

_____ 3+   questions missed = Too hard

Continue to next assessment level passage? _____ Yes _____ No

Oral Reading Accuracy

_____ 0–1 oral errors = Easy

_____ 2–5 oral errors = Adequate

_____ 6+   oral errors = Too hard

PART IV: LISTENING COMPREHENSION

Directions: If you have decided not to continue to have the student read any other passages, then use this passage to begin assessing the student's listening comprehension (see page 8). Begin by reading the background statement for this passage and then say, "I am going to read this story to you. Please listen carefully because I will be asking you some questions after I finish reading it to you." After reading the passage, ask the student the questions associated with the passage. If the student correctly answers more than six questions, you will need to move to the next level and repeat the procedure.

Listening Comprehension

_____ 0–2 questions missed   = move to the next passage level

_____ more than two questions missed = stop assessment or move down a level

Examiner's Notes:

Diamonds (286 words)

PART I: SILENT READING COMPREHENSION

Background Statement: "The following selection is about diamonds. Read it carefully to find out about how diamonds are made, because I'm going to ask you to tell me all about what you read."

Teacher Directions: Once the student completes the silent reading, say, "Tell me about the story you just read." Answers to the questions below that the student provides during the retelling should be marked "ua" in the appropriate blank to indicate that this response was unaided. Ask all remaining questions not addressed during the retelling and mark those the student answers with an "a" to indicate that the correct response was given after prompting by the teacher.

Questions/Answers	**Expository Grammar Element/ Level of Comprehension**
_____1. Where are the most important diamond fields located? *(India, South America, and Africa)*	description/literal
_____2. What information in the passage supports the idea that diamonds are rare? *(only located in certain areas, and even when present tons of rock must be sorted through)*	problem resolution attempts/ inferential
_____3. Where were the first diamonds found? *(sand and gravel in stream beds)*	description/literal
_____4. On what four things is the quality of a diamond based? *(purity, color, weight, and cut)*	description/literal
_____5. What causes the brilliance of a diamond? *(the way it is cut, or number of facets)*	causation/literal
_____6. What two factors lower the purity of a diamond? *(uncrystallized carbon and foreign substances)*	causation/inferential
_____7. Explain how artificial diamonds are made. *(they result from carbon being placed under high pressure and temperature)*	collection/inferential
_____8. Describe where natural diamonds are found. *(in rock formations that look like volcanoes)*	description/literal

PART II: ORAL READING AND ANALYSIS OF MISCUES

Directions: Say, "Now I would like to hear you read this story out loud." Have the student read orally until the 100-word sample is completed. Follow along on the Miscue Grid, marking any oral reading errors as appropriate. *Remember to count miscues only up to the point in the story containing the oral reading stop-marker (//).* Then complete the Developmental/Performance Summary to determine whether to continue the assessment. (*Note:* The Miscue Grid should be completed *after* the assessment session has been concluded in order to minimize stress for the student.)

	MIS-PRONUN.	SUB-STITUTION	OMISSION	INSERTION	TCHR. ASSIST.	SELF-CORRECT.	MEANING DISRUPTION
Diamonds							
A diamond is one of the							
most beautiful treasures that nature							
ever created, and one							
of the rarest. It takes thousands							
of years for nature to transform							
a chunk of carbon into a rough							
diamond. Only three important							
diamond fields have been found in the							
world—in India, South America,							
and Africa. The first diamonds							
were found in the sand and gravel of							
stream beds. These types of diamonds							
are called alluvial diamonds.							
Later, diamonds were found deep							
in the earth in rock formations called							
pipes. These formations resemble							
extinct volcanoes. The rock in which							
diamonds are found is							
called // *blue ground.*							
TOTALS							

Examiner's Summary of Miscue Patterns:

PART III: DEVELOPMENTAL/PERFORMANCE SUMMARY

Silent Reading Comprehension

_____ 0–1 questions missed = Easy

_____ 2   questions missed = Adequate

_____ 3+   questions missed = Too hard

Continue to next assessment level passage?   _____ Yes   _____ No

Oral Reading Accuracy

_____ 0–1 oral errors = Easy

_____ 2–5 oral errors = Adequate

_____ 6+   oral errors = Too hard

PART IV: LISTENING COMPREHENSION

Directions: If you have decided not to continue to have the student read any other passages, then use this passage to begin assessing the student's listening comprehension (see page 8). Begin by reading the background statement for this passage and then say, "I am going to read this story to you. Please listen carefully because I will be asking you some questions after I finish reading it to you." After reading the passage, ask the student the questions associated with the passage. If the student correctly answers more than six questions, you will need to move to the next level and repeat the procedure.

Listening Comprehension

_____ 0–2 questions missed   = move to the next passage level

_____ more than two questions missed = stop assessment or move down a level

Examiner's Notes:

Examiner's Summary of Miscue Patterns:

PART III: DEVELOPMENTAL/PERFORMANCE SUMMARY

Silent Reading Comprehension

_____ 0–1 questions missed = Easy

_____ 2 questions missed = Adequate

_____ 3+ questions missed = Too hard

Continue to next assessment level passage? _____ Yes _____ No

Oral Reading Accuracy

_____ 0–1 oral errors = Easy

_____ 2–5 oral errors = Adequate

_____ 6+ oral errors = Too hard

PART IV: LISTENING COMPREHENSION

Directions: If you have decided not to continue to have the student read any other passages, then use this passage to begin assessing the student's listening comprehension (see page 8). Begin by reading the background statement for this passage and then say, "I am going to read this story to you. Please listen carefully because I will be asking you some questions after I finish reading it to you." After reading the passage, ask the student the questions associated with the passage. If the student correctly answers more than six questions, you will need to move to the next level and repeat the procedure.

Listening Comprehension

_____ 0–2 questions missed = move to the next passage level

_____ more than two questions missed = stop assessment or move down a level

Examiner's Notes:

LEVEL 9 ASSESSMENT PROTOCOLS
Visual Illusions (269 words)

PART I: SILENT READING COMPREHENSION

Background Statement: "This selection is about visual illusions. Read it to find out about three specific types of visual illusions. Read it carefully because when you finish I will ask you to tell me about what you have read."

Teacher Directions: Once the student completes the silent reading, say, "Tell me about the story you just read." Answers to the questions below that the student provides during the retelling should be marked "ua" in the appropriate blank to indicate that this response was unaided. Ask all remaining questions not addressed during the retelling and mark those the student answers with an "a" to indicate that the correct response was given after prompting by the teacher.

Questions/Answers	*Expository Grammar Element/ Level of Comprehension*
_____1. What two reasons were given for visual illusions? *(preconceptions and the brain's difficulty in choosing from two or more patterns)*	description/literal
_____2. What is an example of a lateral inhibition illusion? *(a bull's-eye)*	description/literal
_____3. The Gateway Arch in St. Louis is an example of what distortion? *(length distortion)*	description/literal
_____4. Explain why length distortion occurs. *(because the eyes work better side to side than up and down)*	collection/inferential
_____5. What's an example of the visual illusion called "Hermann's Grid?" *(modern buildings)*	description/literal
_____6. How does Hermann's Grid affect what you see visually? *(it causes the eyes to see gray spots at the corners of squares)*	causation/inferential
_____7. Explain why the old axiom "don't believe everything you see" is valid in everyday life. *(examples of visual illusions are all around us, or other plausible response)*	collection/inferential
_____8. How does the tendency of eyes to move more easily from side to side rather than up and down affect the way we perceive tall objects? *(they seem taller than they actually are)*	causation/literal

PART II: ORAL READING AND ANALYSIS OF MISCUES

Directions: Say, "Now I would like to hear you read this story out loud." Have the student read orally until the 100-word sample is completed. Follow along on the Miscue Grid, marking any oral reading errors as appropriate. *Remember to count miscues only up to the point in the story containing the oral reading stop-marker (//).* Then complete the Developmental/Performance Summary to determine whether to continue the assessment. (*Note:* The Miscue Grid should be completed *after* the assessment session has been concluded in order to minimize stress for the student.)

	MIS-PRONUN.	SUB-STITUTION	OMISSION	INSERTION	TCHR. ASSIST.	SELF-CORRECT.	MEANING DISRUPTION
Visual Illusions							
A visual illusion is an unreal							
or misleading appearance or image,							
according to *Webster's* dictionary. In							
other words, visual illusions are							
sometimes caused by ideas one							
holds about what one expects							
to see. In other instances, the							
illusion is caused by the brain's							
difficulty in choosing from two							
or more visual patterns. If you							
look at a bull's-eye and move							
it slowly in circular motions, you							
should see spokes moving. The							
spokes, if you see them, aren't really							
there. This type of visual illusion is							
called lateral inhibition. Another type							
of visual illusion occurs when a person							
tries to // *estimate the height*							
of a vertical object.							
TOTALS							

Notes:

Examiner's Summary of Miscue Patterns:

PART III: DEVELOPMENTAL/PERFORMANCE SUMMARY

Silent Reading Comprehension

_____ 0–1 questions missed = Easy

_____ 2 questions missed = Adequate

_____ 3+ questions missed = Too hard

Continue to next assessment level passage? _____ Yes _____ No

Oral Reading Accuracy

_____ 0–1 oral errors = Easy

_____ 2–5 oral errors = Adequate

_____ 6+ oral errors = Too hard

PART IV: LISTENING COMPREHENSION

Directions: If you have decided not to continue to have the student read any other passages, then use this passage to begin assessing the student's listening comprehension (see page 8). Begin by reading the background statement for this passage and then say, "I am going to read this story to you. Please listen carefully because I will be asking you some questions after I finish reading it to you." After reading the passage, ask the student the questions associated with the passage. If the student correctly answers more than six questions, you will need to move to the next level and repeat the procedure.

Listening Comprehension

_____ 0–2 questions missed = move to the next passage level

_____ more than two questions missed = stop assessment or move down a level

Examiner's Notes:

EXPOSITORY PASSAGES
LEVELS 10–12

form **D**

Stereo Speakers

Almost everyone has listened to music at one time or another, yet few understand how stereo loudspeakers work. Simply put, all stereo loudspeakers are transducers that change electrical signals from an amplifier into sound waves. Beyond this simplistic explanation, stereo speakers diverge into many different types that even the most enthusiastic music lover can find perplexing. In general, all speakers can be placed into one of two major categories, depending on how the electrical signal is converted to sound.

The most prevalent type of speaker uses *dynamic drivers,* those familiar cones and domes found in both low-cost and expensive models. Basically, this type of speaker has air-exciting diaphragms (cones and domes) that are driven by an electromagnetic component made up of a voice coil and magnet. As an electrical signal is sent from the amplifier, the component moves back and forth. The cone or dome fixed to the voice coil moves with it, resulting in sound waves in the air in front and behind.

The other type of speaker, which produces sound differently from dynamic speakers, is often referred to as a *planar-designed speaker.* This type of speaker, which generally costs substantially more than the dynamic driver type, abandons the use of the voice coil and magnet component in lieu of a flat surface or a long ribbon-like strip that is directly driven by the audio signal from the amplifier to create sound waves. Since most people rarely encounter this type of speaker, the remainder of this discussion will focus on the two major types of dynamic driver speaker.

All dynamic speakers need an enclosure to help prevent something called back wave cancellation. Since all dynamic drivers radiate sound behind as well as in front, if there is no way to control the back wave it will literally cancel out the front wave, resulting in little or no sound. Thus, the enclosure of a stereo speaker serves to deal with this sonic problem.

The most common type of speaker is the acoustic suspension, or sealed box, speaker, which was developed in the 1950s. In this type of speaker, the woofer (dome) is mounted in an airtight enclosure so that its forward surface radiates freely into the room, while its back wave is lost in the internal volume of the sealed box. Since the back wave cannot radiate out into the room, there is no risk of front wave cancellation and it is possible to get powerful bass from a rather diminutive box. The one limitation of this design is that half its acoustical potential (back wave) is lost. Therefore, an acoustic suspension speaker requires more amplifier power than an equivalent unsealed box to achieve a given level of sound.

The other major type of dynamic speaker is called the bass reflex design. This design uses an enclosure that has a carefully designed opening, or vent, which allows the woofer's back wave to escape into the listening area. This type of design tries to capitalize on the back wave by manipulating it so that it reaches the listening area in phase with the front wave. Thus the overall sound is reinforced rather than degraded. This approach produces a more efficient speaker so that, all other things being equal, vented speakers can produce more volume per amplifier watt than acoustic suspension speakers.

Regardless of design, today's speakers far outdistance those of ten years ago in terms of quality of sound per dollar invested. Since no two speakers sound alike regardless of design specifications, the ultimate concern when purchasing a speaker should probably not be design but how it sounds to the individual buyer.

Changing the Way We Look

Cosmetic surgery, once available only to the rich and famous, is a multimillion-dollar-a-year business in the United States. The rapid growth of this type of surgery has occurred even though patients must bear much of the cost, because most cosmetic surgery is not covered by insurance. The cost is considerable, ranging from $1,000 to over $10,000, depending on the procedure, the doctor who does the surgery, and the geographical location in which the procedure is done. Some types of surgery are done on an outpatient basis, while others require several days in the hospital that add to the cost of the procedure.

Most cosmetic surgery is done to modify an individual's facial features. For removal of fine wrinkles around the mouth, brow, and eyes, dermabrasion is often chosen. Dermabrasion requires the physician to use skin planing tools to literally sand off the wrinkled areas after first injecting them with local anesthetic. Smoother skin results, but the patient has to wait about two weeks for the now pinkened skin to return to its normal color.

Another popular facial technique is skin peeling, or chemosurgery. In this procedure, a form of carbolic acid is applied to the face, the top layer of skin is burned off, and a scab results. About ten days later the scab comes off and there is a new, unblemished layer of skin that may take some weeks to return to its normal color. A proscription against direct exposure to the sun for about six months always accompanies this procedure. Fair-skinned individuals are the best candidates because other skin colors may develop irregular pigmentation as a result of this type of surgery.

Eyelid surgery, or blepharoplasty, is done when an individual has excessive skin on the upper lid or bags below the eye. To rid the individual of the "perpetually tired" look, incisions are made in the fold of the lid or just below the lower lash line. Excessive tissue is removed and the incision is stitched. This procedure is usually done on an outpatient basis, and the skin takes only two weeks to return to normal. Although complications are rare, there is always danger of hematomas (puffy areas filled with blood). Also, some people have excessive tearing and some have double vision because of muscle disturbances. Most of these problems either dissipate after several hours or are easily taken care of medically.

light beam hits the window determines whether or not the reflection will bounce back into the flashlight or into your eyes. Whenever light traveling through a material such as optical fiber encounters a material of different density, such as air, some of the light is reflected back toward the light source while the rest continues through the material. In optical fibers these sudden changes occur at the ends of fibers, at fiber breaks, and sometimes at splice joints. Obviously, fiber breaks are of great concern to fiber optic communications companies.

Since fiber optic systems are becoming more expansive and connected over longer distances, it is important to know how much light is lost in a regen, or length, of fiber. It is also important to be able to identify specific points on the fiber that have breaks or signal degradation. Although there are several methods to assess light loss, the most efficient means to pinpoint problems in a regen of fiber is the use of an *optical time domain reflectometer (OTDR)*. An OTDR is an electronic optical instrument that can be used to locate defects and faults and to determine the amount of signal loss at any point in an optical fiber by measuring backscatter levels and Fresnel reflection. The OTDR, unlike other methods, only needs access to one end of a fiber to make thousands of measurements along a fiber. The measurement data points can be between 0.5 and 16 meters apart. The selected data points are displayed on the OTDR screen as a line sloping down from left to right, with distance along the horizontal scale and signal level on the vertical scale. Using any two data points, the OTDR can reveal the distance and relative signal levels between them. Thus the OTDR can help companies that own fiber networks to repair breaks and prevent degradation of their signals: in short, to keep communications clear and repairs efficient.

EXAMINER'S ASSESSMENT PROTOCOLS

form

PART II (OPTIONAL): ORAL READING AND ANALYSIS OF MISCUES

Directions: Say, "Now I would like to hear you read a portion of this passage out loud. Please begin reading with the second paragraph and continue reading until I tell you to stop." Have the student read until the 100-word sample is completed. Follow along on the Miscue Grid, marking any oral reading errors as appropriate. *Remember to count miscues only up to the point of the oral reading stop-marker (///).* Then complete the Developmental/Performance Summary to determine whether to continue the assessment. (Note: The Miscue Grid should be completed *after* the assessment session to save time and reduce stress for the student.)

	MIS-PRONUN.	SUB-STITUTION	OMISSION	INSERTION	TCHR. ASSIST.	SELF-CORRECT.	MEANING DISRUPTION
Stereo Speakers							
The most prevalent type of speaker							
uses dynamic drivers, those familiar							
cones and domes found in both low-							
cost and expensive models. Basically,							
this type of speaker has air-exciting							
diaphragms (cones and domes) that are							
driven by an electromagnetic							
component made up of a voice coil and							
magnet. As an electrical signal is sent							
from the amplifier, the component							
moves back and forth. The cone or							
dome fixed to the voice coil moves							
with it, resulting in sound waves in the							
air in front and behind. The other type							
of speaker, which produces sound							
differently from dynamic speakers, is //							
often referred to as a planar-designed							
speaker.							
TOTALS							

Notes:

Examiner's Summary of Miscue Patterns:

PART III: DEVELOPMENTAL/PERFORMANCE SUMMARY

Silent Reading Comprehension

_____ 0–1 questions missed = Easy

_____ 2   questions missed = Adequate

_____ 3+   questions missed = Too hard

Continue to next assessment level passage? _____ Yes _____ No

Oral Reading Accuracy

_____ 0–1 oral errors = Easy

_____ 2–5 oral errors = Adequate

_____ 6+   oral errors = Too hard

PART IV: LISTENING COMPREHENSION

Directions: If you have decided not to continue to have the student read any other passages, then use this passage to begin assessing the student's listening comprehension (see page 8). Begin by reading the background statement for this passage and then say, "I am going to read this story to you. Please listen carefully because I will be asking you some questions after I finish reading it to you." After reading the passage, ask the student the questions associated with the passage. If the student correctly answers more than six questions, you will need to move to the next level and repeat the procedure.

Listening Comprehension

_____ 0–2 questions missed   = move to the next passage level

_____ more than two questions missed = stop assessment or move down a level

Examiner's Notes:

LEVEL 11 ASSESSMENT PROTOCOLS

Changing the Way We Look (649 words)

PART I: SILENT READING COMPREHENSION

Background Statement: "This passage is about cosmetic surgery. Read it carefully and try to find out some facts about different cosmetic surgery techniques, because I am going to ask you to tell me as much as you can remember about the information in the passage."

Teacher Directions: Once the student completes the silent reading, say, "Tell me about the story you just read." Answers to the questions below that the student provides during the retelling should be marked "ua" in the appropriate blank to indicate that this response was unaided. Ask all remaining questions not addressed during the retelling and mark those the student answers with an "a" to indicate that the correct response was given after prompting by the teacher.

Questions/Answers	*Expository Grammar Element/ Level of Comprehension*
_____1. Describe what is done during dermabrasion. *(the surgeon uses a skin planing tool and scrapes off a layer of skin)*	description/inferential
_____2. What evidence did the passage provide that the number of cosmetic surgery procedures done per year is on the rise? *(it has become a multimillion-dollar business)*	collection/inferential
_____3. How is chemosurgery different from dermabrasion? *(a chemical is used to burn off a layer of skin in chemosurgery while dermabrasion just sands away wrinkles; also chemosurgery results in a scab while dermabrasion does not)*	comparison/inferential
_____4. What are some of the possible complications associated with eyelid surgery? *(hematomas, excessive tearing, and double vision)*	description/literal
_____5. What are three considerations anyone considering plastic surgery should take into account before having it done? *(qualifications of the doctor, cost, and expectations)*	description/literal
_____6. What does the old folk saying suggest about cosmetic surgery? *(Accept responses related to the idea that people should be satisfied with their looks rather than resort to surgery.)*	problem resolution/evaluative
_____7. Besides plastic surgeons, what other kinds of doctors can perform some types of cosmetic surgery? *(dermatologists/skin doctors and otolaryngologists/ ear, nose, and throat doctors)*	collection/literal
_____8. Why does eyelid surgery sometimes accompany a facelift? *(because if a person is having the facial skin tightened, it makes sense to get rid of fatty tissue around the eyes at the same time)*	collection/inferential

PART II (OPTIONAL): ORAL READING AND ANALYSIS OF MISCUES

Directions: Say, "Now I would like to hear you read a portion of this passage out loud. Please begin reading with the third paragraph and continue reading until I tell you to stop." Have the student read until the 100-word sample is completed. Follow along on the Miscue Grid, marking any oral reading errors as appropriate. *Remember to count miscues only up to the point of the oral reading stop-marker (///).* Then complete the Developmental/Performance Summary to determine whether to continue the assessment. (Note: The Miscue Grid should be completed *after* the assessment session to save time and reduce stress for the student.)

	MIS-PRONUN.	SUB-STITUTION	OMISSION	INSERTION	TCHR. ASSIST.	SELF-CORRECT.	MEANING DISRUPTION
Changing the Way We Look							
Another popular facial technique is							
skin peeling, or chemosurgery.							
In this procedure, a form of carbolic							
acid is applied to the face, the top layer							
of skin is burned off, and a scab							
results. About ten days later the scab							
comes off and there is a new,							
unblemished layer of skin that may							
take some weeks to return to its normal							
color. A proscription against direct							
exposure to the sun for about six							
months always accompanies this							
procedure. Fair-skinned individuals							
are the best candidates because other							
skin colors may develop irregular							
pigmentation as a result of this type							
of // *surgery.*							
TOTALS							

Notes:

Examiner's Summary of Miscue Patterns:

PART III: DEVELOPMENTAL/PERFORMANCE SUMMARY

Silent Reading Comprehension

_____ 0–1 questions missed = Easy

_____ 2 questions missed = Adequate

_____ 3+ questions missed = Too hard

Continue to next assessment level passage? _____ Yes _____ No

Oral Reading Accuracy

_____ 0–1 oral errors = Easy

_____ 2–5 oral errors = Adequate

_____ 6+ oral errors = Too hard

PART IV: LISTENING COMPREHENSION

Directions: If you have decided not to continue to have the student read any other passages, then use this passage to begin assessing the student's listening comprehension (see page 8). Begin by reading the background statement for this passage and then say, "I am going to read this story to you. Please listen carefully because I will be asking you some questions after I finish reading it to you." After reading the passage, ask the student the questions associated with the passage. If the student correctly answers more than six questions, you will need to move to the next level and repeat the procedure.

Listening Comprehension

_____ 0–2 questions missed = move to the next passage level

_____ more than two questions missed = stop assessment or move down a level

Examiner's Notes:

LEVEL 12 ASSESSMENT PROTOCOLS
Fiber Optic Communications (760 words)

PART I: SILENT READING COMPREHENSION

Background Statement: "This selection is about fiber optic communications. Read the passage to discover some of the characteristics and problems associated with fiber optic communications. Read it carefully because I am going to ask you to tell me about the entire passage when you finish reading it."

Teacher Directions: Once the student completes the silent reading, say, "Tell me about the story you just read." Answers to the questions below that the student provides during the retelling should be marked "ua" in the appropriate blank to indicate that this response was unaided. Ask all remaining questions not addressed during the retelling and mark those the student answers with an "a" to indicate that the correct response was given after prompting by the teacher.

Questions/Answers	Expository Grammar Element/ Level of Comprehension
_____1. What two advantages does fiber optics have over other forms of communications transmission? *(no interference problems, does not need boosting over long distances, greater capacity, lighter and smaller)*	collection/literal
_____2. What are dopants? *(microscopic particles found in all optic fibers)*	description/literal
_____3. Why is loss of light in optic fiber a major concern of companies that uses it for communication? *(poor signals or even a complete system shutdown)*	problem resolution/evaluative
_____4. What is Rayleigh scattering and why is it always present? *(the light that is reflected back toward its source due to dopants; because of the manufacturing process)*	causation/literal
_____5. Explain the main difference between Rayleigh scattering and Fresnel reflection. *(Rayleigh scattering caused by dopants, Fresnel reflection caused by fiber breaks, splices, or the end of fiber; accept plausible responses even if related to the fog versus light through glass analogy)*	comparison/inferential
_____6. How are a regen and an optical time domain reflectometer related? *(OTDR used to pinpoint light loss in any regen)*	collection/inferential
_____7. What separates the OTDR from other devices designed to pinpoint loss of light in fiber optic cable? *(only need access to one end of a fiber to make measurements)*	comparison/literal
_____8. Why would it be safe to say that OTDRs and other devices will be in greater demand in the future than they are now? *(because of the expansion of fiber optic communications)*	collection/evaluative

PART II (OPTIONAL): ORAL READING AND ANALYSIS OF MISCUES

Directions: Say, "Now I would like to hear you read a portion of this passage out loud. Please begin reading with the third paragraph and continue reading until I tell you to stop." Have the student read until the 100-word sample is completed. Follow along on the Miscue Grid, marking any oral reading errors as appropriate. *Remember to count miscues only up to the point of the oral reading stop-marker (///).* Then complete the Developmental/Performance Summary to determine whether to continue the assessment. (Note: The Miscue Grid should be completed *after* the assessment session to save time and reduce stress for the student.)

	MIS-PRONUN.	SUB-STITUTION	OMISSION	INSERTION	TCHR. ASSIST.	SELF-CORRECT.	MEANING DISRUPTION
Fiber Optic Communications							
The most significant limitation in an							
optical communications system is the							
attenuation of the optical signal as it							
goes through the fiber. As information							
in the light is sent down the fiber, the							
light is attenuated (often called							
insertion lost) due to *Rayleigh*							
scattering. Rayleigh scattering refers							
to an effect created when a pulse of							
light is sent down a fiber and part of							
the pulse is blocked by dopants—							
microscopic particles in the glass—							
and scattered in all directions. Some of							
the light, about 0.0001 percent, is							
scattered back in the opposite direction							
of the pulse; this is called the //							
backscatter.							
TOTALS							

Notes:

Examiner's Summary of Miscue Patterns:

PART III: DEVELOPMENTAL/PERFORMANCE SUMMARY

Silent Reading Comprehension

_____ 0–1 questions missed = Easy

_____ 2 questions missed = Adequate

_____ 3+ questions missed = Too hard

Oral Reading Accuracy

_____ 0–1 oral errors = Easy

_____ 2–5 oral errors = Adequate

_____ 6+ oral errors = Too hard

Examiner's Notes:

THE ESPAÑOL
PORTION OF THE EERIC

Instructions for using the Español portion of the EERIC appear on pages 1 through 14. Examples of a completed student assessment protocol and student summary can be found on pages 16 through 20.

Entrevista de interés y actitud

PRIMARY FORM

Student's Name: _____ Age: _____

Date: _____ Examiner: _____

Introductory Statement: [*Student's name*], *antes de que me leas algunos cuentos, me gustaría hacerte algunas preguntas.*

Vida en casa (Home Life)

1. ¿Dónde vives? ¿Sabes tu dirección? ¿Cuál es?

2. ¿Quién vive en tu casa?

3. ¿Qué tipos de trabajos tienes en casa?

4. ¿Qué es una cosa que realmente te gusta hacer en casa?

5. ¿Lees en casa? [*si la respuesta es sí, pregunte:*] ¿Cuándo lees? y ¿qué fue lo último que leíste? [*si la respuesta es no, pregunte:*] ¿Alguien te ha leído algunas veces? [*si es así, pregunte:*] ¿Quién? y ¿con qué frecuencia?

6. ¿Tienes una hora específica de acostarte cuando vas a la escuela? [*si la respuesta es no, pregunte:*] ¿A qué hora te acuestas?

7. ¿Tienes un televisor en tu recámara? ¿Cuánto tiempo pasas viéndolo? ¿Cuáles son tus programas favoritos?

8. ¿Qué te gusta hacer con tus amigos?

9. ¿Tienes mascotas en casa? ¿Te gusta coleccionar cosas? ¿Tomas lecciones en alguna otra área? (natación, tocar instrumento, bailar, etc.)

10. Cuando conoces a un amigo nuevo, ¿qué es algo que ese amigo debe saber acerca de ti?

FORMA A: NIVEL 6

1. Él buscaba la evidencia.

2. Se dio cuenta que la formación rocosa era muy alta.

3. El conservacionista esperaba poder reforestar la montaña.

FORMA A: NIVEL 7

1. Desafortunadamente ella estaba confundida acerca de la siguiente actividad.

2. Las piedras sumergidas eran peligrosas.

3. Ella se desapareció rápidamente al dar la vuelta.

FORMA A: NIVEL 8

1. Escalar la montaña fue rigoroso y peligroso.

2. La barranca nos daba una vista panorámica del valle.

3. El tiempo de incubación duró dos semanas.

FORMA A: NIVEL 9

1. El secuestro hizo a todos sospechosos.

2. El detective estaba rodeado por la comunidad.

3. Su complexión pálida la hacía verse vieja.

NARRATIVE PASSAGES......forma A

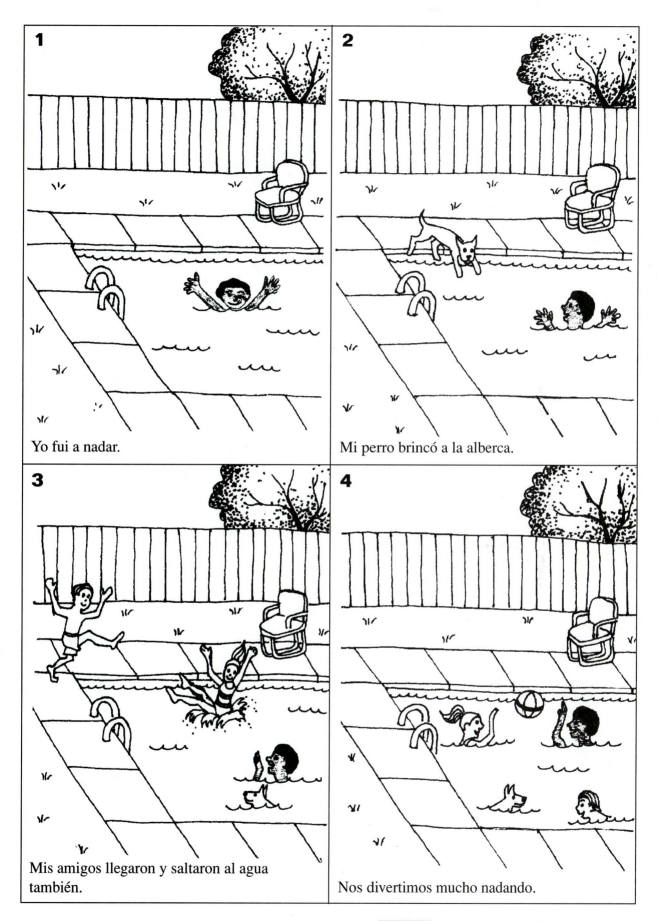

1 Yo fui a nadar.

2 Mi perro brincó a la alberca.

3 Mis amigos llegaron y saltaron al agua también.

4 Nos divertimos mucho nadando.

¡No puedes volar!

Una vez un niño llamado Sam quería volar.

Su mamá y papá dijeron —No puedes volar.

Su hermana dijo —No puedes volar.

Sam trató de saltar desde una caja.

Trató de saltar desde su cama.

Se caía cada vez.

Sam siguió intentando pero no pudo volar.

Entonces, un día llegó una carta para Sam.

La carta decía —Ven a verme, Sam, en el próximo vuelo.

Era de parte de su abuelo.

Sam fue a su familia y leyó la carta.

Sam dijo —Ahora puedo volar.

Sam y su familia se rieron juntos.

El cochino y la víbora

Un día como todos, el señor Cochino daba un paseo hacia el pueblo.

De repente vio un gran hoyo en el camino.

Una enorme víbora estaba en el hoyo.

—¡Socorro, auxilio! —decía la víbora, —Si me ayudas seré tu amiga.

—No puedo —le contestó el cochino—, si te ayudo a salir, me morderás después.

Y la víbora lloraba más.

De todas maneras, el señor Cochino la sacó del hoyo.

Luego la víbora le dijo —Ahora sí te voy a morder, Señor Cochino.

—¿Cómo es posible que me vayas a morder después que te ayudé a salir del hoyo? —le dijo el señor Cochino.

La víbora le contestó, —¡tu ya sabías que yo era una víbora cuando me sacaste!

Ropa nueva

Roberto era el más joven de su familia. No le gustaba ser el más joven porque no podía quedarse despierto viendo televisión en la noche. Lo menos que le gustaba era vestirse con la ropa usada de su hermano.

Un día Roberto le dijo a su mamá, —Mamá, ya me cansé de ponerme la ropa vieja de Brad. ¿Por qué no puedo tener ropa nueva este año escolar?— Su mamá contestó, —Roberto, sabes que no tenemos dinero para comprar ropa nueva para todos. Además, la mayoría de la ropa de Brad parece nueva. Pero si tu puedes encontrar una manera de ganar dinero, creo que puedo ayudarte a comprar unas cosas.—

Roberto pensó y pensó. Finalmente tuvo una idea. Tanto Brad como su hermana Sara, tenían trabajos fuera de casa, pero siempre se metían en problemas porque no cumplían con sus quehaceres. ¿Qué tal si él hacía algo de sus quehaceres a cambio de un pequeño pago?

Roberto les dijo a Brad y Sara su idea. Les gustó la idea. Estaban de acuerdo con pagar a Roberto por limpiar sus cuartos, arreglar sus camas y levantar su ropa. Le dijeron que tenía que limpiar diariamente. Si no, no le pagarían ni un centavo.

Cada día durante cuatro semanas Roberto arregló los cuartos de su hermano y hermana. Finalmente, el último sábado antes de que empezara la escuela, la mamá de Roberto lo llevó a una tienda local. Roberto escogió un par de pantalones holgados de mezclilla y un par de camisas nuevas. El primer día de la escuela, Roberto lució orgulloso con su ropa nueva. Su mamá estaba aún más orgullosa.

Un fuego en la montaña

Una tarde en agosto, Beto y Kiko fueron por una caminata con sus padres al monte Holyoak. El papá de Beto iba en busca de datos acerca de los pumas. Mucha gente temía que los pumas estuvieran extintos en el monte Holyoak. Los muchachos se alborotaron mucho cuando descubrieron lo que parecían huellas de puma cerca de un arroyo. Pero conforme pasó el tiempo ya no volvieron a encontrar otras huellas.

Después de haberse comido su almuerzo, el papá de Beto mandó a los muchachos a explorar río arriba mientras que él rodeaba por el oeste. Les dijo a los muchachos que regresaran en una hora. A los cuarenta y cinco minutos, los muchachos encontraron la fuente del arroyo y ya no lo pudieron seguir. Decidieron buscar huellas cerca del arroyo, antes de comenzar la marcha de regreso. Vieron estructuras interesantes de piedra, nidos de águilas en lo alto de las rocas y por último, dos huellas frescas de puma. Los dos muchachos se alborotaron mucho hasta que se dieron cuenta que no podían oir el ruido del arroyo. Andaban perdidos.

Por más de una hora los muchachos buscaron el arroyo sin encontrarlo. Ya cansados y sucios, también estaban preocupados. Beto decidió hacer una fogata con las esperanzas de que su papá viera el humo. Kiko le advirtío a Beto del peligro de tener fuego en el bosque pero finalmente le ayudó a recoger ramas secas. Tan pronto que Beto prendió el cerillo en el aire seco de la montaña y trató de prender las ramas, la lumbre explotó. En pocos minutos los árboles a su alrededor se prendieron. El fuego se esparció por todas las montañas. Los muchachos corrieron hasta abajo muy rápido.

Antes que el día se acabara, cuadrillas de expertos, aviones cargando retardadores de fuego y helicópteros estaban allí tratando de apagar el fuego. El fuego duró varios días sin embargo, y al apagarse se quemaron más de 45,000 acres de árboles.

Por varios años Beto y Kiko ayudaron a repoblar de árboles la montaña. Un día un guarda bosques comentó, —Muchachos, parece que todo está bien otra vez.— Beto miró al suelo y tristemente respondió,— Tal vez, pero desde entonces no se han visto nuevas huellas de pumas.—

El águila

Existe una vieja leyenda Nativa Americana acerca de un águila que creía que era un pollo. Parece ser que un granjero Hopi y su único hijo decidieron subir a una montaña cercana, para observar el nido del águila. El viaje les tomaría todo el día, así que ellos llevaron raciones y un poco de agua para su caminata. El padre y el hijo cruzaron los enormes campos de maíz y frijol hasta las faldas de las montañas.

Pronto ellos estaban subiendo la montaña y la subida se hizo más peligrosa y dura. Ocasionalmente ellos miraban hacia atrás, hacia su casa y la vista panorámica del valle entero. Finalmente, el padre y el hijo llegaron a la cumbre de la montaña. Colocada en la punta más alta, en una orilla, estaba el nido del águila. El padre metió su mano al nido, después de darse cuenta de que la madre había salido en busca de comida. Sacó lo más valioso, el huevo del águila.

Lo metió en su túnica y los dos descendieron de la montaña. El huevo fue colocado en un nido de pollos para incubarlo. Pronto se salió del cascarón un águila. El aguilucho creció con los pollitos y adoptó sus hábitos para buscar comida en el patio de la casa; tal como escarbar por la comida que el granjero les tiraba.

Un tiempo después, un guerrero anasazi pasó por el área y vio este enorme águila café escarbando y caminando por el patio. Él se bajó de su caballo y fue con el granjero. —¿Por qué tiene usted un águila que actúa como pollo? No está bien —indagó el guerrero noble.

—No es un águila, es un pollo —replicó el granjero. —¿No puede ver que escarba por su comida como los otros pollos? No, es ciertamente un pollo —exclamó el granjero.

—Le mostraré que éste es un águila —dijo el guerrero.

El guerrero cogió el águila en sus brazos y subió al techo del establo. Y entonces diciendo, —Tú eres un águila, la más noble de las aves. ¡Vuela como es tu destino! —él tiró el águila desde el establo. Entonces, la sorprendida águila aleteó hacia el piso y empezó a picotear en busca de comida.

—Ve —dijo el granjero, —Le dije que es un pollo.

El guerrero contestó, —Le enseñaré que ésta es una águila. Está muy claro lo que debo hacer.

Otra vez el guerrero llevó el águila en sus brazos y empezó a caminar hacia la montaña. Él subió todo el día hasta que alcanzó la parte más alta que daba al valle. Entonces, el guerrero extendió su brazo, sostuvo el ave y dijo, —Tú eres una águila, la más noble de las aves. Vuela como es tu destino.

Justo entonces, la brisa de las montañas cruzó por el águila. Sus ojos se abrillantaron al sentir la escencia de la libertad. En un momento el águila extendió sus alas y dejó escapar un gran grito. Saltando del brazo del guerrero, el águila voló hasta lo más alto del cielo oeste.

El águila vio más del mundo en ese gran momento que lo que sus amigos del patio de la granja descubrirían en una vida entera.

EXAMINER'S ASSESSMENT PROTOCOLS

forma **A**

PREPRIMER (PP) LEVEL ASSESSMENT PROTOCOLS
El accidente (Wordless picture story)

PART I: WORDLESS PICTURE STORY READING

Background Statement: "Estos dibujos cuentan acerca una niña y algo que le pasó. Mira cada dibujo según te lo vaya enseñando y piensa acerca la historia que cuentan estos dibujos. Después, te pediré que me cuentes el cuento usando los dibujos."

Teacher Directions: Refer the student to each picture slowly and in order as numbered. Do not comment on the pictures. Then repeat the procedure, asking the student to tell the story in the student's own words. Record the student's reading using a tape recorder, and transcribe the reading as it is being dictated. Replay the recording later to make sure that your transcription is accurate and complete.

PART II: EMERGENT READING BEHAVIOR CHECKLIST

Directions: Following are emergent reading behaviors identified through research and grouped according to broad developmental stages. Check all behaviors you have observed. *If the student progresses to Stage 3 or 4, continue your assessment using the Primer Level (P) passage.*

Stage 1: Early Connections to Reading—Describing Pictures

_____ Attends to and describes (labels) pictures in books

_____ Has a limited sense of story

_____ Follows verbal directions for this activity

_____ Uses oral vocabulary appropriate for age/grade level

_____ Displays attention span appropriate for age/grade level

_____ Responds to questions in an appropriate manner

_____ Appears to connect pictures (sees as being interrelated)

Stage 2: Connecting Pictures to Form Story

_____ Attends to pictures and develops oral stories across the pages of the book

_____ Uses only childlike or descriptive (storyteller) language to tell the story, rather than book language (i.e., Once upon a time . . .; There once was a little boy . . .)

Stage 3: Transitional Picture Reading

_____ Attends to pictures as a connected story

_____ Mixes storyteller language with book language

Stage 4: Advanced Picture Reading

_____ Attends to pictures and develops oral stories across the pages of the book

_____ Speaks as though reading the story (uses book language)

Examiner's Notes:

Vamos a nadar (22 words)

PART I: PICTURE STORY READING—ORAL READING AND ANALYSIS OF MISCUES

Background Statement: "Éste es un cuento acerca de un niño divirtiéndose. Miremos cada dibujo primero. Ahora, lee el cuento para ti mismo. Después voy a pedirte que me leas el cuento."

Teacher Directions: Refer the student to each frame of the story slowly and in order as numbered. Do not read the story or comment on the pictures. After the student has read the story silently, ask the student to read the story aloud. Record the student's reading using a tape recorder, and mark any miscues on the Miscue Grid provided. Following the oral reading, complete the Emergent Reading Behavior Checklist. Assessment information obtained from both the Miscue Grid and the Emergent Reading Behavior Checklist will help you determine whether to continue your assessment. If the student is unable to read the passage independently the first time, read it aloud, then ask the student to try to read the story again. This will help you understand whether the student is able to memorize and repeat text, an important developmental milestone (see the *Instructions for Administering the Preprimer (PP) and Primer (P) Passages* section in the front of this book for more information). The assessment should stop after this activity, if the child is unable to read the text independently. (*Note:* The Miscue Grid should be completed *after* the assessment session has been concluded in order to minimize stress for the student.)

	MIS-PRONUN.	SUB-STITUTION	OMISSION	INSERTION	TCHR. ASSIST.	SELF-CORRECT.	MEANING DISRUPTION
Vamos a nadar							
Yo fui a nadar. Mi perro							
brincó a la alberca. Mis							
amigos llegaron y saltaron							
al agua también. Nos							
divertimos mucho							
nadando.							
TOTALS							

Notes:

PART II: EMERGENT READING BEHAVIOR CHECKLIST

Directions: Following are emergent reading behaviors identified through research and grouped according to broad developmental stages. After the student has completed the oral reading, check each behavior observed below to help determine development level and whether to continue the assessment. *If the student seems to be at Stage 6 or 7 and the oral reading scored at an Easy or Adequate level, continue the assessment using the Level 1 passage.*

Stage 5: Early Print Reading

_____ Tells a story using the pictures

_____ Knows print moves from left to right, top to bottom

_____ Creates part of the text using book language and knows some words on sight

Stage 6: Early Strategic Reading

_____ Uses context to guess at some unknown words (guesses make sense)

_____ Notices beginning sounds in words and uses them in guessing unknown words

_____ Seems to sometimes use syntax to help identify words in print

_____ Recognizes some word parts, such as root words and affixes

Stage 7: Moderate Strategic Reading

_____ Sometimes uses context and word parts to decode words

_____ Self-corrects when making an oral reading miscue

_____ Retells the passage easily and may embellish the storyline

_____ Shows some awareness of vowel sounds

Examiner's Notes:

Examiner's Summary of Miscue Patterns:

PART III: DEVELOPMENTAL/PERFORMANCE SUMMARY

Oral Reading Accuracy

_____ 0–1   oral errors = Easy

_____ 2–5   oral errors = Adequate

_____ 6+   oral errors = Too hard

Continue to next assessment level passage?   _____ Yes   _____ No

Examiner's Notes:

 **NIVEL 1 REGISTRO INFORMATIVO**

¡No puedes volar! (90 words)

PART I: SILENT READING COMPREHENSION

Background Statement: "¿Has deseado poder volar? En este cuento, Sam quiere volar. Lee este cuento para ver si Sam logra volar. Léelo con cuidado porque cuando termines voy a pedir que me lo cuentes."

Teacher Directions: Once the student completes the silent reading, say "Dime acerca de lo que acabas de leer." Answers to the questions below that the student provides during the retelling should be marked "ua" in the appropriate blank to indicate that this response was unaided. Ask all remaining questions not addressed during the retelling and mark those the student answers with an "a" to indicate that the correct response was given after prompting by the teacher.

Questions/Answers	*Story Grammar Element/ Level of Comprehension*
_____1. ¿Cómo se llama el niño del cuento? *(Sam)*	character-characterization/ literal
_____2. ¿Qué quería hacer Sam? *(Sam quería volar, pero no podía.)*	story problem(s)/literal
_____3. ¿Cuáles fueron las dos maneras que Sam trató de volar? *(saltando de su cama y saltando de una caja)*	problem resolution attempts/ literal
_____4. ¿Cómo se resolvió finalmente el problema de Sam? *(Sam voló en un avión)*	problem resolution/ inferential
_____5. ¿Qué hizo la familia y Sam después de que él leó la carta? *(se rieron)*	problem resolution attempts/ literal
_____6. ¿Dónde se llevó acabo el cuento? *(la casa de Sam y su familia)*	setting/inferential
_____7. ¿Qué aprendió Sam acerca de aprender a volar? *(las personas no pueden volar excepto en un avión)*	theme/evaluative
_____8. ¿Cuáles palabras usarías para contarle a alguien qué tipo de niño era Sam? *(responses will vary; accept plausible responses)*	character-characterization/ evaluative

PART II: ORAL READING AND ANALYSIS OF MISCUES

Directions: Say, "Ahora me gustaría oirte leer este cuento en voz alta. Por favor, empieza desde el principio y continúa hasta que te diga." Have the student read orally until the oral reading stop-marker (//) is reached. Follow along on the Miscue Grid, marking any oral reading errors as appropriate. Then complete the Developmental/Performance Summary to determine whether to continue the assessment. (*Note:* The Miscue Grid should be completed *after* the assessment session has been concluded in order to minimize stress for the student.)

	MIS-PRONUN.	SUB-STITUTION	OMISSION	INSERTION	TCHR. ASSIST.	SELF-CORRECT.	MEANING DISRUPTION
¡No puedes volar!							
Una vez un niño llamado Sam							
quería volar. Su mamá y papá							
dijeron —No puedes volar.							
Su hermana dijo —No puedes volar.							
Sam trató de saltar desde una caja.							
Trató de saltar desde su cama.							
Se caía cada vez. Sam siguió							
intentando pero no pudo volar.							
Entonces, un día llegó una carta							
para Sam. La carta decía —Ven							
a verme, Sam, en el próximo vuelo.							
Era de parte de su abuelo.							
Sam fue a su familia y leyó la carta.							
Sam dijo —Ahora puedo volar.							
Sam y su familia se rieron juntos.							
TOTALS							

Notes:

Examiner's Summary of Miscue Patterns:

PART III: DEVELOPMENTAL/PERFORMANCE SUMMARY

Silent Reading Comprehension

_____ 0–1 questions missed = Easy

_____ 2 questions missed = Adequate

_____ 3+ questions missed = Too hard

Oral Reading Accuracy

_____ 0–1 oral errors = Easy

_____ 2–5 oral errors = Adequate

_____ 6+ oral errors = Too hard

Continue to next assessment level passage? _____ Yes _____ No

Examiner's Notes:

forma A

NIVEL 2 REGISTRO INFORMATIVO
El cochino y la víbora (110 words)

PART I: SILENT READING COMPREHENSION

Background Statement: "Lee el cuento para que puedas saber lo que le pasó al señor Cochino cuando trató de ayudar a la víbora. Lee el cuento con cuidado porque se te va a preguntar sobre el cuento."

Teacher Directions: Once the student completes the silent reading, say, "Dime algo sobre el cuento que acabas de leer." Answers to the questions below that the student provides during the retelling should be marked "ua" in the appropriate blank to indicate that this response was unaided. Ask all remaining questions not addressed during the retelling and mark those the student answers with an "a" to indicate that the correct response was given after prompting by the teacher.

Questions/Answers	*Story Grammar Element/ Level of Comprehension*
_____1. ¿Dónde se desarrolló el cuento? *(camino al pueblo)*	setting/literal
_____2. Cuáles fueron los animales del cuento? *(el cochino y una víbora)*	character-characterization/ literal
_____3. ¿Cuál era el problema de la víbora? *(la víbora estaba metida en un hoyo y necesitaba ayuda para salir)*	story problem(s)/literal
_____4. ¿Cómo resolvió el problema la víbora? *(hizo que el cochino le ayudara prometiendo que no lo mordería)*	problem resolution/ inferential
_____5. ¿Cuáles palabras usarías para describir a la víbora? *(muy viva y mentirosa)*	character-characterization/ evaluative
_____6. ¿Qué aprendió el cochino? *(varias respuestas, "no debe uno creer lo que le diga")*	theme/evaluative
_____7. ¿Cómo se sintió el señor Cochino después de ayudar a la víbora a salir del hoyo? *(sorprendido, triste, etc...)*	character-characterization/ inferential
_____8. ¿Qué fue una cosa que la víbora hizo para que el señor Cochino le ayudara a salir del hoyo? *(llorar y decir que sería su amiga)*	problem resolution attempts/ literal

PART II: ORAL READING AND ANALYSIS OF MISCUES

Directions: Say, "Ahora yo quiero que leas el cuento en voz alta." Have the student read orally until the 100-word sample is completed. Follow along on the Miscue Grid, marking any oral reading errors as appropriate. *Remember to count miscues only up to the point in the story containing the oral reading stop-marker (//).* Then complete the Developmental/Performance Summary to determine whether to continue the assessment. (*Note:* The Miscue Grid should be completed *after* the assessment session has been concluded in order to minimize stress for the student.)

	MIS-PRONUN.	SUB-STITUTION	OMISSION	INSERTION	TCHR. ASSIST.	SELF-CORRECT.	MEANING DISRUPTION
El cochino y la víbora							
Un día como todos, el señor Cochino							
daba un paseo hacia el pueblo.							
De repente vio un gran hoyo							
en el camino. Una enorme víbora							
estaba en el hoyo. —¡Socorro, auxilio!							
—decía la víbora, —Si me ayudas							
seré tu amiga. —No puedo —							
le contestó el cochino—, si te ayudo							
a salir, me morderás después.							
Y la víbora lloraba más. De todas							
maneras, el señor Cochino la sacó							
del hoyo. Luego la víbora le dijo							
—Ahora sí te voy a morder, Señor							
Cochino. —¿Cómo es posible que me							
vayas a morder después							
que te// *ayudé a salir del hoyo?*							
—le dijo el señor Cochino.							
TOTALS							

Notes:

Examiner's Summary of Miscue Patterns:

PART III: DEVELOPMENTAL/PERFORMANCE SUMMARY

Silent Reading Comprehension   *Oral Reading Accuracy*

_____ 0–1 questions missed = Easy   _____ 0–1 oral errors = Easy

_____ 2   questions missed = Adequate _____ 2–5 oral errors = Adequate

_____ 3+   questions missed = Too hard _____ 6+   oral errors = Too hard

Continue to next assessment level passage?   _____ Yes   _____ No

Examiner's Notes:

NIVEL 3 REGISTRO INFORMATIVO
El lobo grande y feroz (109 words)

PART I: SILENT READING COMPREHENSION

Background Statement: "¿Ha habido alguien que haya dicho algo acerca de ti que no era verdad? El sr. Lobo cree que a él sí. Lee para saber lo que realmente pasó. Léelo con cuidado porque cuando termines voy a pedir que me cuentes la historia."

Teacher Directions: Once the student completes the silent reading, say, "Dime acerca de lo que leíste." Answers to the questions below that the student provides during the retelling should be marked "ua" in the appropriate blank to indicate that this response was unaided. Ask all remaining questions not addressed during the retelling and mark those the student answers with an "a" to indicate that the correct response was given after prompting by the teacher.

Questions/Answers	*Story Grammar Element/ Level of Comprehension*
_____1. ¿De quién se trató el cuento? *(Sr. Lobo, Abuelita, el leñador, una niña)*	character-characterization/ literal
_____2. ¿Dónde estaba el sr. Lobo cuando vio la casa? *(en el bosque)*	setting/literal
_____3. ¿Por qué le fue necesario al sr. Lobo entrar en la casa? *(estaba mojado y congelado)*	story problem(s)/literal
_____4. ¿Por qué pensó el sr. Lobo que estaba bien entrar a la casa? *(la nota en la puerta)*	problem resolution attempts/ inferential
_____5. ¿Qué hizo el sr. Lobo después de entrar a la casa? *(empezó a calentarse y se cambió a una bata de dormir)*	problem resolution attempts/ literal
_____6. ¿Por qué el sr. Lobo tuvo que correr para salvar su vida? *(el leñador lo iba a matar)*	problem resolution attempts/ literal
_____7. ¿Qué lección aprendió el sr. Lobo? *(algo acerca de no hacer cosas sin tener permiso)*	theme/evaluative
_____8. ¿Qué dijo la sra. Lobo que te hace pensar que ella no tiene confianza en los humanos? *(que los humanos iban a fabricar un cuento acerca de su esposo)*	character-characterization/ inferential

PART II: ORAL READING AND ANALYSIS OF MISCUES

Directions: Say, "Ahora me gustaría oírte leer este cuento en voz alta." Have the student read orally until the 100-word sample is completed. Follow along on the Miscue Grid, marking any oral reading errors as appropriate. *Remember to count miscues only up to the point in the story containing the oral reading stop-marker (//).* Then complete the Developmental/Performance Summary to determine whether to continue the assessment. (*Note:* The Miscue Grid should be completed *after* the assessment session has been concluded in order to minimize stress for the student.)

	MIS-PRONUN.	SUB-STITUTION	OMISSION	INSERTION	TCHR. ASSIST.	SELF-CORRECT.	MEANING DISRUPTION
El lobo grande y feroz							
Un día el sr. Lobo caminaba por							
el bosque. Disfrutaba de una							
caminata por la tarde y no estaba							
molestando a nadie. De repente							
empezó a llover, se mojó y le							
dio frío. Justo cuando el sr.							
Lobo se iba a morir de frío, vio							
una choza en el bosque. Salía							
humo de la chimenea así que							
tocó a la puerta. Nadie se							
encontraba en casa, pero una							
nota en la puerta decía: Entra y							
caliéntate. Regreso a las 2:00 p.m.							
Con cariño, Abuelita							
El pobre lobo mojado entró y							
empezó a calentarse junto a la							
fogata. Vio una de// *las batas de*							
dormir de Abuelita en la cama.							
TOTALS							

Notes:

Examiner's Summary of Miscue Patterns:

PART III: DEVELOPMENTAL/PERFORMANCE SUMMARY

Silent Reading Comprehension

_____ 0–1 questions missed = Easy

_____ 2 questions missed = Adequate

_____ 3+ questions missed = Too hard

Oral Reading Accuracy

_____ 0–1 oral errors = Easy

_____ 2–5 oral errors = Adequate

_____ 6+ oral errors = Too hard

Continue to next assessment level passage? _____ Yes _____ No

Examiner's Notes:

Examiner's Summary of Miscue Patterns:

PART III: DEVELOPMENTAL/PERFORMANCE SUMMARY

Silent Reading Comprehension

_____ 0–1 questions missed = Easy

_____ 2 questions missed = Adequate

_____ 3+ questions missed = Too hard

Oral Reading Accuracy

_____ 0–1 oral errors = Easy

_____ 2–5 oral errors = Adequate

_____ 6+ oral errors = Too hard

Continue to next assessment level passage? _____ Yes _____ No

Examiner's Notes:

NIVEL 5 REGISTRO INFORMATIVO
Los zapatos de moda (103 words)

PART I: SILENT READING COMPREHENSION

Background Statement: "Este cuento es sobre los sentimientos de un grupo de muchachos hacia sus zapatos deportivos. Lee este cuento para saber la importancia de usar zapatos especiales para jugar deportes. Lee el cuento con mucho cuidado porque te voy a hacer preguntas sobre él."

Teacher Directions: Once the student completes the silent reading, say, "Dime algo del cuento que leíste." Answers to the questions below that the student provides during the retelling should be marked "ua" in the appropriate blank to indicate that this response was unaided. Ask all remaining questions not addressed during the retelling and mark those the student answers with an "a" to indicate that the correct response was given after prompting by the teacher.

Questions/Answers	*Story Grammar Element/ Level of Comprehension*
_____1. ¿Dónde se desarrolló el cuento? (*en la escuela Valdez*)	setting/literal
_____2. Quiénes son los personajes principales del cuento? (*Rudy y Juan*)	character-characterization/ literal
_____3. ¿Cuál era el problema entre Rudy y Juan? (*Rudy no creía que Juan podía jugar bien con sus tenis baratos*)	story problem(s)/inferential
_____4. ¿Cómo resolvió Juan el problema que tenía con los otros? (*Juan jugó mejor que todos*)	problem resolution/ inferential
_____5. ¿Qué clase de persona era Rudy? (*presumido, se creía la gran cosa*)	character-characterization/ evaluative
_____6. ¿Qué pasó después del juego? (*se juntaron con Juan para preguntarle su secreto*)	problem resolution attempts/ literal
_____7. ¿Por qué se rieron todos cuando Juan dijo, —Mucha práctica y tenis baratos? (*porque todo era a causa de sus zapatos deportivos*)	problem resolution attempts/ inferential
_____8. ¿Qué lección aprendimos en este cuento? (*no es lo que uno se pone, sino como uno lo aplica*)	theme/evaluative

PART II: ORAL READING AND ANALYSIS OF MISCUES

Directions: Say, "Ahora quiero que leas este cuento en voz alta." Have the student read orally until the 100-word sample is completed. Follow along on the Miscue Grid, marking any oral reading errors as appropriate. *Remember to count miscues only up to the point in the story containing the oral reading stop-marker (//).* Then complete the Developmental/Performance Summary to determine whether to continue the assessment. (*Note:* The Miscue Grid should be completed *after* the assessment session has been concluded in order to minimize stress for the student.)

Un fuego en la montaña (272 words)

PART I: SILENT READING COMPREHENSION

Background Statement: "Este cuento se trata de dos muchachos quienes están perdidos en una montaña. Lee el cuento para saber qué hicieron para encontrar su ruta a casa y los resultados de sus acciones. Léelo con cuidado porque voy a pedir que me lo cuentes."

Teacher Directions: Once the student completes the silent reading, say, "Dime acerca de lo que leíste." Answers to the questions below that the student provides during the retelling should be marked "ua" in the appropriate blank to indicate that this response was unaided. Ask all remaining questions not addressed during the retelling and mark those the student answers with an "a" to indicate that the correct response was given after prompting by the teacher.

Questions/Answers	***Story Grammar Element/ Level of Comprehension***
_____1. ¿Dónde tomó lugar el cuento? *(en el monte Holyoak)*	setting/literal
_____2. ¿Quiénes eran los muchachos? *(Beto y Kiko)*	character-characterization/ literal
_____3. ¿Por qué mandó el papá a los muchachos río arriba? *(para buscar huellas de puma)*	problem resolution attempts/ inferential
_____4. ¿Cuál era el problema que Beto y Kiko tuvieron río arriba? *(se perdieron)*	story problem(s)/literal
_____5. ¿Qué hicieron los muchachos para que los encontraran? *(prendieron una lumbre)*	problem resolution/ literal
_____6. ¿Qué ocurrió cuando ya no pudieron controlar el fuego? *(la gente ayudó a apagar la fogata)*	problem resolution attempts/ literal
_____7. Después que se apagó el fuego, ¿qué hicieron los muchachos? *(ayudaron a repoblar de árboles las montañas)*	problem resolution attempts/ literal
_____8. ¿Qué nuevo problema resultó a causa de este fuego forestal? *(ya no hay pumas en esa área)*	story problem(s)/inferential

PART II: ORAL READING AND ANALYSIS OF MISCUES

Directions: Say, "Ahora me gustaría oirte leer en voz alta." Have the student read orally until the 100-word sample is completed. Follow along on the Miscue Grid, marking any oral reading errors as appropriate. *Remember to count miscues only up to the point in the story containing the oral reading stop-marker (//).* Then complete the Developmental/Performance Summary to determine whether to continue the assessment. (*Note:* The Miscue Grid should be completed *after* the assessment session has been concluded in order to minimize stress for the student.)

	MIS-PRONUN.	SUB-STITUTION	OMISSION	INSERTION	TCHR. ASSIST.	SELF-CORRECT.	MEANING DISRUPTION
Un fuego en la montaña							
Un tarde en agosto, Beto y Kiko							
fueron por una caminata con sus							
padres al monte Holyoak. El papá							
de Beto iba en busca de datos							
acerca de los pumas. Mucha gente							
temía que los pumas estuvieran							
extintos en el monte Holyoak. Los							
muchachos se alborotaron mucho							
cuando descubrieron lo que parecían							
huellas de puma cerca de un							
arroyo. Pero conforme pasó el							
tiempo ya no volvieron a encontrar							
otras huellas. Después de haberse							
comido su almuerzo, el papá de							
Beto mandó a los muchachos a							
explorar río arriba mientras que él							
rodeaba por el oeste. Les dijo a los							
// muchachos que regresaran en							
una hora.							
TOTALS							

Notes:

	MIS-PRONUN.	SUB-STITUTION	OMISSION	INSERTION	TCHR. ASSIST.	SELF-CORRECT.	MEANING DISRUPTION
Un viaje en canoa							
A Katarina y a su familia les gusta							
acampar durante sus vacaciones.							
Frecuentemente ellos van a las							
montañas del parque nacional							
"Great Smoky" o al parque							
nacional "Yellowstone." Como han							
ido a acampar varios años, ahora							
son muy adeptos. Katarina puede							
encender una fogata con pedernal y							
acero, construir un cobertizo y							
encontrar comida en el bosque para							
sostenerse. La actividad favorita de							
Katarina es ir en canoa. Aunque							
ella puede manejar una canoa muy							
bien, hay un viaje que nunca							
olvidará. Fue un viaje en canoa que							
hizo con su familia y su amiga,							
Amelia, a través del Río Madison							
cerca del oeste de "Yellowstone."							
Katarina y Amelia estaban // *juntas*							
en una canoa, siguiendo a sus							
padres por el río.							
TOTALS							

Notes:

Examiner's Summary of Miscue Patterns:

PART III: DEVELOPMENTAL/PERFORMANCE SUMMARY

Silent Reading Comprehension

_____ 0–1 questions missed = Easy

_____ 2 questions missed = Adequate

_____ 3+ questions missed = Too hard

Oral Reading Accuracy

_____ 0–1 oral errors = Easy

_____ 2–5 oral errors = Adequate

_____ 6+ oral errors = Too hard

Continue to next assessment level passage? _____ Yes _____ No

Examiner's Notes:

Examiner's Summary of Miscue Patterns:

PART III: DEVELOPMENTAL/PERFORMANCE SUMMARY

Silent Reading Comprehension

_____ 0–1 questions missed = Easy

_____ 2 questions missed = Adequate

_____ 3+ questions missed = Too hard

Oral Reading Accuracy

_____ 0–1 oral errors = Easy

_____ 2–5 oral errors = Adequate

_____ 6+ oral errors = Too hard

Continue to next assessment level passage? _____ Yes _____ No

Examiner's Notes:

NIVEL 9 REGISTRO INFORMATIVO
El caso de Angela Valdez (414 words)

PART I: SILENT READING COMPREHENSION

Background Statement: "Este cuento es de la desaparición de una joven. Lee el cuento con cuidado porque voy a pedir que me lo repitas cuando termines."

Teacher Directions: Once the student completes the silent reading, say, "Dime algo sobre el cuento que acabas de leer." Answers to the questions below that the student provides during the retelling should be marked "ua" in the appropriate blank to indicate that this response was unaided. Ask all remaining questions not addressed during the retelling and mark those the student answers with an "a" to indicate that the correct response was given after prompting by the teacher.

Questions/Answers	*Story Grammar Element/ Level of Comprehension*
_____1. ¿En qué estación del año tomó lugar el cuento? *(en el otoño)*	setting/literal
_____2. ¿Cuál es el problema principal del cuento? *(la desaparición de Karina Gómez)*	story problem(s)/inferential
_____3. ¿Qué esfuerzos para resolver el problema pusieron las autoridades cuando recibieron la llamada anónima? *(obtuvieron un permiso para catear la casa de la señora Valdez)*	problem resolution attempts/ literal
_____4. Cómo se resolvió al final el caso de Karina Gómez? *(la encontraron en California)*	problem resolution/literal
_____5. ¿Cómo reaccionó la señora Valdez cuando la policía quería catear su casa? *(los dejó que lo hicieran)*	problem resolution attempts/ literal
_____6. ¿Qué clase de persona era la señora Valdez? *(buena gente, amable, cuidadosa, solitaria)*	character-characterization/ inferential
_____7. ¿Qué hizo la gente de la vecindad después que la señora Valdez fue encontrada inocente? *(hablaban más con ella)*	problem resolution attempts/ literal
_____8. ¿Qué puede aprender uno de este cuento? *(no hay que juzgar a los demás por lo que vemos)*	theme/evaluative

PART II: ORAL READING AND ANALYSIS OF MISCUES

Directions: Say, "Ahora me gustaría que leas el cuento en voz alta." Have the student read orally until the 100-word sample is completed. Follow along on the Miscue Grid, marking any oral reading errors as appropriate. *Remember to count miscues only up to the point in the story containing the oral reading stop-marker (//).* Then complete the Developmental/Performance Summary to determine whether to continue the assessment. (*Note:* The Miscue Grid should be completed *after* the assessment session has been concluded in order to minimize stress for the student.)

	MIS-PRONUN.	SUB-STITUTION	OMISSION	INSERTION	TCHR. ASSIST.	SELF-CORRECT.	MEANING DISRUPTION
El caso de Angela Valdez							
Angela Valdez era una señora que vivía							
en nuestra vecindad. Algunas personas							
la veían sospechosamente. Casi nunca							
salía de su casa, que era de estilo							
victoriano, más que a recoger sus							
cartas del buzón . Su cara descolorida							
y su manera anticuada de vestir							
la hacían verse como un fantasma.							
Los niños de la vecindad especulaban							
que ella era una bruja.							
Parecía que la señora Angela							
no había tenido ningún contacto							
con el mundo. Un día de otoño,							
se extendió por la vecindad la noticia							
de que una de las porristas de la prepa,							
Karina Gómez, había desaparecido.							
Se creía// *que había sido secuestrada.*							
TOTALS							

Notes:

Examiner's Summary of Miscue Patterns:

PART III: DEVELOPMENTAL/PERFORMANCE SUMMARY

Silent Reading Comprehension   *Oral Reading Accuracy*

_____ 0–1 questions missed = Easy   _____ 0–1 oral errors = Easy

_____ 2   questions missed = Adequate   _____ 2–5 oral errors = Adequate

_____ 3+   questions missed = Too hard   _____ 6+   oral errors = Too hard

Continue to next assessment level passage?   _____ Yes   _____ No

Examiner's Notes:

SENTENCES FOR INITIAL PASSAGE SELECTION

forma **B**

FORMA B: NIVEL 1

1. Hoy es mi cumpleaños.

2. Quería tener una fiesta.

3. Ella se paró por los árboles.

FORMA B: NIVEL 2

1. Tenemos hojas extras para recoger.

2. Necesito más dinero.

3. Ella me oyó en la cocina.

FORMA B: NIVEL 3

1. Me comenzó a dar miedo.

2. Él podía oír la voz acercándose.

3. Mañana terminaré mi trabajo.

FORMA B: NIVEL 4

1. Ella caminó con cuidado hacia la oscuridad.

2. Yo sé que es importante comer verduras.

3. Él se resbaló cuando trató de alcanzar el roble.

FORMA B: NIVEL 5

1. El árbol se secó después de la tormenta.

2. La vecindad estaba asustada después del incendio.

3. Me espantó mi sueño.

FORMA B: NIVEL 6

1. Pasó difícilmente de grado por falta de participación.

2. Les di tiempo extra a los alumnos superdotados.

3. El éxito académico es el resultado de una buena instrucción.

FORMA B: NIVEL 7

1. Hice una cita para comprar la bicicleta.

2. La cubierta de plástico protectora que cubría la solicitud era especialmente gruesa.

3. Sus piernas robustas hicieron la diferencia en su fuerza física.

FORMA B: NIVEL 8

1. Lo provocaron porque era bajo de estatura.

2. Las burlas familiares causaron la pelea.

3. Su ego herido nunca se recuperó.

FORMA B: NIVEL 9

1. Su aparencia mejoró con su falta de vestirse tradicionalmente.

2. La carta anónima no fue tomada en serio.

3. Él parecía ser una persona formidable, aún con un abrigo barrato.

NARRATIVE PASSAGES......forma B

Mi cumpleaños en el zoológico

Era domingo.

Me levanté y fui a comer.

Mamá me dijo, — Hoy es tu cumpleaños, Patricia.
¿Qué te gustaría hacer?

Yo quería una fiesta, pero no le dije a mi mamá.

Dije, —Nada más quiero jugar.

Mamá dijo, — Ven conmigo a pasear en el coche.

Subí al coche y pronto llegamos a la ciudad.

El coche se detuvo. Salimos.

Caminando, pasamos unos árboles y vi una señal que
decía "Zoológico de la Ciudad."

Todos mis amigos estaban por la puerta.

Yo estaba sonriendo mucho. Mi mamá había planeado
una fiesta para mí.

Fue el mejor cumpleaños.

La bicicleta nueva de María

María quería una bicicleta. En su casa ayudaba mucho para ahorrar dinero. También María le ayudaba a su papá a recoger las hojas que caían de los árboles para ahorrar dinero. Pero de todos modos no tenía dinero para comprar la bicicleta nueva de diez velocidades que había visto en una tienda de bicicletas.

Un día su Tía Nacha llegó a visitar a la familia de María. Tía Nacha se dió cuenta que María quería comprar una bicicleta. Tía Nacha le pidió a María que le fuera a ayudar a limpiar su casa y que ella le pagaría. Al día siguiente María fue a la casa de su Tía Nacha.

Tía Nacha puso a María a trapear el piso de la cocina, la puso a limpiar los muebles, a barrer el garaje y también la puso a doblar la ropa lavada. Hizo tantas cosas que aunque se cansó, el tiempo se le pasó muy rápido. Cuando su Tía Nacha le pagó, le dio un abrazo y se fue de prisa a su casa para darles la buena noticia a sus padres. El papá y la mamá también se pusieron muy contentos con su hija y le dijeron que estaban muy orgullosos de ella.

Al siguiente día María se fue a la tienda.

Tiempo de dormir

La puesta del sol se veía. El aire estaba caliente y Wild Willie tenía miedo. Nunca había estado en un lugar tan seco y caliente. Su caballo, Wizard, intentaba encontrar algo de pasto. Wild Willie empezó a dormirse a causa de haber estado despierto tanto tiempo. Entonces oyó el ruido otra vez; el mismo sonido que había estado oyendo durante varios días. ¿Qué será? ¿Por qué lo estaban siguiendo? ¿Cómo podría saber qué o quién era?

Wizard se volteó despacito. Willie se paró en los estribos para ver sobre el cerro de arena. No vio a nadie. Oyó el sonido otra vez. Esta vez se oía desde atrás. El sonido era lento y bajo. Se bajó de su caballo. Tomó su arma, se alistó. Despacio, el sonido llegó más y más cerca. Willie levantó su arma....

Entonces, el televisor se apagó y una voz dijo, —Beth, es tiempo de acostarse. Mañana hay que ir a la escuela y ya es tarde. —Oh, Mamá, ¿puedo terminar de ver el programa? —pregunté. —No, lo puedes ver otro día —respondió mi mamá.

Mientras subía lentamente las escaleras, me preguntaba, ¿qué habría visto Wild Willie? Quizás habrá sido algún animal o una persona en una carreta. Pero, a lo mejor era el fantasma del viento de arena. Sí, eso tenía que ser. Algunos dicen que lo han visto. Pero no voy a saber hasta que pasen el programa otra vez.

En otra época

Marlo vivía en otra época y en otro lugar. Él vivía en una época de oscuridad y tristeza. Vivía en una choza con sus padres, quienes eran pobres. Él no tenía bastante ropa ni tampoco tenía mucho que comer. Pero estas cosas no eran las que le preocupaban. Para Marlo solamente existía una cosa que él deseaba. Pero no podía obtenerla, porque el jefe de la comarca no dejaba que nadie la tuviera. Lo más importante para él era saber leer. Hoy en día, es posible que aprender a leer no sea de mucha importancia, pero en los tiempos de Marlo sí lo era.

Un día el papá de Marlo lo mandó al castillo con una carreta de legumbres. En el camino Marlo se encontró con un viejito que tenía una mirada muy extraña. El viejito llevaba un capuchón pero sus ojos azules brillaban. El viejito le preguntó a Marlo si le podía dar unas legumbres para comer porque tenía hambre. Marlo, que era muy benévolo, le dio de comer sabiendo que su papá lo iba a regañar. Cuando el viejito acabó de comerse lo que Marlo le había dado, le dijo, —ve al roble esta noche y allí te ofreceré el futuro.— Marlo se fue pensando en lo que el viejito le había dicho.

Esa noche Marlo salió de su choza sin pedir permiso. Corrió hacia el roble y encontró al viejito sentado en el suelo recargado en el roble.

El viejito se levantó y le dio a Marlo una caja. Le dijo, —dentro de esta caja está lo que has andado buscando, tu vida cambiará de hoy en adelante.—

Fue justar
que se le pres
atrás, llamanc
rápidamente.
reacostó bajo

El hermar
que debes reg
tener. Ella le
lo que él dijo

Esa noche
el nombre "E

Marlo tomó la cajita, la miró sin abrirla y de pronto se dio cuenta de que el viejito se había desaparecido. Marlo corrió a su choza. Abrió la caja cuidadosamente. Bajo la luz de una velita vio lo que había en la caja. Era un libro.

Niño láser

Mi nombre es Roberto y soy maestro. Hace varios años conocí a un estudiante de quien me gustaría contarte.

Mateo era un niño de 13 años que nunca salió bien en la escuela. Algunos dicen que era un inadaptado—una persona que no es aceptado por los otros niños de su edad. Además, Mateo tenía problemas en la escuela casi toda su vida. No cumplía sus tareas aunque eran muy fáciles. Por causa de no participar en clase, no entregar su tarea y hacer solo más o menos bien en los exámenes, Mateo apenas pasaba siempre.

Un día cuando Mateo iba en séptimo grado su maestro decidió encontrar cuál era su problema con la escuela. El maestro le mandó para que lo examinaran y un maestro de necesidades especiales le dijo que ¡Mateo era excepcional en las áreas de ciencia y matemáticas! La maestra de necesidades especiales dijo, — A veces los estudiantes que no tienen éxito en la escuela son muy excepcionales. Nada más que nadie les ha dado la oportunidad de demostrar lo que pueden hacer. También, algunos no tienen muchas habilidades en temas escolares. Pero, tienen excelentes habilidades en música, trabajando con cosas mecánicas o también atléticas.

Después de que hicieron el descubrimiento de Mateo, le preguntaron lo que a él le gustaría estudiar. Mateo contestó que quería estudiar los rayos láser. El resto del año Mateo leyó todo lo que encontró en la biblioteca de la universidad acerca de la tecnología de los rayos láser. Más tarde, se encontraron un profesor en California que era experto en la tecnología de los rayos láser. El profesor asintió en hablar con Mateo regularmente para ayudar a contestar preguntas o resolver problems que tenía Mateo.

Durante la última parte del séptimo grado, Mateo trabajó en un proyecto de ciencia especial. Construyó un modelo de un láser. ¡Era fantástico! El modelo de Mateo era correcto hasta el último detalle. Todo el mundo se impresionó con su proyecto. Todos los niños empezaron a llamarlo "niño láser." Encontró nuevos amigos y su vida en la escuela y en casa mejoró mucho.

Desde que conocí al "niño láser," he visto diferente a los estudiantes que tienen problemas. Estoy convencida de que todos tienen talentos escondidos. Nada más tenemos que descubrir cuáles son.

Ramón y Leonardo

A veces Leonardo se sentía como el niño menos popular en toda la escuela. No importaba lo que hacía, sus compañeros constantemente se burlaban de él. Sería que era un niño bajo de estatura y que usaba bifocales gruesos. O quizás era porque no le gustaban los deportes. Posiblemente era porque no podía comprar la ropa de moda que los otros niños valoraban tanto. De todos modos, Leonardo se sentía menospreciado y no estaba contento con su situación.

Un día, mientras ponía sus libros en su gabeta, empezaron las burlas familiares. Una banda chica de compañeros se puso enfrente de él. Cada uno empezó a burlarse de él y a decirle nombres. La mayoría de ellos lo hicieron después de que Ramón Guzmán tiró los libros de Leonardo. Todos ellos se rieron y lo llamaron "payaso," "tonto" y "baboso." Pero Leonardo se aguantó; esto fue, hasta que Ramón dijo cosas horribles acerca de la familia de Leonardo, particularmente de su mamá. Leonardo no lo pudo resistir. Él se avalanzó hacia Ramón pero Ramón era mucho más grande y el ataque de Leonardo terminó en desastre. Ramón lo estrelló contra las gabetas, cogió a Leonardo por el cuello e hizo que Leonardo gritara "Perdóname," en signo de sumisión total.

Cuando el grupo se desbandó para no llegar tarde a su siguiente clase, Lorena Rodríguez se acercó a Leonardo. Ella se disculpó por el comportamiento del grupo y trató de consolar a Leonardo. Ella dijo —Lo que ellos te hagan, a ellos les pasará.— Pero ese consuelo no le ayudó en nada al lastimado ego de Leonardo.

Después de veinte años, Leonardo logró ser el presidente del banco más grande de la ciudad. Él era bien conocido y respetado en la comunidad. Y también era muy generoso cuando se trataba de proyectos cívicos. Aunque nunca se había casado, él había empezado a salir con Lorena Rodríguez, su vieja compañera de clase.

Un viernes por la noche, Leonardo y Lorena estaban comiendo en un restaurante lujoso. Ellos habían terminado su comida y se dirigían a la puerta cuando un limosnero se les acercó. El limosnero les pidió dinero para comprar comida. Había algo raro acerca del limosnero que Leonardo no podía entender. Pero siendo tan generoso, Leonardo le dio al hombre diez dólares. El limosnero estaba tan sorprendido por la valiosa suma de dinero que apretó con fuerza la mano de Leonardo antes de dirigirse hacia la calle. Lorena le gritó que tuviera cuidado, pero fue demasiado tarde. El limosnero se había cruzado enfrente de un camión y fue atropellado. Leonardo y Lorena esperaron a la ambulancia para que se llevaran al hombre.

En los periódicos de la mañana siguiente, imprimieron el incidente del limosnero. El había muerto temprano esa mañana de heridas internas. Mientras Leonardo leía los detalles, dejó caer de pronto el periódico y palideció. El nombre del limosnero era Ramón Guzmán.

La noche larga

Después de haber tenido contratiempos en San Luís, llegué tarde al Aeropuerto Internacional de Nueva Orleans. La noche comenzaba a cubrir la ciudad mientras entraba al taxi que me llevaría al centro de la ciudad. Mientras el taxi se dirigía a la ciudad, la chófer comenzó a platicarme de la ciudad de Nueva Orleans que se conoce como la ciudad de la luna creciente. La chófer era una dama con un acento como si fuera de una isla y su vestido de muchos colores que no era nada tradicional. Después de decirle que quería ir a la calle Rampart, ella de pronto dio vuelta a la izquierda y continuó al suroeste. Quince minutos después y sin ninguna palabra, me bajé del taxi y seguí rumbo a Rampart. Sin haber caminado más de dos cuadras me di cuenta que un hombrecillo malvado me seguía. Dije hombrecillo malvado porque, bajo la luz de la calle al verlo, me pareció como que si algo malo y cruel le hubiera ocurrido durante su vida. ¿Sabes?, algo así como, una apariencia que no era natural. Cuando yo paraba, él paraba. Si caminaba aprisa, él caminaba aprisa. Para asegurarme de que no me estaba siguiendo, me metí por una puerta desconocida. Cuando se me acercó, sin darse cuenta que lo estaba esperando, lo agarré del cuello y le pregunté por qué me estaba siguiendo. Lo único que hizo fue sollozar y me dio una nota escrita en un papel arrugado. Al tratar de leer la notita, el hombrecillo se me fue y corrió hacia la neblina que se acercaba.

La notita decía, —La muerte te sigue. Corre, si valoras tu vida. — Ni siquiera lo pensé. Corrí inmediatamente. Al dar la vuelta en la esquina Rampart y Royal, me topé con un policía. Me sentí protegido y le conté lo que me había ocurrido. El policía se rió sin tomarme en serio. Mientras que el policía se alejaba, noté un par de ojos detrás de un bote de basura en un callejón oscuro y volví a correr otra vez.

Al cruzar corriendo por el callejón, dos seres extraños me acozaron y me dijeron que Nero los había mandado. Me preguntaron que dónde había puesto el paquete. Les contesté que no tenía la menor idea de lo que me estaban hablando. Me levantaron en peso y me llevaron a un edificio sucio.

Tan pronto mis ojos se ajustaron a las luces, vi a un hombre gordo y grande al lado de una mesa. Se veía enorme y me hicieron que me sentara frente a él. Se me acercó y al instante pude ver su cara. Una cara de monstruo que me estudió cuidadosamente y luego volteó a ver a sus cómplices y les dijo, —idiotas, éste no es "El Rata," sáquenlo de aquí.— Me cubrieron los ojos con una venda y me sacaron por otro lado del edificio. Una hora más tarde estaba solo en una calle desierta.

Dos días después salí de la ciudad de la luna creciente. A nadie le dije lo que me había pasado y nunca he regresado a esa ciudad.

EXAMINER'S ASSESSMENT PROTOCOLS

forma B

PREPRIMER (PP) LEVEL ASSESSMENT PROTOCOL
Ojos en mi armario (Wordless picture story)

PART I: WORDLESS PICTURE STORY READING

Background Statement: "Estos dibujos cuentan acerca un niño que se va a acostar. Mira cada dibujo según te lo vaya enseñando y piensa acerca la historia que cuentan estos dibujos. Después, te pediré que me cuentes el cuento usando los dibujos."

Teacher Directions: Refer the student to each picture slowly and in order as numbered. Do not comment on the pictures. Then repeat the procedure, asking the student to tell the story in the student's own words. Record the student's reading using a tape recorder, and transcribe the reading as it is being dictated. Replay the recording later to make sure that your transcription is accurate and complete.

PART II: EMERGENT READING BEHAVIOR CHECKLIST

Directions: Following are emergent reading behaviors identified through research and grouped according to broad developmental stages. Check all behaviors you have observed. *If the student progresses to Stage 3 or 4, continue your assessment using the Primer Level (P) passage.*

Stage 1: Early Connections to Reading—Describing Pictures

_____ Attends to and describes (labels) pictures in books

_____ Has a limited sense of story

_____ Follows verbal directions for this activity

_____ Uses oral vocabulary appropriate for age/grade level

_____ Displays attention span appropriate for age/grade level

_____ Responds to questions in an appropriate manner

_____ Appears to connect pictures (sees as being interrelated)

Stage 2: Connecting Pictures to Form Story

_____ Attends to pictures and develops oral stories across the pages of the book

_____ Uses only childlike or descriptive (storyteller) language to tell the story, rather than book language (i.e., Once upon a time . . .; There once was a little boy . . .)

Stage 3: Transitional Picture Reading

_____ Attends to pictures as a connected story

_____ Mixes storyteller language with book language

Stage 4: Advanced Picture Reading

_____ Attends to pictures and develops oral stories across the pages of the book

_____ Speaks as though reading the story (uses book language)

Examiner's Notes:

PART I: PICTURE STORY READING—ORAL READING AND ANALYSIS OF MISCUES

Background Statement: "Éste es un cuento de un niño que está jugando un juego. Vamos a ver cada dibujo primero. Ahora, lee el cuento para ti mismo—en silencio. Después, te voy a pedir que me leas el cuento."

Teacher Directions: Refer the student to each frame of the story slowly and in order as numbered. Do not read the story or comment on the pictures. After the student has read the story silently, ask the student to read the story aloud. Record the student's reading using a tape recorder, and mark any miscues on the Miscue Grid provided. Following the oral reading, complete the Emergent Reading Behavior Checklist. Assessment information obtained from both the Miscue Grid and the Emergent Reading Behavior Checklist will help you to determine whether to continue your assessment. If the student is unable to read the passage independently the first time, read it aloud, then ask the student to try to read the story again. This will help you to understand whether the student is able to memorize and repeat text, an important developmental milestone (see the *Instructions for Administering the Preprimer (PP) and Primer (P) Passages* section in the front of this book for more information). The assessment should stop after this activity, if the child is unable to read the text independently. (Note: The Miscue Grid should be completed *after* the assessment session has been concluded in order to minimize stress for the student.)

Examiner's Summary of Miscue Patterns:

Beis
Me ;
en la
juga
El ú
lo di
que
TOT

Note:

PART III: DEVELOPMENTAL/PERFORMANCE SUMMARY

Silent Reading Comprehension

_____ 0–1 questions missed = Easy

_____ 2   questions missed = Adequate

_____ 3+   questions missed = Too hard

Oral Reading Accuracy

_____ 0–1 oral errors = Easy

_____ 2–5 oral errors = Adequate

_____ 6+   oral errors = Too hard

Continue to next assessment level passage? _____ Yes _____ No

Examiner's Notes:

NIVEL 1 REGISTRO INFORMATIVO
Mi cumpleaños en el zoológico (96 words)

PART I: SILENT READING COMPREHENSION

Background Statement: "¿Qué te gusta hacer en tu cumpleaños? Lee este cuento con cuidado para encontrar qué cosa especial una niña quería para su cumpleaños. Voy a pedir que me cuentes acerca de la historia cuando termines de leer."

Teacher Directions: Once the student completes the silent reading, say, "Dime acerca del cuento que leíste." Answers to the questions below that the student provides during the retelling should be marked "ua" in the appropriate blank to indicate that this response was unaided. Ask all remaining questions not addressed during the retelling and mark those the student answers with an "a" to indicate that the correct response was given after prompting by the teacher.

Questions/Answers	*Story Grammar Element/ Level of Comprehension*
_____1. ¿Quiénes eran las personas en el cuento? *(Patricia y su mamá)*	character-characterization/ literal
_____2. ¿Qué era el deseo de Patricia? *(quería una fiesta)*	story problem(s)/literal
_____3. ¿Qué dijo Patricia que quería hacer para su cumpleaños? *(nada más jugar)*	problem resolution attempts/ literal
_____4. ¿Le llegó a Patricia su deseo? ¿Cómo sabes? *(le dieron una fiesta en el zoológico)*	problem resolution/ literal
_____5. ¿Cómo llegaron Patricia y su mamá al zoológico? *(en coche)*	problem resolution attempts/ literal
_____6. ¿Cuáles palabras usarían para describir cómo se sintió Patricia en el zoológico? *(sorprendida, feliz...)*	character-characterization/ inferential
_____7. ¿Dónde estaba Patricia cuando empezó el cuento? *(en su recámara, o en su casa)*	setting/inferential
_____8. ¿Cúando supo Patricia que iba a tener una fiesta? *(cuando llegó al zoológico y vio a sus amigas)*	problem resolution attempts/ inferential

PART II: ORAL READING AND ANALYSIS OF MISCUES

Directions: Say, "Ahora, me gustaría oirte leer este cuento en voz alta." Have the student read orally until the word sample is completed. Follow along on the Miscue Grid, marking any oral reading errors as appropriate. *Remember to count miscues only up to the point in the story containing the oral reading stop-marker (//).* Then complete the Developmental/Performance Summary to determine whether to continue the assessment. (*Note:* The Miscue Grid should be completed *after* the assessment session has been concluded in order to minimize stress for the student.)

NIVEL 2 REGISTRO INFORMATIVO
La bicicleta nueva de María (212 words)

PART I: SILENT READING COMPREHENSION

Background Statement: "¿Has tratado alguna vez de ahorrar dinero para comprar algo? Lee este cuento para que sepas cómo María pudo ahorrar dinero para comprar algo. Lee con cuidado porque te voy a preguntar sobre el cuento cuando termines."

Teacher Directions: Once the student completes the silent reading, say, "Dime algo sobre el cuento que acabas de leer." Answers to the questions below that the student provides during the retelling should be marked "ua" in the appropriate blank to indicate that this response was unaided. Ask all remaining questions not addressed during the retelling and mark those the student answers with an "a" to indicate that the correct response was given after prompting by the teacher.

Questions/Answers	*Story Grammar Element/ Level of Comprehension*
_____1. ¿Acerca de quién era el cuento? (de María)	character-characterization/ literal
_____2. ¿Cuál era el problema de María en el cuento? (quería una bicicleta nueva pero no tenía dinero)	story problem(s)/literal
_____3. ¿Qué había hecho María antes para ahorrar dinero? (recoger hojas, ayudar en casa)	problem resolution attempts/ literal
_____4. ¿Además de María, qué otros personajes estaban en el cuento? (Tía Nacha y la familia de María)	character-characterization/ literal
_____5. ¿Cómo resolvió María su problema? (trabajó para su Tía Nacha y ahorró dinero)	problem resolution/ inferential
_____6. ¿Cuáles fueron dos cosas que María hizo para su Tía Nacha? (trapeó el piso, barrió el garaje, limpió los muebles, dobló la ropa)	problem resolution attempts/ literal
_____7. ¿Qué lección aprendió María sobre cómo conseguir algo que se quiere de verdad? (se necesita trabajar duro y ser paciente)	theme/evaluative
_____8. ¿Para qué fue María a la tienda al día siguiente? (para comprar su bicicleta)	problem resolution attempts/ inferential

PART II: ORAL READING AND ANALYSIS OF MISCUES

Directions: Say, "Ahora quiero que leas el cuento en voz alta." Have the student read orally until the 100-word sample is completed. Follow along on the Miscue Grid, marking any oral reading errors as appropriate. *Remember to count miscues only up to the point in the story containing the oral reading stop-marker (//).* Then complete the Developmental/Performance Summary to determine whether to continue the assessment. (*Note:* The Miscue Grid should be completed *after* the assessment session has been concluded in order to minimize stress for the student.)

	MIS-PRONUN.	SUB-STITUTION	OMISSION	INSERTION	TCHR. ASSIST.	SELF-CORRECT.	MEANING DISRUPTION
La bicicleta nueva de María							
María quería una bicicleta. En su							
casa ayudaba mucho para ahorrar							
dinero. También María le ayudaba							
a su papá a recoger las hojas que							
caían de los árboles para ahorrar							
dinero. Pero de todos modos no							
tenía dinero para comprar la							
bicicleta nueva de diez							
velocidades que había visto en							
una tienda de bicicletas. Un día su							
Tía Nacha llegó a visitar a la							
familia de María. Tía Nacha se							
dio cuenta que María quería							
comprar una bicicleta. Tía Nacha							
le pidió a María que le fuera a ayudar							
a limpiar su casa y que ella le							
pagaría. Al día// *siguiente María*							
fue a la casa de su Tía Nacha.							
TOTALS							

Notes:

	MIS-PRONUN.	SUB-STITUTION	OMISSION	INSERTION	TCHR. ASSIST.	SELF-CORRECT.	MEANING DISRUPTION
Tiempo de dormir							
La puesta del sol se veía. El aire							
estaba caliente y Wild Willie tenía							
miedo. Nunca había estado en un							
lugar tan seco y caliente. Su							
caballo, Wizard, intentaba							
encontrar algo de pasto. Wild							
Willie empezó a dormirse a causa							
de haber estado despierto tanto							
tiempo. Entonces oyó el ruido otra							
vez; el mismo sonido que había							
estado oyendo durante varios días.							
¿Qué será? ¿Por qué lo estaba							
siguiendo? ¿Cómo podría saber qué							
o quién era? Wizard se volteó							
despacito. Willie se paró en los							
estribos para ver sobre el cerro de							
arena. No vio a nadie.							
Oyó// *el sonido otra vez.*							
TOTALS							

Notes:

Examiner's Summary of Miscue Patterns:

PART III: DEVELOPMENTAL/PERFORMANCE SUMMARY

Silent Reading Comprehension

_____ 0–1 questions missed = Easy

_____ 2 questions missed = Adequate

_____ 3+ questions missed = Too hard

Oral Reading Accuracy

_____ 0–1 oral errors = Easy

_____ 2–5 oral errors = Adequate

_____ 6+ oral errors = Too hard

Continue to next assessment level passage?   _____ Yes   _____ No

Examiner's Notes:

NIVEL 4 REGISTRO INFORMATIVO
En otra época (317 words)

PART I: SILENT READING COMPREHENSION

Background Statement: "Este cuento es acerca de un niño que vivía en otra época. Lee el cuento para que sepas lo que Marlo quería y por qué no lo podía tener. Léelo con mucho cuidado porque te voy a preguntar sobre el cuento cuando termines."

Teacher Directions: Once the student completes the silent reading, say, "Dime acerca del cuento que acabas de leer." Answers to the questions below that the student provides during the retelling should be marked "ua" in the appropriate blank to indicate that this response was unaided. Ask all remaining questions not addressed during the retelling and mark those the student answers with an "a" to indicate that the correct response was given after prompting by the teacher.

Questions/Answers	*Story Grammar Element/ Level of Comprehension*
_____1. ¿Dónde vivía Marlo? *(en una choza)*	setting/literal
_____2. ¿Qué problema tenía Marlo? *(quería saber como leer)*	story problem(s)/literal
_____3. ¿Qué hizo Marlo para que el anciano lo ayudara? *(le dio algunas legumbres)*	problem resolution attempts/ inferential
_____4. ¿Dónde quedó Marlo de ver al anciano? *(en el roble)*	setting/literal
_____5. ¿Cómo se resolvió el problema de Marlo? *(el anciano le dio un libro para que aprendiera a leer)*	problem resolution attempts/ inferential
_____6. ¿Cómo describirías a Marlo? *(buena gente, noble, agradecido)*	character-characterization/ evaluative
_____7. ¿Cómo sabes que este cuento se desarrolló en otra época y no en nuestra época? *(castillo, choza, uso de una carreta, la gente no sabía leer)*	setting/inferential
_____8. ¿Por qué el tema de "ser bueno con otros" es un buen tema para este cuento? *(algo como: Marlo recibió su deseo por ser una persona bondadosa)*	theme/evaluative

PART II: ORAL READING AND ANALYSIS OF MISCUES

Directions: Say, "Ahora, quiero que leas el cuento en voz alta." Have the student read orally until the 100-word sample is completed. Follow along on the Miscue Grid, marking any oral reading errors as appropriate. *Remember to count miscues only up to the point in the story containing the oral reading stop-marker (//).* Then complete the Developmental/Performance Summary to determine whether to continue the assessment. (*Note:* The Miscue Grid should be completed *after* the assessment session has been concluded in order to minimize stress for the student.)

	MIS-PRONUN.	SUB-STITUTION	OMISSION	INSERTION	TCHR. ASSIST.	SELF-CORRECT.	MEANING DISRUPTION
En otra época							
Marlo vivía en otra época y en							
otro lugar. Él vivía en una época							
de oscuridad y tristeza. Vivía en							
una choza con sus padres							
quienes eran pobres. Él no tenía							
bastante ropa ni tampoco tenía							
mucho que comer. Pero estas							
cosas no eran las que le							
preocupaban. Para Marlo							
solamente existía una cosa que él							
deseaba. Pero no podía obtenerla,							
porque el jefe de la comarca no							
dejaba que nadie la tuviera. Lo							
más importante para él era saber							
leer. Hoy en día, es posible que							
aprender a leer no sea de mucha							
importancia, pero en los tiempos							
de// *Marlo sí lo era.*							
TOTALS							

Notes:

Examiner's Summary of Miscue Patterns:

PART III: DEVELOPMENTAL/PERFORMANCE SUMMARY

Silent Reading Comprehension

_____ 0–1 questions missed = Easy

_____ 2 questions missed = Adequate

_____ 3+ questions missed = Too hard

Oral Reading Accuracy

_____ 0–1 oral errors = Easy

_____ 2–5 oral errors = Adequate

_____ 6+ oral errors = Too hard

Continue to next assessment level passage?   _____ Yes   _____ No

Examiner's Notes:

NIVEL 5 REGISTRO INFORMATIVO
Un paseo por la tarde (410 words)

PART I: SILENT READING COMPREHENSION

Background Statement: "Este cuento se trata de una joven que va caminando en un bosque supuestamente embrujado. Lee el cuento para ver que le pasa a Alicia cuando entra al bosque. Leélo con cuidado porque voy a pedir que me lo cuentes."

Teacher Directions: Once the student completes the silent reading, say, "Dime acerca de lo que leíste." Answers to the questions below that the student provides during the retelling should be marked "ua" in the appropriate blank to indicate that this response was unaided. Ask all remaining questions not addressed during the retelling and mark those the student answers with an "a" to indicate that the correct response was given after prompting by the teacher.

Questions/Answers	*Story Grammar Element/ Level of Comprehension*
_____1. ¿Quién es el personaje principal del cuento? *(Alicia)*	character-characterization/ literal
_____2. ¿Dónde estaba Alicia cuando conoció a la viejita? *(en el bosque, bajo un árbol)*	setting/literal
_____3. ¿Dónde llevó la viejita a Alicia? *(a su choza)*	setting/literal
_____4. ¿Cuál fue el problema de Alicia con la viejita? *(escaparse antes de que la vendiera al enano o no parecer cansada)*	story problem(s)/inferential
_____5. ¿Cómo se escapó Alicia de la viejita? *(corrió por la puerta mientras la viejita buscaba su perro)*	problem resolution/literal
_____6. ¿Qué pasó cuando Alicia ya no pudo correr y se durmió? *(su hermano la despertó)*	problem resolution attempts/ literal
_____7. ¿Qué pasó cuando Alicia ya estaba segura en casa otra vez? *(ella encontró un pedazo de metal con el nombre "Espíritu" imprimido)*	problem resolution attempts/ literal
_____8. ¿Por qué Alicia siempre le decía a la viejita que no estaba cansada? *(porque no quería que la vendiera)*	problem resolution attempts/ inferential

PART II: ORAL READING AND ANALYSIS OF MISCUES

Directions: Say, "Ahora, me gustaría oirte leer este cuento en voz alta." Have the student read orally until the 100-word sample is completed. Follow along on the Miscue Grid, marking any oral reading errors as appropriate. *Remember to count miscues only up to the point in the story containing the oral reading stop-marker (//).* Then complete the Developmental/Performance Summary to determine whether to continue the assessment. (*Note:* The Miscue Grid should be completed *after* the assessment session has been concluded in order to minimize stress for the student.)

NIVEL 6 REGISTRO INFORMATIVO
Niño láser (379 words)

PART I: SILENT READING COMPREHENSION

Background Statement: "Este cuento se trata de un niño con problemas en la escuela. Lee el cuento y encuentra cómo solucionaron los problemas. Léelo con cuidado porque te voy a pedir que me lo cuentes después."

Teacher Directions: Once the student completes the silent reading, say, "Dime acerca del cuento que leíste." Answers to the questions below that the student provides during the retelling should be marked "ua" in the appropriate blank to indicate that this response was unaided. Ask all remaining questions not addressed during the retelling and mark those the student answers with an "a" to indicate that the correct response was given after prompting by the teacher.

Questions/Answers	*Story Grammar Element/ Level of Comprehension*
_____1. ¿Quién era el personaje principal? *(Mateo)*	character-characterization/ literal
_____2. ¿Qué era su problema? *(no iba bien en la escuela)*	story problem(s)/inferential
_____3. ¿Qué decidió hacer su maestra acerca de su problema? *(hacerle un examen para ver si tenía necesidades especiales)*	problem resolution attempts/ literal
_____4. Describe lo que la escuela descubrió acerca del problema de Mateo. *(tenía habilidades altas en matemáticas y ciencias)*	problem resolution/inferential
_____5. ¿Cómo trató la escuela de resolver su problema? *(permitió que Mateo estudiara lo que le interesaba)*	problem resolution attempts/ inferential
_____6. ¿Cómo afectó a Mateo poder estudiar lo que le interesaba? *(mejoró como estudiante e hizo amigos)*	character-characterization/ inferential
_____7. ¿Cómo afectó al autor la historia de Mateo? *(le hizo creer que todos tienen talentos especiales, si uno los busca)*	theme/evaluative
_____8. ¿Por qué arreglaron para Mateo las llamadas telefónicas con un professor? *(para que pudiera preguntar acerca de rayos láseres cuando necesitara)*	problem resolution attempts/ literal

PART II: ORAL READING AND ANALYSIS OF MISCUES

Directions: Say, "Me gustaría oirte leer este cuento en voz alta." Have the student read orally until the 100-word sample is completed. Follow along on the Miscue Grid, marking any oral reading errors as appropriate. *Remember to count miscues only up to the point in the story containing the oral reading stop-marker (//).* Then complete the Developmental/Performance Summary to determine whether to continue the assessment. (*Note:* The Miscue Grid should be completed *after* the assessment session has been concluded in order to minimize stress for the student.)

	MIS-PRONUN.	SUB-STITUTION	OMISSION	INSERTION	TCHR. ASSIST.	SELF-CORRECT.	MEANING DISRUPTION
Niño láser							
Mi nombre es Roberto y soy							
maestro. Hace varios años conocí a							
un estudiante de quien me gustaría							
contarte. Mateo era un niño de 13							
años que nunca salió bien en la							
escuela. Algunos dicen que era un							
inadaptado, alguien quien no cabe							
con los otros niños de su edad.							
Además, Mateo tenía problemas en							
la escuela casi toda su vida. No							
cumplía sus tareas aunque eran muy							
fáciles. Por causa de no participar en							
clase, no entregar su tarea y hacer							
solo más o menos bien en los							
exámenes, Mateo apenas pasaba							
siempre. Un día cuando Mateo iba							
en // *séptimo grado su maestro*							
decidió encontrar cuál era su							
problema con la escuela.							
TOTALS							

Notes:

	MIS-PRONUN.	SUB-STITUTION	OMISSION	INSERTION	TCHR. ASSIST.	SELF-CORRECT.	MEANING DISRUPTION
La entrega de periódicos							
Salvador tuvo la oportunidad de							
ganar dinero por primera vez. Para							
solicitar un empleo como repartidor							
de periódicos, fue a ver al Sr.							
Murillo, el gerente de distribución.							
El Sr. Murillo era una persona baja							
y gorda que tenía una voz fuerte.							
Después de revisar la solicitud de							
trabajo de Salvador le dijo, —Tú							
pareces ser un joven responsable.							
¿Están de acuerdo tus padres en							
que tú entregues periódicos? —¡Si							
Señor,— respondió Salvador, —y							
mi papá le escribió una carta							
diciéndole eso. —El trabajo es							
tuyo,— le dijo el Sr. Murillo.							
—Pero tienes que darte cuenta que							
ésta es una// *ruta muy larga y te*							
tienes que levantar muy temprano.							
TOTALS							

Notes:

Examiner's Summary of Miscue Patterns:

PART III: DEVELOPMENTAL/PERFORMANCE SUMMARY

Silent Reading Comprehension

_____ 0–1 questions missed = Easy

_____ 2 questions missed = Adequate

_____ 3+ questions missed = Too hard

Oral Reading Accuracy

_____ 0–1 oral errors = Easy

_____ 2–5 oral errors = Adequate

_____ 6+ oral errors = Too hard

Continue to next assessment level passage? _____ Yes _____ No

Examiner's Notes:

Examiner's Summary of Miscue Patterns:

PART III: DEVELOPMENTAL/PERFORMANCE SUMMARY

Silent Reading Comprehension

_____ 0–1 questions missed = Easy

_____ 2 questions missed = Adequate

_____ 3+ questions missed = Too hard

Oral Reading Accuracy

_____ 0–1 oral errors = Easy

_____ 2–5 oral errors = Adequate

_____ 6+ oral errors = Too hard

Continue to next assessment level passage? _____ Yes _____ No

Examiner's Notes:

La noche larga (507 words)

PART I: SILENT READING COMPREHENSION

Background Statement: "Este cuento es de una identidad equivocada, leélo cuidadosamente porque te voy a pedir que me platiques el cuento cuando hayas terminado."

Teacher Directions: Once the student completes the silent reading, say, "Dime algo sobre el cuento que leíste." Answers to the questions below that the student provides during the retelling should be marked "ua" in the appropriate blank to indicate that this response was unaided. Ask all remaining questions not addressed during the retelling and mark those the student answers with an "a" to indicate that the correct response was given after prompting by the teacher.

Questions/Answers	*Story Grammar Element/ Level of Comprehension*
_____1. ¿En dónde y a qué horas tomó lugar este cuento? *(en Nueva Orleans, en la noche)*	setting/literal
_____2. ¿Cuál fue el problema que tuvo el escritor de este cuento mientras caminaba por la calle Rampart? *(alguien lo seguía y le dio una nota diciéndole que iba a morir)*	story problem(s)/inferential
_____3. ¿Cómo reaccionó el policía al oír la historia del escritor? *(no le creyó)*	problem resolution attempts/ literal
_____4. ¿Qué pasó después que dejó al policía? *(dos hombres lo llevaron a un edificio)*	problem resolution attempts/ literal
_____5. ¿Cómo solucionó, el escritor de este cuento, el problema? *(fue un caso de confundir la identidad)*	problem resolution/ inferential
_____6. ¿Quién era Nero y cómo lo describirías? *(era el jefe, criminal y mala gente)*	character-characterization/ inferential
_____7. ¿Qué serie de eventos le causó problemas a la persona de este cuento? *(retraso de su avión, el caminar a solas, parecerse a otra persona)*	story problem(s)/inferential
_____8. ¿Qué hizo el escritor después que lo dejaron ir? *(permaneció dos días más en Nueva Orleans pero nunca regresó otra vez)*	problem resolution attempts/ literal

PART II: ORAL READING AND ANALYSIS OF MISCUES

Directions: Say, "Ahora me gustaría oirte leer el cuento en voz alta." Have the student read orally until the 100-word sample is completed. Follow along on the Miscue Grid, marking any oral reading errors as appropriate. *Remember to count miscues only up to the point in the story containing the oral reading stop-marker (//).* Then complete the Developmental/Performance Summary to determine whether to continue the assessment. (*Note:* The Miscue Grid should be completed *after* the assessment session has been concluded in order to minimize stress for the student.)

	MIS-PRONUN.	SUB-STITUTION	OMISSION	INSERTION	TCHR. ASSIST.	SELF-CORRECT.	MEANING DISRUPTION
La noche larga							
Despúes de haber tenido							
contratiempos en San Luís, llegué							
tarde al Aeropuerto Internacional de							
Nueva Orleans. La noche comenzaba							
a cubrir la ciudad mientras entraba al							
taxi que me llevaría al centro de la							
ciudad. Mientras el taxi se dirigía a							
la ciudad, la chófer comenzó a							
platicarme de la ciudad de Nueva							
Orleans que se conoce como la							
ciudad de la luna creciente. La							
chófer era una dama con un acentó							
como si fuera de una isla y su							
vestido de muchos colores que no							
era nada tradicional. Después de							
decirle que quería ir a la calle							
Rampart, ella // *de pronto dio vuelta*							
a la izquierda y continuó al suroeste.							
TOTALS							

Notes:

Examiner's Summary of Miscue Patterns:

PART III: DEVELOPMENTAL/PERFORMANCE SUMMARY

Silent Reading Comprehension

_____ 0–1 questions missed = Easy

_____ 2 questions missed = Adequate

_____ 3+ questions missed = Too hard

Continue to next assessment level passage? _____ Yes _____ No

Oral Reading Accuracy

_____ 0–1 oral errors = Easy

_____ 2–5 oral errors = Adequate

_____ 6+ oral errors = Too hard

Examiner's Notes:

SENTENCES FOR INITIAL PASSAGE SELECTION

forma C

FORMA C: NIVEL 6

1. Lo consideró cuidadosamente, pero era muy caro.

2. El nuevo método de aumentar la temperatura dio buenos resultados.

3. Lo que es común hoy es el resultado de muchos años de experiencia.

FORMA C: NIVEL 7

1. Los científicos esperan transformar la zona industrial antes del fin del año.

2. Minerales ajenos al caso son usados para desarrollar minerales manejables.

3. La presencia de impurezas baja el valor de las gemas.

FORMA C: NIVEL 8

1. Para mejorar el mundo, los científicos constantemente están buscando nuevos adelantos.

2. El lugar arreglado de antemano fue eliminado.

3. Compresionar cientos de alambres en uno es conocido como "fibra óptica."

FORMA C: NIVEL 9

1. Se movió en una forma circular y luego corrió lateralmente.

2. El objeto vertical no se podía ver fácilmente.

3. Una serie de accidentes ocurrieron en el cruce.

EXPOSITORY PASSAGES......forma

El cielo nocturno

Levanta la vista hacia el cielo. Si es una noche clara, verás las estrellas. ¿Cuántas estrellas hay? Nadie sabe con certeza. Pero hay una estrella que conoces por su nombre. Se puede ver durante el día. Es nuestro sol. El sol es una estrella. Todas las estrellas son soles. Nuestro sol está tan cerca de la tierra que no podemos ver otras estrellas durante el día. Podemos ver otros soles sólamente en la noche.

Las estrellas están hechas de un gas muy caliente y parece que titilean porque el aire pasa por ellas. Aunque no siempre se pueden ver, siempre están en el cielo, aún durante el día.

Flores voladoras

Hay muchos tipos de insectos. Hay grandes, chicos, feos, los que muerden y los que ayudan. Pero hay un tipo que la mayoría de la gente cree que es el más hermoso. A este insecto algunas veces se le llama "la flor voladora." Es la mariposa.

Las mariposas son insectos que tienen dos pares de alas. Las alas están cubiertas con escamas muy pequeñas. Las escamas son de diferentes colores. Estas escamas dan a la mariposa sus colores hermosos. Las mariposas huelen y oyen usando sus antenas largas y delgadas. Las mariposas no pueden morder o masticar. Usan largas lenguas, como tubos, para alcanzar la comida en las flores.

Las mariposas empiezan como huevitos. Luego, salen como orugas. Las orugas forman un capullo. Cuando el capullo se abre, sale la mariposa con sus alas coloridas. Las mariposas adultas tienen que poner huevos pronto. Ellas no viven por mucho tiempo.

Las mariposas y las polillas son diferentes. A las mariposas les gusta el día. A las polillas la noche. Las polillas no son tan brillantes como las mariposas. Los cuerpos de las mariposas son delgados, mientras que las polillas generalmente tienen cuerpos largos y gruesos. Las polillas forman capullos antes de convertirse en insectos con alas. La mayoría de mariposas no forman capullos.

La historia de la Coca-Cola

Por todo el mundo mucha gente ha oído del refresco Coca-Cola. Pero no mucha gente sabe la verdadera historia de cómo fue inventada esta bebida.

La Coca-Cola fue la invención de un Señor John Pemberton. Aunque no era doctor, sus conocidos lo llamaban Dr. Pemberton. Él era un boticario de un pueblo en el sur de los Estados Unidos. Al Dr. Pemberton le gustaba inventar cosas. El vivió durante el tiempo de la guerra civil.

Un día el Dr. Pemberton decidió hacer una medicina para curar el dolor de cabeza. Él hizo esta medicina mezclando nueces, frutas y hojas. También agregó las drogas necesarias para curar un dolor de cabeza. El Dr. Pemberton ahora pensó que tenía algo con buen sabor para vender.

Durante el verano de 1886, el Dr. Pemberton llevó una jarra de su medicina mezclada a una de las mejores boticas de la ciudad de Atlanta, Georgia. Le dijo al gerente que la mezclara con agua y que se la recetara a personas con dolor de cabeza. No se vendió mucho, pero un día, un trabajador en la botica vendió la nueva medicina a un cliente que traía un dolor de cabeza. En vez de usar agua natural, por accidente usó agua gaseosa. El agua gaseosa hace burbujas. A todos les gustó este nuevo cambio y hasta la fecha se usa agua gaseosa en la Coca-Cola.

Con el transcurso del tiempo, la mayoría de la medicina que cura los dolores de cabeza fue eliminada de la Coca-Cola. Sin embargo, la bebida del Dr. Pemberton todavía es una de las bebidas favoritas del mundo.

Palomitas

Hay tres tipos de maíz que se cosechan en los Estados Unidos. El primero es el que la gente come. Se llama elote dulce por su sabor. El segundo es el elote que se usa para alimentar ganado, su nombre es elote de campo. A algunas personas les gusta comer elote de campo. Este maíz no es tan dulce como el primero y los dientes de este elote no son tan grandes. Al tercer tipo de maíz se le refiere como maíz indio, es el que se usa para hacer palomitas. Éste se cosecha a nivel industrial en los Estados Unidos porque cada persona come un promedio de un kilogramo de palomitas al año.

Cuando Cristóbal Colón llegó a las Américas, la gente indígena ya tenía muchos años comiendo palomitas. Preparaban las palomitas de diferentes formas. Una forma era la de poner un elote en un palo y quemarlo. Cualquier diente del elote que se separaba del elote ya cocido se recogía y se lo comían. Otra forma de preparalo era de quitarle todos los dientes al elote y echarlos al fuego. Los dientes ya cocidos que saltaban del fuego se los comían. Ya que estas formas de cocer maíz limitaban el número de dientes del elote que se podían comer, los indígenas empezaron a usar casuelas de barro en donde calentaban arena. Cuando la arena estaba muy caliente, ponían los dientes del elote en las casuelas y esperaban a que se cocieran.

Las palomitas se hacen palomitas por el agua que cada diente de elote tiene. Los expertos están de acuerdo de que cada diente de elote debe tener por lo menos un catorce por ciento de agua para que se pueda convertir en palomita. Si un diente de elote tiene menos de un doce por ciento de agua, el diente de maíz no se hará palomita.

Cocinando sin fuego: El micro-ondas

Cocinando con micro-ondas es muy común hoy. Pero, es una invención muy moderna. El horno de micro-ondas que uno usa hoy se desarrolló de una invención del tubo MAGNETRON en 1940. La invención del tubo MAGNETRON, por el Sr. John Randall y el Dr. H. A. Boot, fue una parte importante de la defensa con radar de Inglaterra durante la Segunda Guerra Mundial. Después de inventarla, ninguno de los hombres la consideraba como una manera de preparar la comida.

No fue hasta los últimos años de los años 1940 que el Dr. Percy Spencer descubrió la habilidad del MAGNETRON para calentar y cocinar comida desde adentro hacia afuera. Spencer experimentó con muchas comidas diferentes, todas con el mismo resultado: el interior se calentaba primero.

La compañía donde Spencer trabajaba tomó muchos años para desarrollar lo que hoy conocemos como horno de micro-ondas. Una persona no podía comprar un horno de micro-ondas para uso doméstico hasta 1952 y entonces se llamaba horno de radar. Estos modelos eran caros y abultados.

Los hornos de micro-ondas de hoy son baratos y vienen con una variedad de atracciones. Éstas incluyen: descongelar, guardar la temperatura constante y recalentado automático. Cocinar con micro-ondas, dicen algunos, fue el primer nuevo método de cocinar comida desde que los humanos descubrieron el fuego. ¿Por qué? Porque con micro-ondas no se requiere fuego o elemento de fuego para cocinar la comida. La comida se cocina con energía electromagnética.

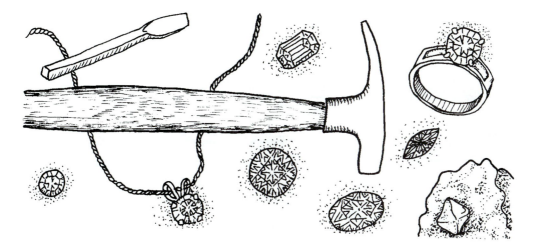

Diamantes

Un diamante es una de las joyas más hermosas creadas por la naturaleza y una de las más raras. Toma miles de años para transformar un pedazo de carbón en diamante en bruto. Solamente tres minas de diamantes importantes han sido encontradas en todo el mundo — India, Suramérica y Africa.

Los primeros diamantes se encontraron en la arena y grava de arroyos. Estos tipos de diamantes se llaman diamantes aluviales. Después, encontraron diamantes en la tierra profunda, en formaciones de piedra llamadas "pipas." Estas formaciones parecen volcanes extinguidos. La piedra en que se encuentran los diamantes se llama "tierra azul." Aún cuando hay muchos diamantes, requiere escavar y buscar a través de toneladas de roca y grava para encontrar suficientes diamantes para un anillo de un carate.

La calidad de gemas diamantinas está basada en peso, color, pureza y tallado. El peso de un diamante es medido en carates. Su pureza está determinada por la presencia o ausencia de impurezas tales como materiales ajenos y carbón no cristalizado. El color de los diamantes puede variar, pero la mayoría tienen tinta amarilla o café. El tallado de un diamante también se toma encuenta para valorizarlo. Un diamante tallado completamente, llamado "sin fallas," podría tener cincuenta y ocho facetas. Las facetas o lados causan el brillo producida cuando un diamante refleja la luz.

Los humanos han aprendido como hacer diamantes artificiales. Los diamantes fabricados son puestos en una máquina que crea la misma presión que existe a doscientas cincuenta millas bajo de la superficie de la tierra. Además de la presión intensa, los compuestos de carbón son calentados a temperaturas de más de cinco mil grados Fahrenheit. Desafortunadamente, los diamantes fabricados son pequeños y se usan principalmente en lugares industriales. Como gemas, no tienen valor.

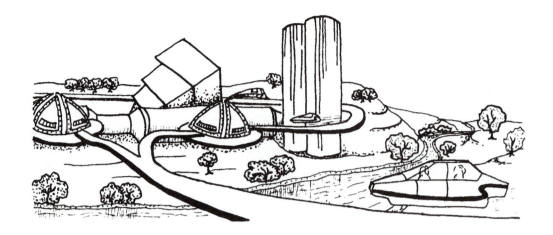

Ya está aquí el futuro

¿Qué traerá el siglo veintiuno en cuanto a invenciones nuevas y tecnologías ultramodernas? Nadie sabe de seguro. Pero los científicos, los inventores y los futuristas predicen una variedad de invenciones nuevas. Estos nuevos avances afectarán cómo vivimos y jugamos. Algunos de ellos ya están en la mesa de diseño.

Un ejemplo es el vehículo de levitación. La idea de un vehículo que se puede levantar y bajar verticalmente y también se maneja en la carretera es la invención de Paul Moeller. Él nombró su versión de este tipo de vehículo Moeller 400. La gente involucrada en este tipo de tecnología ve aumentos en población y carreteras apretadas como razones de que un vehículo de levitación sea necesario. Imagínese volando a la ciudad, llegando a un sitio predeterminado, bajando y entonces manejando el resto del camino a su trabajo.

Otra innovación que será mejorada durante los años 1990 es el rayo láser dental. Los investigadores han desarrollado un láser con el que esperan reemplazar el muy temido taladro dental. El láser básicamente vaporiza las carias sin afectar el esmalte dental. Como ganancia, con el láser se elimina la necesidad de dar una inyección para anestesiar el área en cuestión.

Probablemente una de las tecnologías más significantes que afectará a la gente en el futuro es el uso de fibras ópticas. Las fibras ópticas se componen de cientos de alambres en uno, lo cual permite que cantidades enormes de información se transfieran atravées de alambres muy delgados. Un ejemplo de la aplicación de fibras ópticas será el desarrollo de videoteléfonos con color y movimiento. Estos teléfonos serán importantes, particularmente para la gente sorda.

Otro avance en el horizonte es la televisión de alta definición. El consumidor normal podrá mejorar dramáticamente su manera de ver televisión cuando este tipo de televisor esté al alcance de todos. Estos televisores tendrán el color tan vívido como el de una película de 35 milímetros y la calidad de sonido de disco compacto. Este refinamiento nos llevará al mejoramiento de películas caseras y juegos de video, de las cuales ambos serán accesibles en forma tri-dimensional.

A pesar de los nuevos avances en tecnología, la gente tendrá que estar preparada para enfrentar los retos del futuro; el saber ayudarnos a medida que el tiempo pasa y ayudarnos a preservar nuestro hogar, La Tierra.

Ilusiones visuales

Según el diccionario, una ilusión visual aparenta una imagen que no es real. En otras palabras, ilusiones visuales son causadas por ideas que una persona tiene acerca de algo que esa persona desea ver. Algunas veces la ilusión visual ocurre por la dificultad que el cerebro tiene de escoger de dos o más modelos visuales.

Si uno ve en un blanco y si ese blanco se mueve en forma circular, uno podría ver alambres moviéndose. Estos alambres, si se ven, en realidad no existen. A este tipo de ilusión visual se le llama inhibición lateral.

Otro tipo de ilusión visual ocurre cuando una persona trata de calcular la altura de un objeto vertical. A esto se le refiere como "distorción de longitud." El famoso Arco "Gateway" de la ciudad de San Luis es un ejemplo de distorción de longitud, porque el arco se ve más alto que ancho. En realidad, la altura y la anchura del arco son idénticos. La distorción de longitud ocurre porque los ojos se mueven más fácilmente de lado a lado que de arriba a abajo. El esfuerzo de ver hacia arriba hace que el cerebro no pueda interpretar la altura de objetos verticales.

Si una persona ve una serie de cuadros, esa persona notará pequeñas manchas grises en cada intersección. Si la persona ve directamente hacia una intersección del cuadro, las manchas se desaparecen. Esta ilusión visual es conocido como cuadrícula de Hermann, la que se ve seguido en rascacielos modernos. Muchos de estos rascacielos tienen ventanas separadas con tiras de metal o de cemento.

Lo que aquí se cubrió son sólo tres ejemplos de tanta cosa que nuestros ojos ven que no es verdad. Pero sí refuerzan el dicho "No creer todo lo que se vea."

EXAMINER'S ASSESSMENT PROTOCOLS

forma C

NIVEL 1 REGISTRO INFORMATIVO
Osos (102 words)

PART I: SILENT READING COMPREHENSION

Background Statement: "Este cuento se trata de los osos. Lee el cuento para encontrar información acerca de los diferentes osos. Léelo con cuidado porque voy a pedir que me cuentes la historia."

Teacher Directions: Once the student completes the silent reading, say, "Dime acerca de lo que leíste." Answers to the questions below that the student provides during the retelling should be marked "ua" in the appropriate blank to indicate that this response was unaided. Ask all remaining questions not addressed during the retelling and mark those the student answers with an "a" to indicate that the correct response was given after prompting by the teacher.

Questions/Answers	*Expository Grammar Element/ Level of Comprehension*
_____1. ¿Acerca qué clases de osos leíste? (*café, negro, polar, "grizzly"*)	collection/literal
_____2. ¿Qué tipo de oso es el más grande? (*"grizzly"*)	description/literal
_____3. Explica por qué no es prudente estar cerca de los osos. (*algo como son animales salvajes, no les gustan los humanos, corren rápido, suben árboles*)	problem resolution attempts/ inferential
_____4. ¿Cuáles son algunas cosas que los osos hacen muy bien? (*oler, oír, correr o subirse a los árboles*)	collection/literal
_____5. ¿Cómo encuentran los osos su comida? (*oliendo y oyendo*)	problem resolution attempts/ inferential
_____6. ¿Por qué están tan hambrientos después del invierno? (*duermen la mayoría del invierno*)	causation/inferential
_____7. ¿Puedes nombrar dos cosas que comen los osos? (*plantas, moras y animales chicos*)	collection/literal
_____8. ¿Dónde dice en el cuento cuál es el lugar más seguro para estar cerca de los osos? (*en el zoológico*)	description/literal

PART II: ORAL READING AND ANALYSIS OF MISCUES

Directions: Say, "Ahora me gustaría oirte leer este cuento en voz alta." Have the student read orally until the passage is completed. Follow along on the Miscue Grid, marking any oral reading errors as appropriate. Then complete the Developmental/Performance Summary to determine whether to continue the assessment. (*Note:* The Miscue Grid should be completed *after* the assessment session has been concluded in order to minimize stress for the student.)

	MIS-PRONUN.	SUB-STITUTION	OMISSION	INSERTION	TCHR. ASSIST.	SELF-CORRECT.	MEANING DISRUPTION
Osos							
Hay muchas clases de osos. Algunos							
osos son cafés. Otros son negros.							
Aún otros son blancos y se llaman							
osos polares. Los más grandes se							
llaman osos "grizzly." Los osos							
pueden oler y oír muy bien.							
Los osos tienen ojos chicos y no							
pueden ver muy bien. Comen todo							
tipo de comida. Ellos comen							
animales chicos, plantas y moras.							
La mayoría de los osos duermen							
durante el invierno. Cuando							
despiertan tienen mucha hambre.							
Los osos corren muy rápido. Pueden							
subirse a los árboles. No es prudente							
estar cerca de ellos. El mejor lugar							
para estar cerca de los osos es //							
el zoológico.							
TOTALS							

Notes:

Examiner's Summary of Miscue Patterns:

PART III: DEVELOPMENTAL/PERFORMANCE SUMMARY

Silent Reading Comprehension

_____ 0–1 questions missed = Easy

_____ 2 questions missed = Adequate

_____ 3+ questions missed = Too hard

Continue to next assessment level passage? _____ Yes _____ No

Oral Reading Accuracy

_____ 0–1 oral errors = Easy

_____ 2–5 oral errors = Adequate

_____ 6+ oral errors = Too hard

Examiner's Notes:

El cielo nocturno (108 words)

PART I: SILENT READING COMPREHENSION

Background Statement: "Este cuento es acerca de las estrellas. Léelo y trata de recordar algunos de los hechos importantes de las estrellas porque te voy a preguntar acerca de lo que hayas leído."

Teacher Directions: Once the student completes the silent reading, say, "Dime lo que aprendiste sobre las estrellas." Answers to the questions below that the student provides during the retelling should be marked "ua" in the appropriate blank to indicate that this response was unaided. Ask all remaining questions not addressed during the retelling and mark those the student answers with an "a" to indicate that the correct response was given after prompting by the teacher.

Questions/Answers	Expository Grammar Element/ Level of Comprehension
_____1. ¿Cuál es la mejor noche para ver estrellas? *(una noche clara)*	description/literal
_____2. ¿De qué están hechas las estrellas? *(de gases calientes)*	description/literal
_____3. ¿Cuál estrella se puede ver solamente durante el día? *(el sol)*	causation/literal
_____4. ¿Por qué titilean las estrellas? *(por el aire que pasa por ellas)*	causation/literal
_____5. ¿Por qué la gente en la tierra no puede ver otras estrellas durante el día? *(el sol está muy cerca y muy brillante)*	collection/literal
_____6. Si alguna noche voltearas al cielo y no pudieras ver estrellas, ¿cuál sería la razón? *(la noche estaría nublada)*	problem resolution attempts/ evaluative
_____7. Explica por qué el decir — "mira todos los soles en el cielo nocturno" — puede ser correcto. *(porque toda estrella es un sol)*	causation/literal
_____8. ¿Puedes dar una razón por qué el planeta Tierra no puede llamarse estrella? *(no está compuesto de gases calientes, es un planeta no una estrella, tiene agua, etc.)*	comparison/evaluative

PART II: ORAL READING AND ANALYSIS OF MISCUES

Directions: Say, "Ahora quiero que leas el cuento en voz alta." Have the student read orally until the 100-word sample is completed. Follow along on the Miscue Grid, marking any oral reading errors as appropriate. *Remember to count miscues only up to the point in the story containing the oral reading stop-marker (//).* Then complete the Developmental/Performance Summary to determine whether to continue the assessment. (*Note:* The Miscue Grid should be completed *after* the assessment session has been concluded in order to minimize stress for the student.)

	MIS-PRONUN.	SUB-STITUTION	OMISSION	INSERTION	TCHR. ASSIST.	SELF-CORRECT.	MEANING DISRUPTION
El cielo nocturno							
Levanta la vista hacia el cielo. Si es							
una noche clara, verás las estrellas.							
¿Cuántas estrellas hay? Nadie sabe							
con certeza. Pero hay una estrella							
que conoces por su nombre. Se							
puede ver durante el día. Es nuestro							
sol. El sol es una estrella. Todas las							
estrellas son soles. Nuestro sol está							
tan cerca de la tierra que no							
podemos ver otras estrellas durante							
el día. Podemos ver otros soles							
sólamente en la noche. Las estrellas							
están hechas de un gas muy caliente y							
parece que titilean							
porque el aire pasa por ellas.							
Aunque no siempre se pueden ver,							
siempre // *están en el cielo, aún*							
durante el día.							
TOTALS							

Notes:

Examiner's Summary of Miscue Patterns:

PART III: DEVELOPMENTAL/PERFORMANCE SUMMARY

Silent Reading Comprehension

_____ 0–1 questions missed = Easy

_____ 2 questions missed = Adequate

_____ 3+ questions missed = Too hard

Oral Reading Accuracy

_____ 0–1 oral errors = Easy

_____ 2–5 oral errors = Adequate

_____ 6+ oral errors = Too hard

Continue to next assessment level passage? _____ Yes _____ No

Examiner's Notes:

NIVEL 3 REGISTRO INFORMATIVO
Flores voladoras (222 words)

PART I: SILENT READING COMPREHENSION

Background Statement: "Esta selección es acerca de un insecto muy especial. Es acerca de las mariposas. Lee esta selección para encontrar información interesante acerca de las mariposas. Voy a pedir que me cuentes de lo que leíste, así que lee con cuidado."

Teacher Directions: Once the student completes the silent reading, say, "Dime acerca de lo que leíste." Answers to the questions below that the student provides during the retelling should be marked "ua" in the appropriate blank to indicate that this response was unaided. Ask all remaining questions not addressed during the retelling and mark those the student answers with an "a" to indicate that the correct response was given after prompting by the teacher.

Questions/Answers	*Expository Grammar Element/ Level of Comprehension*
_____1. ¿De qué tipo de insecto se trató la selección? *(mariposas)*	description/literal
_____2. ¿Por qué le dicen a las mariposas "flores voladoras"? *(por sus varios colores)*	collection/inferential
_____3. ¿Qué les da a las mariposas sus colores? *(escamas)*	causation/literal
_____4. ¿Puedes nombrar dos maneras en que la mariposa y la polilla son diferentes? *(a las mariposas les gusta el día, tienen más colores, son más delgadas, la mayoría no forman capullos, — las polillas son lo opuesto)*	comparison/literal
_____5. ¿Puedes nombrar dos maneras en que la mariposa y la polilla son similares? *(vuelan, ponen huevos, tienen escamas, tienen alas, etc.)*	comparison/inferential
_____6. ¿Para qué usan las antenas? *(oler y oír)*	collection/literal
_____7. ¿Por qué las mariposas adultas tienen que poner sus huevos lo más pronto posible? *(no viven mucho tiempo)*	problem resolution attempts/ inferential
_____8. ¿Qué pasa después de que un huevo de mariposa se hace oruga? *(forma una piel dura que tiene que romper para salir)*	causation/literal

PART II: ORAL READING AND ANALYSIS OF MISCUES

Directions: Say, "Ahora me gustaría oirte leer esta selección en voz alta." Have the student read orally until the 100-word sample is completed. Follow along on the Miscue Grid, marking any oral reading errors as appropriate. *Remember to count miscues only up to the point in the story containing the oral reading stop-marker (//).* Then complete the Developmental/Performance Summary to determine whether to continue the assessment. (*Note:* The Miscue Grid should be completed *after* the assessment session has been concluded in order to minimize stress for the student.)

	MIS-PRONUN.	SUB-STITUTION	OMISSION	INSERTION	TCHR. ASSIST.	SELF-CORRECT.	MEANING DISRUPTION
Flores voladoras							
Hay muchos tipos de insectos.							
Hay grandes, chicos, feos, los que							
muerden y los que ayudan. Pero hay							
un tipo que la mayoría de la gente cree							
que es el más hermoso. A este							
insecto algunas veces se le llama							
"la flor voladora." Es la mariposa.							
Las mariposas son insectos que tienen							
dos pares de alas. Las alas están							
cubiertas con escamas muy pequeñas.							
Las escamas son de diferentes colores.							
Estas escamas dan a la mariposa							
sus colores hermosos. Las mariposas							
huelen y oyen usando sus antenas							
largas y delgadas. Las mariposas no							
pueden morder o masticar. Usan							
largas lenguas, // *como tubos, para*							
alcanzar la comida en las flores.							
TOTALS							

Notes:

Examiner's Summary of Miscue Patterns:

PART III: DEVELOPMENTAL/PERFORMANCE SUMMARY

Silent Reading Comprehension

_____ 0–1 questions missed = Easy

_____ 2 questions missed = Adequate

_____ 3+ questions missed = Too hard

Continue to next assessment level passage? _____ Yes _____ No

Oral Reading Accuracy

_____ 0–1 oral errors = Easy

_____ 2–5 oral errors = Adequate

_____ 6+ oral errors = Too hard

Examiner's Notes:

NIVEL 4 REGISTRO INFORMATIVO

La historia de la Coca-Cola (169 words)

PART I: SILENT READING COMPREHENSION

Background Statement: "Este cuento es sobre la historia de Coca-Cola. Léelo con cuidado porque me vas a contar acerca de lo que leíste."

Teacher Directions: Once the student completes the silent reading, say, "Dime algo de lo que acabas de leer sobre la Coca-Cola." Answers to the questions below that the student provides during the retelling should be marked "ua" in the appropriate blank to indicate that this response was unaided. Ask all remaining questions not addressed during the retelling and mark those the student answers with an "a" to indicate that the correct response was given after prompting by the teacher.

Questions/Answers	*Expository Grammar Element/ Level of Comprehension*
_____ 1. ¿Quién inventó la Coca-Cola? *(Sr./Dr. Pemberton)*	causation/literal
_____ 2. ¿Qué es lo que el Dr. Pemberton estaba tratando de inventar cuando inventó la Coca-Cola? *(medicina para el dolor de cabeza)*	description/literal
_____ 3. Además de agregar medicinas para dolor de cabeza, ¿cuáles otras cosas agregó el Dr. Pemberton a su medicina? *(hojas, frutas, nueces)*	description/literal
_____ 4. ¿Por qué al principio no se vendió mucho esta medicina? *(porque la miel estaba mezclada con agua regular)*	causation/inferential
_____ 5. ¿Por qué puede uno decir que la Coca-Cola se hizo muy popular por accidente? *(porque por accidente se mezcló la miel con agua gaseosa)*	problem resolution attempts/ inferential
_____ 6. ¿En qué ciudad se hizo famosa la Coca-Cola original? *(Atlanta)*	description/literal
_____ 7. Explica la diferencia entre la Coca-Cola de hoy y la original. *(no es medicina para el dolor de cabeza u otra respuesta aparente)*	comparison/inferential
_____ 8. ¿Cuál es la diferencia entre agua regular y agua gaseosa? *(el agua regular no tiene burbujas)*	comparison/inferential

PART II: ORAL READING AND ANALYSIS OF MISCUES

Directions: Say, "Ahora me gustaría que leas el cuento en voz alta." Have the student read orally until the 100-word sample is completed. Follow along on the Miscue Grid, marking any oral reading errors as appropriate. *Remember to count miscues only up to the point in the story containing the oral reading stop-marker (//).* Then complete the Developmental/Performance Summary to determine whether to continue the assessment. (*Note:* The Miscue Grid should be completed *after* the assessment session has been concluded in order to minimize stress for the student.)

La historia de la Coca-Cola	MIS-PRONUN.	SUB-STITUTION	OMISSION	INSERTION	TCHR. ASSIST.	SELF-CORRECT.	MEANING DISRUPTION
Por todo el mundo mucha gente ha							
oído del refresco Coca-Cola. Pero no							
mucha gente sabe la verdadera historia							
de cómo fue inventada esta bebida.							
La Coca-Cola fue la invención de un							
Señor John Pemberton. Aunque no era							
doctor, sus conocidos lo llamaban							
Dr. Pemberton. Él era un boticario de							
un pueblo en el sur de los Estados							
Unidos. Al Dr. Pemberton le gustaba							
inventar cosas. El vivió durante el							
tiempo de la guerra civil. Un día el							
Dr. Pemberton decidió hacer una							
medicina para curar el dolor de							
cabeza. Él hizo esta medicina							
mezclando nueces, frutas y hojas. //							
TOTALS							

Notes:

Examiner's Summary of Miscue Patterns:

PART III: DEVELOPMENTAL/PERFORMANCE SUMMARY

Silent Reading Comprehension   **Oral Reading Accuracy**

_____ 0–1 questions missed = Easy   _____ 0–1 oral errors = Easy

_____ 2   questions missed = Adequate   _____ 2–5 oral errors = Adequate

_____ 3+   questions missed = Too hard   _____ 6+   oral errors = Too hard

Continue to next assessment level passage? _____ Yes _____ No

Examiner's Notes:

NIVEL 5 REGISTRO INFORMATIVO
Palomitas (306 words)

PART I: SILENT READING COMPREHENSION

Background Statement: "Esta selección se trata de maíz y palomitas en particular. Lee la selección para descubrir información interesante acerca del maíz. Léelo con cuidado porque voy a pedir que me lo cuentes después."

Teacher Directions: Once the student completes the silent reading, say, "Dime acerca del cuento que leíste." Answers to the questions below that the student provides during the retelling should be marked "ua" in the appropriate blank to indicate that this response was unaided. Ask all remaining questions not addressed during the retelling and mark those the student answers with an "a" to indicate that the correct response was given after prompting by the teacher.

Questions/Answers	*Expository Grammar Element/ Level of Comprehension*
_____1. ¿Qué clase de maíz se menciona en este cuento? *(maíz para palomitas)*	description/inferential
_____2. Explica la diferencia de elote dulce y el elote de campo. *(el elote dulce no se da a los animales, es más dulce y más grande)*	comparison/inferential
_____3. ¿Qué hace que el maíz se vuelva en palomita? *(agua en el diente)*	causation/inferential
_____4. ¿Qué significa "no estallar" refiriéndose a las palomitas? *(que no se hace palomitas)*	description/literal
_____5. ¿Cuál era el método más efectivo de cocer palomitas para los indígenas? *(uso de cazuelas de barro con arena)*	problem resolution attempts/ inferential
_____6. ¿Cuál es el promedio de palomitas que la gente come por años en los Estados Unidos? *(un kilogramo)*	description/literal
_____7. ¿Cuánto hace que la gente ha comido palomitas? *(miles de años)*	description/literal
_____8. ¿Cuál es el problema asociado con las tres maneras de cocer palomitas de los indígenas? *(perdían dientes de elotes)*	problem resolution attempts/ inferential

PART II: ORAL READING AND ANALYSIS OF MISCUES

Directions: Say, "Ahora me gustaría oirte leer el cuento en voz alta." Have the student read orally until the 100-word sample is completed. Follow along on the Miscue Grid, marking any oral reading errors as appropriate. *Remember to count miscues only up to the point in the story containing the oral reading stop-marker (//).* Then complete the Developmental/Performance Summary to determine whether to continue the assessment. (*Note:* The Miscue Grid should be completed *after* the assessment session has been concluded in order to minimize stress for the student.)

	MIS-PRONUN.	SUB-STITUTION	OMISSION	INSERTION	TCHR. ASSIST.	SELF-CORRECT.	MEANING DISRUPTION
Palomitas							
Hay tres tipos de maíz que se							
cosechan en los Estados Unidos.							
El primero es el que la gente come.							
Se llama elote dulce por su sabor.							
El segundo es el elote que se usa							
para alimentar ganado, su nombre							
es elote de campo. A algunas							
personas les gusta comer elote de							
campo. Este maíz no es tan dulce							
como el primero y los dientes de							
este elote no son tan grandes. Al							
tercer tipo de maíz se le refiere							
como maíz indio, es el que se usa							
para hacer palomitas. Éste se							
cosecha a nivel industrial en los							
Estados Unidos // *porque cada*							
persona come un promedio de un							
kilogramo de palomitas al año.							
TOTALS							

Notes:

Examiner's Summary of Miscue Patterns:

PART III: DEVELOPMENTAL/PERFORMANCE SUMMARY

Silent Reading Comprehension

_____ 0–1 questions missed = Easy

_____ 2 questions missed = Adequate

_____ 3+ questions missed = Too hard

Oral Reading Accuracy

_____ 0–1 oral errors = Easy

_____ 2–5 oral errors = Adequate

_____ 6+ oral errors = Too hard

Continue to next assessment level passage? _____ Yes _____ No

Examiner's Notes:

PART I: SILENT READING COMPREHENSION

Background Statement: "Esta selección es acerca del horno de micro-ondas. Lee la selección para ver cómo el horno de micro-ondas se desarrolló. Léelo con cuidado porque voy a pedir que me cuentes la historia después."

Teacher Directions: Once the student completes the silent reading, say, "Dime acerca de lo que leíste." Answers to the questions below that the student provides during the retelling should be marked "ua" in the appropriate blank to indicate that this response was unaided. Ask all remaining questions not addressed during the retelling and mark those the student answers with an "a" to indicate that the correct response was given after prompting by the teacher.

Questions/Answers	*Expository Grammar Element/ Level of Comprehension*
_____1. ¿Cuál invención precipitó el desarrollo del horno de micro-ondas? *(el tubo MAGNETRON)*	causation/literal
_____2. ¿Para qué usaron el tubo MAGNETRON primero? *(radar)*	description/literal
_____3. ¿Qué descubrió el Dr. Percy Spencer acerca del tubo MAGNETRON? *(podía calentar comida desde adentro hacia afuera)*	description/literal
_____4. ¿Cómo se llamaba el primer horno de micro-ondas? *(horno de radar)*	description/literal
_____5. Menciona dos maneras en que los hornos de micro-ondas de hoy son diferentes a los primeros. *(no tan grande, más atracciones, menos costo)*	comparison/inferential
_____6. Explica por qué alguna gente cree que cocinar con micro-ondas es el método más nuevo de cocinar desde el descubrimiento del fuego. *(no requiere fuego, ni elemento de fuego para cocinar la comida)*	causation/literal
_____7. ¿Qué tipo de energía se usa en el horno de micro-ondas para cocinar la comida? *(electromagnética)*	description/literal
_____8. ¿Cuáles son dos atracciones que se encuentran en la mayoría de hornos de micro-ondas, según la selección? *(descongelar, guardar la temperatura constante y recalentado)*	description/literal

PART II: ORAL READING AND ANALYSIS OF MISCUES

Directions: Say, "Ahora, lee esta selección en voz alta." Have the student read orally until the 100-word sample is completed. Follow along on the Miscue Grid, marking any oral reading errors as appropriate. *Remember to count miscues only up to the point in the story containing the oral reading stop-marker (//).* Then complete the Developmental/Performance Summary to determine whether to continue the assessment. (*Note:* The Miscue Grid should be completed *after* the assessment session has been concluded in order to minimize stress for the student.)

	MIS-PRONUN.	SUB-STITUTION	OMISSION	INSERTION	TCHR. ASSIST.	SELF-CORRECT.	MEANING DISRUPTION
Cocinando sin fuego:							
El micro-ondas							
Cocinando con micro-ondas es							
muy común hoy. Pero, es una							
invención muy moderna. El horno							
de micro-ondas que uno usa hoy se							
desarrolló de una invención del							
tubo MAGNETRON en 1940. La							
invención del tubo MAGNETRON,							
por el Sr. John Randall y el Dr. H. A.							
Boot, fue una parte importante de							
la defensa con radar de Inglaterra							
durante la Segunda Guerra							
Mundial. Después de inventarla,							
ninguno de los hombres la							
consideraba como una manera de							
preparar la comida. No fue hasta							
los últimos años de los años 1940							
que el Dr. Percy Spencer descubrió							
la habilidad del MAGNETRON para //							
calentar y cocinar comida desde							
adentro hacia afuera.							
TOTALS							

Notes:

Examiner's Summary of Miscue Patterns:

PART III: DEVELOPMENTAL/PERFORMANCE SUMMARY

Silent Reading Comprehension

_____ 0–1 questions missed = Easy

_____ 2   questions missed = Adequate

_____ 3+   questions missed = Too hard

Continue to next assessment level passage?   _____ Yes   _____ No

Oral Reading Accuracy

_____ 0–1 oral errors = Easy

_____ 2–5 oral errors = Adequate

_____ 6+   oral errors = Too hard

Examiner's Notes:

NIVEL 7 REGISTRO INFORMATIVO
Diamantes (295 words)

PART I: SILENT READING COMPREHENSION

Background Statement: "La siguiente selección es acerca de los diamantes. Léelo con cuidado para ver cómo los diamantes son hechos, porque voy a pedir que me cuentes acerca de lo que leíste."

Teacher Directions: Once the student completes the silent reading, say, "Dime acerca de lo que leíste." Answers to the questions below that the student provides during the retelling should be marked "ua" in the appropriate blank to indicate that this response was unaided. Ask all remaining questions not addressed during the retelling and mark those the student answers with an "a" to indicate that the correct response was given after prompting by the teacher.

Questions/Answers	*Expository Grammar Element/ Level of Comprehension*
_____1. ¿ Dónde están las minas de diamantes más importantes? *(India, Suramérica, Africa)*	description/literal
_____2. En la selección, ¿cuál información apoya la idea de que los diamantes son raros? *(sólo se encuentran en áreas particulares y aunque estén presentes, tienen que buscarse en toneladas de roca)*	problem resolution attempts/ inferential
_____3. ¿Dónde se encontraron los primeros diamantes? *(en arena y grava de arroyos)*	description/literal
_____4. ¿Cuáles son las cuatro características de calidad de los diamantes? *(pureza, color, peso, corte)*	description/literal
_____5. ¿Qué causa que brille un diamante? *(cómo está cortado, número de facetas)*	causation/literal
_____6. ¿Cuáles dos factores bajan la pureza de un diamante? *(carbón no cristalizado, sustancias ajenas)*	causation/inferential
_____7. Explica cómo se hacen los diamantes artificiales. *(resultan de carbón bajo presión a temperaturas altas)*	collection/inferential
_____8. Describe dónde se encuentran los diamantes naturales. *(formaciones de roca que parecen volcanes)*	description/literal

PART II: ORAL READING AND ANALYSIS OF MISCUES

Directions: Say, "Ahora, lee esta selección en voz alta." Have the student read orally until the 100-word sample is completed. Follow along on the Miscue Grid, marking any oral reading errors as appropriate. *Remember to count miscues only up to the point in the story containing the oral reading stop-marker (//).* Then complete the Developmental/Performance Summary to determine whether to continue the assessment. (*Note:* The Miscue Grid should be completed *after* the assessment session has been concluded in order to minimize stress for the student.)

	MIS-PRONUN.	SUB-STITUTION	OMISSION	INSERTION	TCHR. ASSIST.	SELF-CORRECT.	MEANING DISRUPTION
Diamantes							
Un diamante es una de las joyas							
más hermosas creadas por la							
naturaleza y una de las más raras.							
Toma miles de años para transformar							
un pedazo de carbón en diamante en							
bruto. Solamente tres minas de							
diamantes importantes han sido							
encontradas en todo el mundo —							
India, Suramérica y Africa. Los							
primeros diamantes se encontraron							
en la arena y grava de arroyos. Estos							
tipos de diamantes se llaman							
diamantes aluviales. Después,							
encontraron diamantes en la tierra							
profunda, en formaciones de piedra							
llamadas "pipas." Estas formaciones							
parecen volcanes extinguidos. La							
piedra en que se encuentran los							
diamantes se llama "tierra azul."							
TOTALS							

Notes:

Examiner's Summary of Miscue Patterns:

PART III: DEVELOPMENTAL/PERFORMANCE SUMMARY

Silent Reading Comprehension

_____ 0–1 questions missed = Easy

_____ 2 questions missed = Adequate

_____ 3+ questions missed = Too hard

Oral Reading Accuracy

_____ 0–1 oral errors = Easy

_____ 2–5 oral errors = Adequate

_____ 6+ oral errors = Too hard

Continue to next assessment level passage? _____ Yes _____ No

Examiner's Notes:

Ya está aquí el futuro (384 words)

PART I: SILENT READING COMPREHENSION

Background Statement: "Esta selección se trata de algunas invenciones que afectarán a la gente en el futuro. Léelo con cuidado para encontrar cuales son las invenciones y las maneras en que afectarán a la gente, porque voy a pedir que me cuentes acerca de lo que leíste."

Teacher Directions: Once the student completes the silent reading, say, "Dime acerca de lo que leíste." Answers to the questions below that the student provides during the retelling should be marked "ua" in the appropriate blank to indicate that this response was unaided. Ask all remaining questions not addressed during the retelling and mark those the student answers with an "a" to indicate that the correct response was given after prompting by the teacher.

Questions/Answers	*Expository Grammar Element/ Level of Comprehension*
_____1. ¿Qué es un vehículo de levitación? *(una máquina que es parte avión y parte automóvil)*	collection/inferential
_____2. ¿Por qué están desarrollando este tipo de vehículo? *(las carreteras están llenas de coches y el incremento de población)*	causation/literal
_____3. Explica cómo trabaja un láser dental. *(destruye las caries sin dolor)*	description/inferential
_____4. Explica cómo un videoteléfono con color y movimiento beneficiaría a los sordos. *(podrían llamar a la gente que saben hablar por señas y comunicarse con ellos)*	causation/inferential
_____5. ¿Qué pueden hacer las fibras ópticas que no puede hacer la tecnología tradicional? *(permite transmitir mucha información a través de alambres muy delgados)*	comparison/inferential
_____6. ¿Cuáles dos áreas de tu televisor serán aumentadas cuando la televisión de alta definición se vuelva común? *(sonido y video)*	description/literal
_____7. ¿A qué se compara la calidad de sonido y video en una televisión de alta definición? *(discos compactos y película de 35 milímetros)*	comparison/literal
_____8. ¿Qué sabemos, según la selección, acerca de cómo las nuevas invenciones afectarán a la gente? *(las respuestas pueden variar, pero puede ser algo acerca de ayudando a la gente enfrentar los obstáculos del futuro)*	causation/inferential

PART II: ORAL READING AND ANALYSIS OF MISCUES

Directions: Say, "Ahora lee esta selección en voz alta." Have the student read orally until the 100-word sample is completed. Follow along on the Miscue Grid, marking any oral reading errors as appropriate. *Remember to count miscues only up to the point in the story containing the oral reading stop-marker (//).* Then complete the Developmental/Performance Summary to determine whether to continue the assessment. (*Note:* The Miscue Grid should be completed *after* the assessment session has been concluded in order to minimize stress for the student.)

	MIS-PRONUN.	SUB-STITUTION	OMISSION	INSERTION	TCHR. ASSIST.	SELF-CORRECT.	MEANING DISRUPTION
Ya está aquí el futuro							
¿Qué traerá el siglo veintiuno en							
cuanto a invenciones nuevas y							
tecnologías ultramodernas? Nadie							
sabe de seguro. Pero los científicos,							
los inventores y los futuristas							
predicen una variedad de							
invenciones nuevas. Estos nuevos							
avances afectarán cómo vivimos y							
jugamos. Algunos de ellos ya están							
en la mesa de diseño. Un ejemplo							
es el vehículo de levitación. La idea							
de un vehículo que se puede							
levantar y bajar verticalmente y							
también se maneja en la carretera							
es la invención de Paul Moeller. Él							
nombró su versión de este tipo de							
vehículo Moeller 400. La gente							
involucrada en este tipo de							
tecnología // *ve aumentos en*							
población y carreteras apretadas							
como razones de que un vehículo							
de levitación sea necesario.							
TOTALS							

Notes:

Examiner's Summary of Miscue Patterns:

PART III: DEVELOPMENTAL/PERFORMANCE SUMMARY

Silent Reading Comprehension

_____ 0–1 questions missed = Easy

_____ 2   questions missed = Adequate

_____ 3+   questions missed = Too hard

Oral Reading Accuracy

_____ 0–1 oral errors = Easy

_____ 2–5 oral errors = Adequate

_____ 6+   oral errors = Too hard

Continue to next assessment level passage?   _____ Yes   _____ No

Examiner's Notes:

NIVEL 9 REGISTRO INFORMATIVO
Ilusiones visuales (282 words)

PART I: SILENT READING COMPREHENSION

Background Statement: "Esta selección es sobre ilusiones visuales. Léela para que sepas algo acerca de tres tipos de ilusiones visuales. Léela con cuidado porque cuando termines te voy a preguntar sobre lo que leíste."

Teacher Directions: Once the student completes the silent reading, say, "Dime algo sobre la selección que acabas de leer." Answers to the questions below that the student provides during the retelling should be marked "ua" in the appropriate blank to indicate that this response was unaided. Ask all remaining questions not addressed during the retelling and mark those the student answers with an "a" to indicate that the correct response was given after prompting by the teacher.

Questions/Answers	*Expository Grammar Element/ Level of Comprehension*
_____1. ¿Cuáles fueron las dos razones dadas para las ilusiones visuales? *(preconcepción y la inabilidad del cerebro de escoger de dos o más modelos)*	description/literal
_____2. ¿Cuál es un ejemplo de ilusión de inhibición lateral? *(un blanco)*	description/literal
_____3. ¿El Arco "Gateway" de San Luis es un ejemplo de cuál distorción? *(distorción de longitud)*	description/literal
_____4. Explica cómo ocurre la distorción de longitud. *(la vista trabaja mejor de lado a lado que de arriba a abajo)*	collection/inferential
_____5. ¿Cuál es un ejemplo de la ilusión visual conocida como "la cuadrícula de Hermann"? *(rascacielos modernos)*	description/literal
_____6. ¿Cómo afecta la cuadrícula de Hermann lo que uno ve visualmente? *(los ojos ven manchas grises en esquinas de cuadros)*	causation/inferential
_____7. Explica por qué el dicho "no creas todo lo que ves" es válido en la vida diaria. *(ejemplos de ilusiones visuales ocurren a nuestro alrededor)*	collection/inferential
_____8. ¿Cómo es que los ojos moviéndose de lado a lado en vez de arriba hacia abajo afectan cómo interpretamos objectos de mucha altura? *(parecen más altos de lo que son actualmente)*	causation/literal

PART II: ORAL READING AND ANALYSIS OF MISCUES

Directions: Say, "Ahora lee la selección en voz alta." Have the student read orally until the 100-word sample is completed. Follow along on the Miscue Grid, marking any oral reading errors as appropriate. *Remember to count miscues only up to the point in the story containing the oral reading stop-marker (//).* Then complete the Developmental/Performance Summary to determine whether to continue the assessment. (*Note:* The Miscue Grid should be completed *after* the assessment session has been concluded in order to minimize stress for the student.)

	MIS-PRONUN.	SUB-STITUTION	OMISSION	INSERTION	TCHR. ASSIST.	SELF-CORRECT.	MEANING DISRUPTION
Ilusiones visuales							
Según el diccionario, una ilusión							
visual aparenta una imagen que no							
es real. En otras palabras, ilusiones							
visuales son causadas por ideas que							
una persona tiene acerca de algo							
que esa persona desea ver. Algunas							
veces la ilusión visual ocurre por la							
dificultad que el cerebro tiene de							
escoger de dos o más modelos							
visuales. Si uno ve en un blanco y							
si ese blanco se mueve en forma							
circular, uno podría ver alambres							
moviéndose. Estos alambres, si se							
ven, en realidad no existen. A este							
tipo de ilusión visual se le llama							
inhibición lateral. Otro tipo de							
ilusión visual // *ocurre cuando una*							
persona trata de calcular la altura							
de un objeto vertical.							
TOTALS							

Notes:

Examiner's Summary of Miscue Patterns:

PART III: DEVELOPMENTAL/PERFORMANCE SUMMARY

Silent Reading Comprehension

_____ 0–1 questions missed = Easy

_____ 2 questions missed = Adequate

_____ 3+ questions missed = Too hard

Oral Reading Accuracy

_____ 0–1 oral errors = Easy

_____ 2–5 oral errors = Adequate

_____ 6+ oral errors = Too hard

Continue to next assessment level passage? _____ Yes _____ No

Examiner's Notes:

EXPOSITORY PASSAGES
NIVELES 10–12

forma **D**

Altoparlantes estereofónicos

Casi todos han escuchado música alguna vez u otra pero pocos entienden cómo funcionan los altoparlantes. Dicho simplemente, casi todos los altoparlantes son transductores que cambian señales eléctricas de un amplificador en ondas sonoras. Más allá de esta simple explicación, los altoparlantes estereofónicos se dividen en tantas variedades que aún el amante de música más entusiástico los encuentra difícil de entender. En general, todos los altoparlantes pueden ser agrupados en dos grandes categorías, dependiendo en la forma en que las señales eléctricas son convertidas en sonido.

La mayor cantidad de altoparlantes usan conductores dinámicos, esos conos y cubiertas familiares que se encuentran en los modelos caros y baratos. Básicamente, este tipo de altoparlante tiene diafragmas (conos y cubiertas) movidos por aire que son conducidos por un componente electromagnético producido por una bobina y un magneto. Cuando una señal eléctrica es enviada desde el amplificador, el componente se mueve de atrás hacia el frente. El cono o la cubierta en conjunción con la bobina se mueven juntos, produciendo así ondas sonoras enfrente y atrás.

El otro tipo de altoparlante, el cual produce el sonido de forma diferente al altoparlante de systema dinámico, es generalmente conocido como altoparlante de sistema plano. Este tipo de altoparlante, el cual cuesta substancialmente más que el de sistema dinámico, abandona el uso de la bobina y magneto por una superficie plana o una tira que es directamente conducida por la señal auditiva del amplificador para crear ondas sonoras. Ya que la mayoría de la gente raramente se encuentra con este tipo de altoparlante, el comentario que sigue se enfocará en los dos tipos más importantes de altoparlantes de sistema dinámico.

Todos los altoparlantes dinámicos necesitan un encajamiento para evitar algo conocido como "contrarresto de ondas posteriores." Debido a que todos los conductores dinámicos producen sonido posterior así como frontal, si no hay forma de controlar la onda posterior, ésta cancelaría completamente la onda frontal, dando como resultado un sonido muy bajo o, en caso extremo, falta de sonido completamente. Por esto, el encajamiento de un altoparlante estereofónico sirve para reducir este problema de sonido.

El tipo más común de altoparlante es el de suspensión acústica, o altoparlante de caja sellada, mismo que fue desarrollado en los años 50. En este tipo de altoparlante, la bocina (cubierta) está montada en una caja sellada para que la superficie frontal irradie libremente hacia la habitación, mientras que la onda posterior se pierde en el volumen interior de la caja sellada. Debido a que la onda posterior no puede irradiar hacia la habitación, no existe el peligro de que la onda frontal se contrarreste y es posible así obtener un fuerte tono bajo de una caja relativamente diminutiva. Una limitación de este diseño es que la mitad del potencial acústico (onda posterior) se pierde. Por eso, un altoparlante de suspensión acústica requiere más fuerza por parte del amplificador que un altoparlante equivalente en caja no sellada para alcanzar un determinado nivel de sonido.

El otro tipo importante de altoparlante dinámico es el de diseño de bajo reflejo. Este diseño usa un encajamiento que tiene una abertura diseñada cuidadosamente, o ventanilla, la cual permite que las ondas posteriores de la bocina escapen hacia la habitación donde se les escucha. Este tipo de diseño trata de capitalizar en la onda posterior, manipulándola de manera que alcance el área donde se les escucha en sincronía con la onda frontal. De esta manera todo el sonido es reforzado en lugar de degradado. Este método produce un altoparlante más eficiente ya que, siendo todas las cosas iguales, los altoparlantes con ventanillas producen más volumen por "watt" que los altoparlantes de suspensión acústica.

Sin importar el diseño, los altoparlantes de hoy sobrepasan por mucho a aquellos de hace diez años en términos de calidad de sonido por dólar invertido. Debido a que dos altoparlantes no suenan igual, no importa que diseño de especificaciones tenga, lo más importante al comprar un altoparlante probablemente no debería ser el diseño sino cómo le suena al comprador.

Cambiando nuestra apariencia

La cirugía cosmética, antes accesible sólamente para los ricos y famosos, es un negocio de multimillones de dólares al año en los Estados Unidos. El crecimiento rápido de este tipo de cirugía ha ocurrido aunque los pacientes tienen que hacer los pagos, porque la mayoría de cirugías cosméticas no están cubiertas por el seguro. El costo es considerable, desde $1.000 hasta más de $10.000, dependiendo en el procedimiento, el doctor que hace la cirugía y el área física en donde el procedimiento se hace. Algunos tipos de cirugías no requieren hospitalización mientras que otros requieren varios días en el hospital, lo que aumenta el costo de dicho procedimiento.

La mayoría de cirugías cosméticas son hechas para modificar las características faciales de individuos. Para remover arrugas finas alrededor de la boca, cejas y ojos, usan un proceso que se llama "raspado." El "raspado" requiere que el médico use herramientas para aplanar el cutis para así, literalmente, lijar las áreas arrugadas después de inyectarlas con anestesia local. El resultado es una piel más suave, pero el paciente tiene que esperar aproximádamente dos semanas para que la piel rosada por el proceso regrese a su color normal.

Otra técnica popular para la cara es quitar el cutis o quimocirugía. En este procedimiento, una forma de ácido carbólico se aplica a la cara, la superficie de la piel se quema y se forma una costra. Después de diez días se quita la costra y queda una piel sin defectos que requiere varias semanas para regresar a su color normal. Una advertencia contra la exposición al sol por seis meses siempre acompaña este proceso. Individuos con la piel clara son los mejores candidatos porque otros colores de piel pueden desarrollar color irregular como resultado de este tipo de cirugía.

La cirugía del párpado o blefaroplastia, se realiza cuando un individuo tiene exceso de piel en el párpado superior o abolsamientos abajo del ojo. Para quitar la apariencia perpetua de estar cansado, se hacen incisiones en el pliegue del párpado o justo abajo de la línea de pestañas inferiores. El exceso de piel es removido y la incisión es cosida. Este procedimiento es usualmente realizado en clínicas y la piel le toma solamente dos semanas para retornar a su estado normal. Aunque son raras las complicaciones, siempre hay peligro de hinchamientos (áreas abultadas por el acumulamiento de sangre). También, algunas personas llegan a tener lagrimeo excesivo y algunas otras tienen doble visión a causa de los músculos atrofiados por la cirugía. Muchos de estos problemas se disipan naturalmente en algunas horas o son médicamente tratadas.

Probablemente la cirugía cosmética de la que la gente ha oído más es la facial. En la última década se han desarrollado técnicas nuevas para que las cirugías faciales puedan ser llevadas acabo en clínicas. El proceso en si, usando anestesia local, así como sedativos preoperacionales, envuelven incisiones abajo de la línea del cabello y alrededor de las orejas. Se quita el tejido graso y la piel floja de la cara y del cuello es estirada. Algunas veces la cirugía de los párpados y el aumento de barbilla acompañan este proceso facial. La convalecencia varía de acuerdo con el individuo pero generalmente dura varias semanas.

Aunque no todos son buenos candidatos para la cirugía cosmética, los que tengan interés en cambiar su apariencia, deberían considerar varias cosas. Primero, se debe escoger un cirujano con experiencia y que tenga buenas recomendaciones. Además de cirujanos plásticos o reconstructivos, los especialistas en dermatología y otorrinolaringología (oído, naríz y garganta), los cuales están certificados por el estado, pueden hacer procedimientos relacionados con sus áreas de especialización. La segunda consideración es lo que usted desea: la cirugía cosmética no produce milagros. Aunque un cambio facial se desea, el cambio que resulta puede o no llenar esos deseos. Converse en serio con su doctor acerca de lo que va a ocurrir y lo que no va a ocurrir con la cirugía. La última consideración es comparar el costo con los resultados esperados. Un viejo dicho sugiere: "si no está dañado, no lo arregles." Parece que mucha gente podría ahorrarse dinero y dolor si considerara con cuidado si un cambio de apariencia realmente es necesario.

Comunicaciones de fibra óptica

Uno de los más importantes avances tecnológicos de los recientes años ha sido la venida de la comunicación através de la fibra óptica. Sea que se use en el sistema de computadoras o en la cadena de televisión interactiva, la fibra óptica ya es parte de la vida americana. Debido a que continuará reemplazando mucho de lo que usamos para comunicarnos, es importante que uno tenga el mayor conocimiento acerca de la fibra óptica.

La comunicación de fibra óptica es simple: una señal eléctrica es convertida en luz, la cual es transmitida mediante una fibra óptica, que está hecha de cristal, a un receptor distante donde es convertida otra vez a su señal eléctrica original. Los beneficios que tiene la comunicación de fibra óptica sobre otras maneras de transmisión son substanciales. Una señal se puede transmitir a distancias más lejanas sin estimulantes y sin problemas de interferencias departe de campos eléctricos cercanos. Adicionalmente, su capacidad es mucho más que la de los sistemas de cables de cobre o coaxiales, y la fibra de cristal es en si, mucho más liviana y pequeña que la de los sistemas de cobre. A pesar de estos beneficios, la comunicación de fibra óptica aun no es libre de problemas.

La limitación más significante de un sistema de comunicaciones de fibra óptica es la atenuación de la señal óptica al atravesar la fibra. Segun vaya pasando la información en la luz por la fibra, la luz es atenuada (a esto se le llama "pérdida de inserción") por razón de la *dispersión de Rayleigh*. La dispersión de Rayleigh se refiere a un efecto creado cuando un pulso de luz es enviado por una fibra y parte de este pulso es bloqueado por "dopants"—partículas microscópicas en el cristal— y son esparcidas en muchas direcciones. Parte de la luz, aproximadamente 0,0001 por ciento, es esparcida en la dirección opuesta del pulso; a esto se le llama disperso de retorno. Puesto que las "dopants" en la fibra óptica son uniformemente distribuidas através de la fibra por razón del proceso manufacturero, este efecto ocurre através de su entera longitud.

El efecto de dispersión de Rayleigh es similar a una linterna encendida en una neblina durante la noche. Uno puede ver la neblina porque las partículas de humedad reflejan pequeñas cantidades de luz hacia uno: los rayos de luz son disparcidos por las partículas de humedad. Una neblina gruesa esparce más de la luz porque hay más partículas que la obstruyen. Las partículas de "dopant" en la fibra actúan como partículas de humedad de la neblina, regresando pequeñas cantidades de luz hacia su origen según la luz les pegue. La dispersión de Rayleigh es el factor mayor de pérdida en las comunicaciones de fibra óptica.

Otra causa de la pérdida de luz en la fibra optical es el *reflejo Fresnel* o "Fresnel reflection." El reflejo Fresnel es anólogo a una linterna encendida en una ventana: la mayoría de la luz pasa por la ventana, pero una poca refleja de retorno. El ángulo en el cual el rayo de luz pega en la ventana determina si el reflejo va a rebotar en la linterna o en los ojos de uno. Cuando la luz que va viajando mediante un material como la fibra óptica se encuentra con un material de diferente densidad, tal como el aire, una poca de esta luz es reflejada hacia el origen de la luz, mientras que el resto de la luz continua viajando por el material. En las fibras ópticas, estos cambios repentinos ocurren en las puntas de las fibras, en las aberturas de las fibras y algunas veces en las uniones de las fibras. Obviamente, estas aberturas en las fibras son razón de mayor preocupación para las compañías de comunicaciones de fibra óptica.

En vista de que las fibras ópticas se están haciendo más expansivas y conectadas por distancias más largas, es importante saber cuánta luz se pierde en un "regen" o longitud, de fibra. Es también importante poder identificar puntos específicos en la fibra que tienen quebraduras o señales de degradación. Aunque existen varios métodos para fijar la pérdida de luz, la manera más eficiente para determinar con gran precisión los problemas en un "regen" de fibra es con el uso del reflejómetro del dominio del tiempo optical (RDTO). Un RDTO es un instrumento optical electrónico que se puede usar para localizar defectos, y para determinar la cantidad de pérdida de una señal en cualquier punto en una fibra óptica al medir los niveles de disperso de retorno y el reflejo Fresnel. El RDTO se distingue a otros métodos en que solamente necesita acceso a una punta de la fibra para hacer miles de medidas através de la fibra. Los datos de los puntos de las medidas pueden ser entre 0,5 y 16 metros apartes. Los puntos de los datos seleccionados son exhibidos en la pantalla RDTO como una línea inclinada de la izquierda a la derecha, con distancia a lo largo de la escala horizontal y el nivel de señal en la escala vertical. Usando cualquiera de dos puntos de los datos, el RDTO puede revelar la distancia y los niveles relativos de la señal entre ellos. Así que, el RDTO puede ayudar a las compañías que son dueñas de las cadenas de fibra para reparar las quebraduras y prevenir degradación de sus señales: en suma, para mantener las comunicaciones claras y las reparaciones eficientes.

EXAMINER'S ASSESSMENT PROTOCOLS

forma **D**

NIVEL 10 REGISTRO INFORMATIVO
Altoparlantes estereofónicos (664 words)

PART I: SILENT READING COMPREHENSION

Background Statement: "Esta selección se trata de altoparlantes estereofónicos. Léela para saber de los diferentes tipos de altoparlantes que usa la gente para escuchar la música. Léela con cuidado porque voy a pedir que me cuentes lo más que puedas acerca de altoparlantes estereofónicos basado en la información de la selección."

Teacher Directions: Once the student completes the silent reading, say, "Dime acerca de lo que acabas de leer acerca de los altoparlantes estereofónicos." Answers to the questions below that the student provides during the retelling should be marked "ua" in the appropriate blank to indicate that this response was unaided. Ask all remaining questions not addressed during the retelling and mark those the student answers with an "a" to indicate that the correct response was given after prompting by the teacher.

Questions/Answers	*Expository Grammar Element/ Level of Comprehension*
_____1. ¿Qué causa que el sonido salga de un altoparlante? *(una señal eléctrica cambiada a ondas de sonido)*	causation/literal
_____2. ¿Cuál es la diferencia entre el altoparlante dinámico y el altoparlante de sistema plano? *(los de sistema plano no usan bobina ni magneto)*	comparison/inferential
_____3. ¿Por qué la onda posterior es un problema para los que fabrican los altoparlantes estereofónicos? *(si el diseño no da forma de controlar la onda posterior, ésta cancelaría completamente la onda frontal y no habría sonido)*	causation/literal
_____4. Describe cómo los altoparlantes de suspensión acústica eliminan el problema de contrarresto de ondas posteriores. *(su diseño guarda el contrarresto de ondas posteriores en el fondo del encajamiento sellado)*	description/inferential
_____5. ¿Cuál es la diferencia entre un diseño de bajo reflejo y un altoparlante de caja sellada? *(altoparlantes de bajo reflejo tienen ventanillas y producen más volumen por "watt")*	comparison/inferential
_____6. ¿Por qué el altoparlante de bajo reflejo puede producir más volumen por "watt"? *(usa las ondas posteriores para producir el sonido en lugar de cancelar las ondas posteriores)*	causation/inferential
_____7. ¿Por qué sugiere la selección que la decisión final en escoger un altoparlante debería ser cómo le suena al comprador y no el diseño? *(porque todos los altoparlantes modernos están bien hechos pero suenan diferente a diferente gente, entonces, una persona debe comprar los que le suenan mejor)*	problem resolution/evaluative
_____8. En cuestión de dónde ponerlo, ¿cuál tipo de altoparlante dinámico sería el mejor para poner junto a una pared? *(siendo todo igual, él de suspensión acústica sería el mejor, porque los de bajo reflejo tienen ventanillas y necesitan estar a distancia de una pared)*	problem resolution/evaluative

PART II (OPTIONAL): ORAL READING AND ANALYSIS OF MISCUES

Directions: Say, "Ahora quiero que leas parte de este pasaje en voz alta. Comienza con el segundo párafo y continua leyendo hasta que te diga que pares." Have the student read until the 100-word sample is completed. Follow along on the Miscue Grid, marking any oral reading errors as appropriate. *Remember to count miscues only up to the point of the oral reading stop-marker (//).* Then complete the Developmental/Performance Summary to determine whether to continue the assessment. (Note: The Miscue Grid should be completed *after* the assessment session to save time and reduce stress for the student.)

	MIS-PRONUN.	SUB-STITUTION	OMISSION	INSERTION	TCHR. ASSIST.	SELF-CORRECT.	MEANING DISRUPTION
Altoparlantes estereofónicos							
La mayor cantidad de altoparlantes							
usan conductores dinámicos, esos							
conos y cubiertas familiares que se							
encuentran en los modelos caros y							
baratos. Básicamente, este tipo de							
altoparlante tiene diafragmas (conos							
y cubiertas) movidos por aire que							
son conducidos por un componente							
electromagnético producido por una							
bobina y un magneto. Cuando una							
señal eléctrica es enviada desde el							
amplificador, el componente se							
mueve de atrás hacia delante. El							
cono o la cubierta en conjunción con							
la bobina se mueven juntos,							
produciendo así ondas sonoras							
enfrente y atrás.							
El otro tipo de altoparlante, el cual							
produce el sonido de forma diferente							
al // *altoparlante de systema*							
dinámico, es generalmente conocido							
como altoparlante de sistema plano.							
TOTALS							

Notes:

Examiner's Summary of Miscue Patterns:

PART III: DEVELOPMENTAL/PERFORMANCE SUMMARY

Silent Reading Comprehension   *Oral Reading Accuracy*

_____ 0–1 questions missed = Easy   _____ 0–1 oral errors = Easy

_____ 2   questions missed = Adequate   _____ 2–5 oral errors = Adequate

_____ 3+   questions missed = Too hard   _____ 6+   oral errors = Too hard

Continue to next assessment level passage?   _____ Yes   _____ No

Examiner's Notes:

PART I: SILENT READING COMPREHENSION

Background Statement: "Esta selección se trata de cirugía cosmética. Léela con cuidado porque voy a pedir que me cuentes acerca de lo que has leído."

Teacher Directions: Once the student completes the silent reading, say, "Dime lo que aprendiste acerca de la cirugía cosmética." Answers to the questions below that the student provides during the retelling should be marked "ua" in the appropriate blank to indicate that this response was unaided. Ask all remaining questions not addressed during the retelling and mark those the student answers with an "a" to indicate that the correct response was given after prompting by the teacher.

Questions/Answers	*Expository Grammar Element/ Level of Comprehension*
_____1. Explica lo que hace el cirujano durante el "raspado." *(el cirujano usa herramientas para aplanar la piel o quitar un nivel de la piel)*	description/inferential
_____2. ¿Qué evidencia se encuentra en la selección sobre el hecho de que la cantidad de cirugías cosméticas está aumentando cada año? *(es un negocio de multimillones de dólares)*	collection/inferential
_____3. ¿Cuál es la diferencia entre quimocirugía y raspado? *(en quimocirugía se usa una substancia química para quemar la superficie de la piel, en el raspado se lijan las áreas arrugadas; en quimocirugía se forma una costra después del tratamiento, con el raspado no hay formación de costra.)*	comparison/inferential
_____4. ¿Cuáles son las complicaciones posibles en la cirugía del párpado? *(hinchamiento, lagrimeo excesivo, doble visión)*	description/literal
_____5. ¿Cuáles son las tres consideraciones que una persona debe tomar en cuenta antes de tener cirugía cosmética? *(calidad del doctor, costo y deseos)*	description/literal
_____6. ¿Qué quiere decir el viejo dicho acerca de cirugía cosmética? *(algo acerca de... personas deben aceptar su apariencia en vez de buscar cirugía para cambiarla)*	problem resolution/evaluative
_____7. Además de cirujanos plásticos, ¿cuáles otros doctores pueden hacer algunos tipos de cirugía cosmética? *(dermatólogos, otorrinolaringólogos)*	collection/literal
_____8. ¿Por qué la cirugía del párpado a veces acompaña la cirugía facial? *(si alguien va a tener la piel de la cara ajustada, parece lógico quitar el exceso de piel alrededor de los ojos, también)*	collection/inferential

PART II (OPTIONAL): ORAL READING AND ANALYSIS OF MISCUES

Directions: Say, "Ahora quiero que leas parte de este pasaje en voz alta. Comienza con el tercer párafo y continua leyendo hasta que te diga que pares." Have the student read until the 100-word sample is completed. Follow along on the Miscue Grid, marking any oral reading errors as appropriate. *Remember to count miscues only up to the point of the oral reading stop-marker (//).* Then complete the Developmental/Performance Summary to determine whether to continue the assessment. (Note: The Miscue Grid should be completed *after* the assessment session to save time and reduce stress for the student.)

	MIS-PRONUN.	SUB-STITUTION	OMISSION	INSERTION	TCHR. ASSIST.	SELF-CORRECT.	MEANING DISRUPTION
Cambiando nuestra apariencia							
Otra técnica popular para la cara es							
quitar el cutis o quimocirugía. En							
este procedimiento, una forma de							
ácido carbólico se aplica a la cara,							
la superficie de la piel se quema y							
se forma una costra. Después de							
diez días se quita la costra y queda							
una piel sin defectos que requiere							
varias semanas para regresar a su							
color normal. Una advertencia							
contra la exposición al sol por seis							
meses siempre acompaña este							
proceso. Individuos con la piel							
clara son los mejores candidatos							
porque otros colores de piel pueden							
desarrollar color irregular como							
resultado de este tipo de // *cirugía*.							
TOTALS							

Notes:

Examiner's Summary of Miscue Patterns:

PART III: DEVELOPMENTAL/PERFORMANCE SUMMARY

Silent Reading Comprehension   **Oral Reading Accuracy**

_____ 0–1 questions missed = Easy   _____ 0–1 oral errors = Easy

_____ 2   questions missed = Adequate   _____ 2–5 oral errors = Adequate

_____ 3+   questions missed = Too hard   _____ 6+   oral errors = Too hard

Continue to next assessment level passage?   _____ Yes   _____ No

Examiner's Notes:

NIVEL 12 REGISTRO INFORMATIVO
Comunicaciones de fibra óptica (912 words)

PART I: SILENT READING COMPREHENSION

Background Statement: "Esta selección se trata de las comunicaciones através de la fibra óptica. Léela para saber acerca de algunas características y problemas asociados con las comunicaciones através de la fibra óptica. Lee con cuidado porque te voy a pedir que me cuentes sobre lo que leíste."

Teacher Directions: Once the student completes the silent reading, say, "Cuéntame acerca de lo que leíste." Answers to the questions below that the student provides during the retelling should be marked "ua" in the appropriate blank to indicate that this response was unaided. Ask all remaining questions not addressed during the retelling and mark those the student answers with an "a" to indicate that the correct response was given after prompting by the teacher.

Questions/Answers	*Expository Grammar Element/ Level of Comprehension*
_____1. ¿Cuáles dos beneficios tienen las fibras ópticas que otros medios para transmitir comunicaciones no tienen? *(no existen problemas de interferencia, no necesita un estimulante para las largas distancias, mayor capacidad, más liviano y más pequeño)*	collection/literal
_____2. ¿Qué son "dopants"? *(partículas microscópicas que se encuentran en todas las fibras ópticas)*	description/literal
_____3. ¿Por qué la pérdida de luz en la fibra óptica es una preocupación mayor de las compañías que la usan para la comunicación? *(señales de calidad inferior, o una cesación de trabajo de un sistema entero)*	problem resolution/evaluative
_____4. ¿Qué es la dispersión de Rayleigh y por qué está siempre presente? *(la luz que es reflejada de retorno hacia su origen causado por los "dopants"; causado por el proceso manufacturero)*	causation/literal
_____5. Explica la diferencia mayor entre la dispersión de Rayleigh y el reflejo Fresnel. *(la dispersión de Rayleigh es causado por "dopants," el reflejo Fresnel es causado por quebraduras en la fibra, los lazamientos o las puntas de la fibra; accept plausible response even if related to the fog versus light through glass analogy)*	comparison/inferential
_____6. ¿Cómo se relacionan un "regen" y un reflejómetro de dominio de tiempo optical? *(un RDTO se usa para determinar la pérdida de luz en un "regen")*	collection/inferential
_____7. ¿Qué separa el RDTO de otros aparatos diseñados para determinar la pérdida de luz en un cable de fibra óptica? *(se necesita solamente una punta de la fibra para tomar las medidas con este aparato)*	comparison/literal
_____8. ¿Por qué se pudiera decir con certidumbre que los RDTOs y otros aparatos estarán en más demanda en el futuro que hoy en día? *(por razón de la expanción de las comunicaciones através de la fibra óptica)*	collection/evaluative

PART II (OPTIONAL): ORAL READING AND ANALYSIS OF MISCUES

Directions: Say, "Ahora quiero que leas parte de este pasaje en voz alta. Comienza con el tercer párafo y continua leyendo hasta que te diga que pares." Have the student read until the 100-word sample is completed. Follow along on the Miscue Grid, marking any oral reading errors as appropriate. *Remember to count miscues only up to the point of the oral reading stop-marker (//).* Then complete the Developmental/Performance Summary to determine whether to continue the assessment. (*Note:* The Miscue Grid should be completed *after* the assessment session to save time and reduce stress for the student.)

	MIS-PRONUN.	SUB-STITUTION	OMISSION	INSERTION	TCHR. ASSIST.	SELF-CORRECT.	MEANING DISRUPTION
Comunicaciones de fibra óptica							
La limitación más significante de un							
sistema de comunicaciones de fibra							
óptica es la atenuación de la señal							
óptica al atravesar la fibra. Segun							
vaya pasando la información en la							
luz por la fibra, la luz es atenuada (a							
esto se le llama "pérdida de							
inserción") por razón de la							
dispersión de Rayleigh. La							
dispersión de Rayleigh se refiere a							
un efecto creado cuando un pulso de							
luz es enviado por una fibra y parte							
de este pulso es bloqueado por							
"dopants"—partículas microscópicas							
en el cristal—y son esparcidas en							
muchas direcciones. Parte de la luz,							
aproximadamente 0,0001 por //							
ciento, es esparcida en la dirección							
opuesta del pulso; a esto se le llama							
disperso de retorno.							
TOTALS							

Notes:

Examiner's Summary of Miscue Patterns:

PART III: DEVELOPMENTAL/PERFORMANCE SUMMARY

Silent Reading Comprehension

_____ 0–1 questions missed = Easy

_____ 2 questions missed = Adequate

_____ 3+ questions missed = Too hard

Oral Reading Accuracy

_____ 0–1 oral errors = Easy

_____ 2–5 oral errors = Adequate

_____ 6+ oral errors = Too hard

Examiner's Notes:

MISCUE
ANALYSIS GRIDS · · · · · · · appendix

MISCUE ANALYSIS GRID

	MIS-PRONUN.	SUB-STITUTION	OMISSION	INSERTION	TCHR. ASSIST.	SELF-CORRECT.	MEANING DISRUPTION
TOTALS							

Notes:

Examiner's Summary of Miscue Patterns:

PART III: DEVELOPMENTAL/PERFORMANCE SUMMARY

Silent Reading Comprehension

_____ 0–1 questions missed = Easy

_____ 2 questions missed = Adequate

_____ 3+ questions missed = Too hard

Continue to next assessment level passage? _____ Yes _____ No

Oral Reading Accuracy

_____ 0–1 oral errors = Easy

_____ 2–5 oral errors = Adequate

_____ 6+ oral errors = Too hard

PART IV: LISTENING COMPREHENSION

Directions: If you have decided not to continue to have the student read any other passages, then use this passage to begin assessing the student's listening comprehension (see page 8). Begin by reading the background statement for this passage and then say, "I am going to read this story to you. Please listen carefully because I will be asking you some questions after I finish reading it to you." After reading the passage, ask the student the questions associated with the passage. If the student correctly answers more than six questions, you will need to move to the next level and repeat the procedure.

Listening Comprehension

_____ 0–2 questions missed = move to the next passage level

_____ more than two questions missed = stop assessment or move down a level

Examiner's Notes:

MISCUE ANALYSIS GRID

	MIS-PRONUN.	SUB-STITUTION	OMISSION	INSERTION	TCHR. ASSIST.	SELF-CORRECT.	MEANING DISRUPTION
TOTALS							

Notes:

Examiner's Summary of Miscue Patterns:

PART III: DEVELOPMENTAL/PERFORMANCE SUMMARY

Silent Reading Comprehension

_____ 0–1 questions missed = Easy

_____ 2 questions missed = Adequate

_____ 3+ questions missed = Too hard

Oral Reading Accuracy

_____ 0–1 oral errors = Easy

_____ 2–5 oral errors = Adequate

_____ 6+ oral errors = Too hard

Continue to next assessment level passage? _____ Yes _____ No

PART IV: LISTENING COMPREHENSION

Directions: If you have decided not to continue to have the student read any other passages, then use this passage to begin assessing the student's listening comprehension (see page 8). Begin by reading the background statement for this passage and then say, "I am going to read this story to you. Please listen carefully because I will be asking you some questions after I finish reading it to you." After reading the passage, ask the student the questions associated with the passage. If the student correctly answers more than six questions, you will need to move to the next level and repeat the procedure.

Listening Comprehension

_____ 0–2 questions missed = move to the next passage level

_____ more than two questions missed = stop assessment or move down a level

Examiner's Notes: